Social media marketing is a continually evolving space. The speed of change challenges professionals to keep pace and bring the most up-to-date thinking to their work. *The Hidden Psychology of Social Networks* provides a timeless approach because it's based on people, not networks. Focusing on how people think and behave in those spaces will help brands bring value to consumers and create visibility for themselves on any network.

—Josh Ehart, former Chief Data Officer,
Energy BBDO

Without Federer's keen insights and thoughtful analysis, you are destined to become an irrelevant, almost clownlike figure in your profession, honking your rubber nose and clanging your marketing cowbell to an increasingly disinterested audience. Buy this book or die a joke.

—Jason Kreher, Creative Director,
Wieden+Kennedy

THE

HIDDEN

PSYCHOLOGY

OF

SOCIAL
NETWORKS

THE
HIDDEN
PSYCHOLOGY
OF
SOCIAL
NETWORKS

HOW BRANDS CREATE
AUTHENTIC ENGAGEMENT
BY UNDERSTANDING WHAT
MOTIVATES US

JOE FEDERER

Mc
Graw
Hill

NEW YORK CHICAGO SAN FRANCISCO ATHENS LONDON
MADRID MEXICO CITY MILAN NEW DELHI
SINGAPORE SYDNEY TORONTO

1 2 3 4 5 6 7 8 9   LCR   25 24 23 22 21 20

ISBN   978-1-260-46022-3
MHID   1-260-46022-3

e-ISBN   978-1-260-46023-0
e-MHID   1-260-46023-1

Library of Congress Cataloging-in-Publication Data

Names: Federer, Joe, author.
Title: The hidden psychology of social networks : how brands create authentic
    engagement by understanding what motivates us / Joe Federer.
Description: 1 Edition. | New York City : McGraw-Hill, 2020. | Includes bibliographical
    references and index.
Identifiers: LCCN 2020022088 | ISBN 9781260460223 (hardback) | ISBN
    9781260460230 (ebook)
Subjects: LCSH: Social networks—Psychological aspects. | Branding (Marketing)—
    Psychological aspects.
Classification: LCC HM741 .F343 2020 | DDC 302.3—dc23
LC record available at https://lccn.loc.gov/2020022088

*To my parents, Joe and Cathy, who filled my first
memories with finger paint coloring experiments,
backyard nature expeditions, and big questions. You've
instilled in me a reverence for curiosity and the pursuit of
interesting ideas that I will carry for the rest of my life.
Thank you for setting me down this path.*

Contents

PART III

SOCIAL MEDIA'S RIGHT AND LEFT BRAINS

Acknowledgments

For as long as I can remember, I've had the privilege of being surrounded by people who were passionate about interesting ideas. I am grateful to have been exposed to such inspiring, driven, curious people for much of my life. This book represents my best attempt to perpetuate this love affair with interesting ideas.

To my professors and teachers, thank you for introducing me to the ideas and thinkers that inspired this book: Brett Desnoyer, Jerry Boyle, Jim Gerker, Mark Laury, Andrew Schmitt, Michael Anthony, Pamela Morris, and many, many more.

To my industry mentors and colleagues, thank you for giving me the opportunity to learn from you and work with you: Kelly Sauter, Ron Culp, Rachel Levy, Zac Rybacki, Leah Gritton, Jacqueline Kohlmann, Abby Lovett, Corinne Gudovic, Ben Foster, Josh Ehart, Troy Hitch, and again, many, many more.

To my publishing team, especially my editor, Casey Ebro, thank you for grappling with these ideas with me and bringing this writing to life.

To the thinkers who inspired this book and their friends and families, your dedication to finding truths beneath the surface continue to inspire generations of curious inquirers: Sigmund Freud, Carl Jung, Joseph Campbell, Jordan B. Peterson, Richard Dawkins, Iain McGilchrist. The list goes on, but this acknowledgments page will not.

Introduction

This book is about the wonderful, strange world of social media as analyzed through the lenses of evolutionary biology and psychology. It's also about how brands, advertisers, influencers, and anyone interested in understanding social media can create better content, drive better engagement, and strategize better campaigns. But I want to start this book with a brief story. It's a story of intrigue, romance, adventure, and betrayal—of mythical creatures, magical powers, and unexplored continents. As you probably guessed, this is the story of my 12-year-old self playing a text-based online role-playing game, long before I'd ever heard the term "social media."

Before *World of Warcraft*, *Counterstrike*, or *Everquest*, there was a genre of online game called a *multiuser dungeon* (MUD). A MUD was unlike any modern video game in that it had no graphics. The characters, the monsters, and everything that constituted the world of *DragonRealms*, my MUD of choice, was text based. As a player, entering a new area conjured intricate descriptions of environments, objects, weapons, armor, and most importantly, other characters. MUDs were the first genre to allow massive numbers of users to come together and discover each other in the world of the game.

In *DragonRealms*, players were expected to role-play as if they truly were part of that world. Players didn't log out, for example. They "went to sleep." Players never spoke in Internet slang or abbreviations. Instead, characters were expected to speak in full, grammatically correct sentences—or, if not grammatically correct, in language that reflected the character being role-played. Players didn't "lol." Their characters laughed. And because this happened solely through text, the experience was that of a massive fantasy novel being told through the perspectives of thousands of players and being written right before our eyes. And yes, if you are wondering, I ~~was~~ am a massive dork.

One night, I logged in to my character, who was stealthy and adept at hiding in the game. Hiding was a skill that could be improved over time so that lower-level players could not perceive the hider in the same room. My in-game love interest was sitting in the room in which I had just "woken up," and she was not alone. *Gasp!* My Ryonia was kissing another man! I stood up from the computer and paced around my parents' office. As an awkward preteen, I hadn't really experienced heartbreak in the outside world, but here it was.

Even in my emotionally raw state, I understood this to be an absurd proposition. I was not this character. I only *played* the character online. However, I had seriously underestimated the amount of self I had invested into this online world. Simply by interfacing with people's characters through my character, I'd gone from feeling like an addict about to get his fix (read: happy) to feeling depressed, betrayed, and heartbroken. While, logically, I could reconcile that this was all very silly, my emotions were not so easily persuaded.

While it took me some time to recover, this experience and emotional fallout led me to a healthy questioning of what it meant to play a character online. What was meant to be a fantastical, fictional character was also a part of me. It was a different "me" than the "me" on AOL Instant Messenger, and it was different from the offline "me" too. But this silly character was, indeed, part of me. Not only were my online and offline personas disjointed, my online persona itself had subdivisions and splinters, depending on with whom I was interacting and where.

I tell this story not to brag about how successful I was in my early love life but to illustrate that in the Internet age, even as young people, we're required to understand very nuanced differences in whom we are expected to be online depending on the context. Social media is not unlike *DragonRealms*. The characters we play are based on us, but they're usually not representative of our full, complex, offline selves. Our online selves and our offline selves are intimately entangled, even if it's not always clear how. Part of this book aims to clarify that very question: what is the relationship between our various online selves?

Social media represents new psychological territory for us. For our brains, Facebook, Instagram, Twitter, and Reddit are real places. We don't just log on to social media. We navigate through it. Throughout this book, you'll see me refer to what people are like "in" different social media spaces rather than "on" them because I believe that's a more accurate way to think about our relationship to social media psychologically.

These social media platforms aren't just websites we visit or apps we open. They're places we enter. If we're interested in engaging people in these spaces, we need to become accustomed to their cultural norms. When we attend a happy hour with our coworkers, we're probably slightly different versions of ourselves than when we go to a music festival with our friends or we are home for Thanksgiving dinner with our families. Likewise, the person we play on Facebook and the person we represent on Twitter may be very different characters. The way we relate to a piece of content on Reddit is likely very different from how we'd relate to that same content on LinkedIn. But enough about that, let's talk about me.

I've been an Internet dork for about as long as I can remember, and I've worked in social media marketing since the industry became an industry. When I was in kindergarten, I wanted a computer like my dad's, so I saved up my allowance and did extra chores for four years until I could buy my own—a refurbished lemon of a laptop bought off the Best Buy floor. In high school, I regularly got in trouble for Photoshopping teachers and other students into memes. When I started working in public relations, I volunteered to help make some last-minute social creative for a client that generated a few thousand organic shares, and I was quickly moved from the new business team on which I was hired to a group of digital specialists. Since then, I've built social creative and strategy teams at major agencies and platforms such as Ketchum Public Relations, Energy BBDO, and Reddit.

For many of my clients, I've achieved orders of magnitude better engagement, and many have been able to attribute their improved engagement to tangible business results. My campaigns have performed in the top 5 percent of third-party Facebook studies for at-shelf sales, and I have helped brands become top performers in Pinterest's advertising alpha. When I joined Reddit in 2016 to build their brand strategy team, I wrote the brand engagement playbook for what many advertisers consider to be the most skeptical community on the Internet. Today, Kantar Millward Brown reports 2.8× better aided awareness, 2× better brand favorability, and 16 percent better purchase intent for campaigns run on Reddit as compared to average.

This book will combine the psychological research and theories that underpin my approach to social media marketing with real brand examples and case studies. For legal reasons and to protect brands' proprietary information, I've removed information about my role in specific examples, but about half of these campaigns are my concepts and executions in action.

Social media feels very new to us, and in many ways, it is. It hasn't been around for long, especially in the grand scheme of human evolution. But what isn't new is us. From the content we share to the people we engage to the posts we *like*, the ways we express ourselves in social media are governed by the same psychological and biological processes that have dictated human social lives for millennia. In broad strokes, that's what this book is about—understanding how social media fits into the innate, essential drives that have dictated our biological and cultural evolution as humans.

At the core of this book is a simple question: why is social media so compelling to us? To answer that question, we'll begin in the world of evolutionary biology, in which the word *meme* was first coined. We'll explore how ideas themselves act like genetic replicators to spread throughout social media, and we'll reverse engineer some of the important qualities that share-driving content tends to exhibit. Then, we'll look to the work of Sigmund Freud, the father of modern psychology, whose Id, Ego, and Superego model has unique application to understanding the different personas we wear online. Finally, we'll explore a more modern understanding of neuroanatomy to explain broader-level trends in how people form and represent their opinions and themselves in social media.

If you're a marketer or advertiser reading this book, you may wonder why that question is so important. After all, the eyeballs are on social media—isn't that all we really need to know? The truth is that in order to effectively reach people in different social media environments, we need to understand what value they derive from participating in those social networks in the first place. Putting on a headdress and donning body glitter may be an effective way to integrate naturally into a music festival, but it's probably not how we want to approach someone at an office happy hour. Social media etiquette is equally nuanced, but it does not have the obvious physical social cues to tell us when we err. By understanding the contexts in which we hope to reach people, we'll make more efficient use of our media buys, establish more thoughtful strategies, develop better creative, and in the end, deliver more effective marketing.

PART I

MEMEOLOGY

WHAT'S IN A MEME?

Meme. It's that hot buzzword about which everyone in advertising, marketing, and communications with any digital sense can't stop talking. Memes seem to arise spontaneously from the ether and from many sources at once. As much as the Internet likes fighting, all corners seem to genuinely agree on how they're used—and, perhaps just as importantly, how they're *not* used. Using a meme incorrectly is the digital equivalent of trying to say "Hello!" in a new language and accidentally calling someone's mother a "ham planet." If you've ever visited a community called r/AdviceAnimals, a shrine of the past era of meme culture still active on Reddit, you know that meme culture has very particular ways of using certain images, phrases, typefaces, backgrounds, and so on.

If you've ever dared post in r/AdviceAnimals without following its customs precisely, it's safe to wager that you've felt the cold shunning of digital social faux pas. And unless you did some excavating yourself, you probably still don't really understand where you went wrong. While to an outsider r/AdviceAnimals is just a collection of pictures with funny text on them, each particular background and corresponding caption follows a very particular structure and formula. So unless you're lucky enough to innovate some new format that the community accepts, you're speaking Mandarin in the middle of Mexico. And not like Chinatown in Mexico City either—you're in Durango, and your phone is out of battery.

For advertisers and marketers, memes are those untouchable, invaluable relics that seem right within reach but crumble at our slightest touch. The truth is that very few of us really understand meme culture from the inside, and like any culture, it's extremely difficult to fool the natives into thinking we're locals. Fortunately for you, dear reader, I am a massive dork and am fluent in this culture. So as we say in the deep Internet, follow me, for I will be your guide.

We're going to start at the very beginning with what is *actually* meant by the word *meme*. When we hear "meme," most of us know what's being discussed. A meme is one of those silly pictures or gifs with text on them. Right? *Meme* is one of those words that is widely used but rarely defined. Even in academic literature about memes— yes, there is academic literature about memes—researchers and authors rarely agree. In fact, the actual coining of the word *meme* tends to be a small footnote in most discussions about memes. Usually when we say "meme," we mean a particularly popular piece of content with qualities of being highly shareable, of having repeated itself in various ways across time, and having particular rawness or lack of polish in the format of the content itself. One of the more prominent researchers on memes, a professor of digital culture named Limor Shifman, has gone as far as to list the specific qualities of memes, their types, what qualifies as a "meme" versus a "trend," and much more.[1] As wonderful as Shifman's insights are into meme culture generally, Shifman and I disagree about one fundamental thing: the definition of the word. That's right, you've just found yourself in the middle of a nerd war, so grab a keyboard and pick a side.

In 1976, an evolutionary biologist named Richard Dawkins wrote a monumental book called *The Selfish Gene*.[2] This work was meant to articulate a modern understanding of the theory of evolution to people without a biology degree, and it's still among the top recommended books about evolution. Because his audience consists mostly of non-biologists, Dawkins takes specific measures to address what we might call a pop culture understanding of evolution. Most of us are probably familiar with the phrase "survival of the fittest." Intuitively that sounds like it means "the plants and animals that are best equipped will survive the longest." In actuality, Dawkins tells us we need to look a level deeper to understand the true meaning of the phrase. In keeping with the title of his book, Dawkins tells us that the "selfish gene" is the driving force of evolution, and its survival doesn't necessarily mean staying alive.

Genes are the most basic units of DNA, and all life on Earth shares the same building blocks of DNA arranged in different orders. The most important and mysterious quality of the gene is its ability to replicate itself. However, in the course of replication, genes sometimes make errors, which we call *mutations*. Most gene mutations aren't beneficial and cause the new gene to die. But every so often, a useful mutation occurs, one that helps the new gene replicate itself more effectively and create a new generation of genes.

Imagine that one specific arrangement of DNA produces a kind of bird that survives by eating grubs that live in thick tree bark. As a whole, the population of birds will have an average beak length, but when you look at individual birds, they probably have slightly different-sized beaks. It may be the case that birds with slightly longer beaks tend to survive long enough to reach sexual maturity more often than birds with shorter beaks. Over the course of many, many generations of birds, we could predict that the average beak size will grow because the genes for longer beaks are better propagators than the genes for shorter beaks. If you can imagine a flip book of snapshots of each bird generation viewed in succession, it would almost appear that a conscious process was molding the birds' beaks to be longer, which is a fascinating illusion created by the combined processes of random gene mutation and natural selection.

Dawkins's broader point is that genes are the true drivers of the evolutionary process. The term *natural selection* is really a personification of nature "selecting" certain genes, when in actuality, nature and the environment simply present a set of circumstances in which particular mutations of genes survive, and others do not. We can lean into this metaphor as long as we remember that it's an abstraction of the actual process.

In the spirit of personification, we could say that genes appear to be doing their best to make their ways into the next generations of genes.

A few billion years ago in the "primordial soup" that made up the first accumulation of life-forms on Earth, simple genes replicated and spread throughout every environment they could manage. But energy sources are finite, and as genes thrived on Earth, the environment became more and more competitive. As genes continued to replicate themselves, some infidelities in copies helped these early genes adapt to new kinds of energy sources or survive in places that other genes couldn't. Eventually, with generations and generations of replication and mutation, genes began to build around themselves what Dawkins calls "gene machines." A gene machine is a plant or an animal—it's a machine the gene builds around itself to help itself propagate a new generation of genes. (Don't worry, I promise this comes back to memes.)

Following Dawkins's model for genes and gene machines, Dawkins turns his focus to humans specifically. He acknowledges that something is clearly different in human evolution. In human evolution, Dawkins identifies a new kind of replicator—the meme, which he defines as a unit of cultural transmission. Things like ideas, songs, fashion, and language are all examples of memes—or, more specifically, groups of memes. Like genes, memes undergo an evolutionary process. When a new idea occurs to me, a physical process happens within my brain. And if I can find a way to articulate that idea to others, that physical process happens within their brains too. The recipient of my meme may even change the meme, akin to a mutation. So the meme isn't just a metaphor. It's not that ideas are *like* genes— they actually undergo a very similar process of replication, mutation, and exposure to selection pressures. The selection pressures imposed on a meme are complex, but they can be largely reduced to how attractive the meme is to other brains. Memes, like genes, don't often exist in isolation, so the memes already encoded in our minds have significant influence on which new memes are appealing to us.

ANY IDEA WITH A CHANCE OF PROPAGATING IS A MEME

Let's say I have an idea for a coffee shop that sells only lukewarm coffee. No hot coffee. No iced coffee. Just lukewarm coffee. That's a meme (well, a set of memes)—a coffee shop that serves only lukewarm coffee.

Now let's say you and I are having a conversation, and I tell you about my idea. You might think to yourself, "Hmm, that's a really bad idea. But what about a coffee shop that sells only iced coffee. . . ." In that case, a meme emerged in me, and I transmitted that idea to you. You received the meme, and in the environment of your brain—your personal meme pool—you evolved the meme. And let's be honest, your evolved meme probably has a much better chance at propagating than my original. This is the process by which Dawkins claims all human culture is shared and formed over time. As ideas occur to us, we share them, and as ideas are shared, they evolve.

What started as a 12-page section in Dawkins's book about evolutionary biology has become a set of disciplines entirely their own. The idea of "memes" as the new replicators caught fire in academia, and in that sense, the "meme" meme was an extremely successful propagator. However, one of Dawkins's own success criteria for evaluating memes was "copy fidelity," and in that sense, the "meme" was a bad meme.

Decades later, different schools of thought still debate what is meant by the word *meme*, and I bet you thought the next few paragraphs were going to drag you through the academic controversy surrounding the definition of memes. God, that sounds boring. Don't worry, I wouldn't do that to you. The only piece of that drama important to this discussion is how broadly we define memes. For Dawkins, a meme was a "unit of cultural transmission, or a unit of imitation and replication." The examples he uses are "tunes, ideas, catch-phrases, clothes fashions, ways of making pots or of building arches." Susan Blackmore, another biologist who wrote a book called *The Meme Machine*, also defines memes as being any type of information that can be copied by imitation.[3] This definition has been criticized for being too broad and, as Limor Shifman puts it, "may lack analytical power." Shifman's definition of a meme is much more specific and focuses more on the way the Internet colloquially uses the term *meme*. She calls memes "digital content units with common characteristics, created with awareness of each other, circulated, imitated, and transformed via the Internet by many users."[4] Catchy, isn't it? To Shifman's credit, she's also called Internet memes the "postmodern folklore," which is so true it hurts.

While I understand the criticism, I side with keeping the definition of *meme* very broad. For the purposes of this book, we'll say that any idea that can be transmitted between brains is a meme. Even simpler—a meme is just an idea. When Dawkins gives examples of memes, he points exclusively to memes that have successfully propagated and spread. That makes sense because he's driving home the point that successful memes spread like successful genes (Figure 1.1). Dawkins doesn't dwell on those memes that aren't successful propagators, so his focus on success has sometimes been interpreted to mean that *only* successful propagators are memes. If we return to the biological gene side of the metaphor, most genetic mutations are actually harmful and fail to help the mutated gene replicate. But those genes that fail to replicate are still genes. Likewise, most ideas don't stick. But fortunately, we humans tend to have lots of ideas, and there are lots of humans, so we play a numbers game to continue evolving good ideas.

Genes are the essential building blocks that make up every plant and animal.

Memes are the essential building blocks that make up broader ideas and cultures.

FIGURE 1.1 **Genes Versus Memes**

When we use *meme* as a reference to particular kinds of Internet content, we're just isolating the most successful replicators. We're also referring to more than just the idea when we talk about Internet memes—we're including the format through which the idea is conveyed. For example, we might stumble upon the idea that budgets are generally tight for people right before they get paid by their employers. But it's not an Internet meme until someone posts a photo of a goldfish cracker sitting on top of sushi rice next to a dab of wasabi and captions it, "When payday is still two days away."[5]

In actuality, within that Internet meme is an entire complex of memes, and that's true of nearly all memes. The simple fact that you can read this text means that not only have you mastered the English language and all of the necessary memes surrounding sentence structure and punctuation but you're also familiar with the network of ideas communicated within each word. Technically, any individual meme we try to identify is a complex of memes networked together, so while we'll continue to isolate particular ideas as individual memes, it's worth remembering that memes rely on a broad cultural net of other memes for context. Our language, cultural knowledge, education, and personal experience all influence how we process memes.

As brands, everything we do revolves around memes. Beyond that, a brand itself is a meme—or a combination of memes. After all, a meme is just an idea. As advertisers, communicators, community managers, influencers—whatever we want to call ourselves—we're in the business of propagating memes. Whether it's "Just do it," "I'm lovin' it," or "Buy my merch, you schmuck," ideas are at the bottom of every marketing and communications discipline. When we talk about Internet memes as "those silly pictures with text on them," what we're really talking about is the format used to communicate different memes.

In following from Dawkins's gene and gene machine framework, we might call these formats "meme machines." For early humans, we had only the meme machines of the sounds we made, the pictures we drew, and then eventually, the languages we invented. Now, as you're reading this, you're (hopefully) extracting memes from this book, and the meme machine is likely the physical pages in your hand, the digital screen on which the text is being displayed, or the audiobook version to which you're listening.

MEME MACHINES EVOLVE TO MOST EFFICIENTLY COMMUNICATE THEIR MEMES

Let's break this down a little more using a favorite example of mine, particularly for those of us with nine-to-fives. Let's talk about the meme "Mondays suck." Inevitably, embedded within the meme "Mondays suck" is an endless thread of more granular memes. To understand what is meant by these two words, we need to understand what Mondays are and the structure of a week. We need to understand the colloquial definition of the word *suck*, and we also need to understand the general cultural phenomenon of the average workweek starting on Mondays. We can continue to excavate more and more granular memes embedded in this phrase, but let's assume we all understand what that means. Mondays suck!

In fact, "Mondays" have sucked for a very long time. Marcus Aurelius even dedicates a section of *Meditations* to how awful "Mondays" are:

> At dawn, when you have trouble getting out of bed, tell yourself: "I have to go to work—as a human being. What do I have to complain of, if I'm going to do what I was born for—the things I was brought into the world to do? Or is this what I was created for? To huddle under the blankets and stay warm?[6]

There are entire movies written about how much Mondays suck. *Office Space* is a personal favorite. The movie came out in 1999, and today the only things that really feel dated about it are the fashion, the cubicles, and the film quality. In *Office Space*, the protagonist Peter can't seem to deal with yet another Monday. He hates his job, and Mondays represent the beginning of his wretched workweek. Perhaps the pinnacle scene demonstrating Peter's hatred for Mondays happens early in the film as he approaches the cubicles of two friends in an attempt to lure them out to lunch early. A colleague sneaks up behind him and, in the cheesiest "office joke" voice possible, says, "Sounds like *somebody's* got a case of the *Mondays*." Peter cringes. His friends cringe. We cringe. The only thing worse than Mondays is clichéd office humor about Mondays. But somehow, millions of people enjoy watching *Office Space,* which at its core, is an hour and a half of jokes about how much Mondays suck. Why?

The meme machine is just as important as the meme itself. The meme can be carried by two entirely different meme machines, and they may show absolutely polar results when we measure their effectiveness at propagating. Great comedians are perfect examples of this principle. A great comedian can tell you a joke about something you've heard a thousand other jokes about but will do so in a way that makes the idea—the meme—feel totally fresh and new. A bad joke teller can start with the most hilarious possible content and absolutely fail to engage an audience.

When we're participating in social media as content creators, we desperately need to understand this principle. In advertising and marketing, we generally spend an enormous amount of time thinking about what we want to say—the meme—but we rarely put equal thought into the meme machines we use to deliver those memes. We have particular formats that tend to be the norms of our industry— 60-second, 30-second, 15-second, and now even 6-second cuts of video—and we force our memes to fit into those machines. Video *can* be the right meme machine to deliver a meme, but it isn't always.

Imagine I'm at a friend's house for movie night, and that friend presents me with a few choices in movies to watch. One of those movies happens to be *Office Space*, and because I like that movie, there's a strong likelihood that I'll pick it. So in the context of a group of movies—a meme pool of movies—*Office Space* is a viable meme carrier for people like me. But we don't always encounter meme machines in their original environments.

If I'm scrolling through a cable TV menu, and I see that *Office Space* is on but halfway over, I probably won't tune in to watch. OK, maybe for like *five minutes.* In the slightly more competitive meme pool of cable TV menus, *Office Space* has the disadvantage of being much longer than an average TV program. But if I love the movie, there's still a chance that I'll tune in anyway.

Now imagine that the movie *Office Space* is sitting in its full length on my Facebook feed. Even if I'm the biggest *Office Space* fan in the world—and I might be by the time I'm done with this paragraph—the likelihood that I'll sit and watch for an hour and a half is pretty low.

Maybe even zero. Why? Because Facebook—and social media feeds in general—are more competitive content environments. Social feeds are algorithmically programmed to deliver more and more interesting content, and they get better over time as they gather engagement data about the stuff with which you're most likely to interact.

This isn't to say that the meme of "Mondays suck!" can't propagate successfully in social feeds though. Remember that *Office Space* is just one of many meme machines that can carry the idea that "Mondays suck!" We know for a fact that our "Mondays suck!" meme can and does propagate in social because there are myriad examples of Internet memes, jokes, videos, and so on that carry similar memes. It's just that the meme machine needs to evolve to survive in these more competitive environments.

A movie is a relatively heavy meme machine. A movie requires that we give our full attention to something for at least an hour and a half. In order to fully absorb the memes from the movie, we not only need to give it our full visual attention but our full auditory attention too. Then, even after we've given our captive visual and auditory attention, we're in a passive state of waiting for the memes to be delivered to us. We don't dictate the speed at which the movie plays, and in a world where more and more media is consumed on mobile devices, we can hardly expect to have a few seconds of undivided attention, let alone a couple of hours. In order for these memes to thrive in a social environment, they must find a way to become lighter. The meme machines we use must be low friction and must be extremely efficient at delivering their memes.

One way the Internet organically evolves meme machines to become lighter is to take a video with spoken dialogue and turn that scene into a screenshot with a caption on it. Suddenly, the meme machine goes from passive to active. When the meme is contained in an image-with-text-on-it meme machine—an *image macro*—we consumers of the content suddenly become active participants in the extraction of the meme. We read through the text, which we process more quickly than when we hear something out loud, we extract the meme from the meme machine, and we continue scrolling through our feeds.

We don't have to enable sound on our phone or put headphones in or click a full-screen button to watch something. We just read and move on to the next things in our feed. Not only that, an image with legible text on it is extremely easy to share. Have you ever seen a funny video in a social feed and wanted to send it to someone who wasn't connected to you on that social network? It's almost impossible for the average person. But if you're trying to share an image, you have a greater ability to save it to your local device or even take a screenshot. Screenshotting an image preserves the meme, while screenshotting a video usually loses the original meme. That's in large part why efficiency is such an important driver of sharing online—the lightness of a meme machine is an important determinant of how well the meme it carries can propagate. The meme machine is vital to the meme's survival.

THE MEME MACHINE IS AS IMPORTANT AS THE MEME ITSELF

There is a particular kind of meme machine that dominated Internet meme culture during the late 2000s and early 2010s. Those of you who browsed Reddit or 4chan regularly probably already know where this is going. The Internet collectively agreed on Impact font as the universal meme font. But not just Impact font—white Impact font with a black outline.

The consistency in the use of this font and format for memes is striking when we look back through this period of meme culture. And it's no accident. Impact font is particularly thick, and it stands up to even chaotic imagery. Combined with a black outline, this font is legible on nearly any kind of background. Not only that, when this format was screenshotted and lost resolution, Impact generally stood up to the image degradation. The meme was still extractable. In some sense, we could say that this font style was evolved for the ultimate efficiency of the meme machine. A large, clear font that helps to deliver a meme more efficiently is a helpful trait for the survival of the meme it carries.

Very few brands leverage this meme machine, and I think the reason for that is summed up nicely in a piece of feedback I once received from an art director I worked with: "But it's *ugly*!" It's not an unfair critique, and I don't disagree—white Impact font with a black outline isn't exactly chic. But the problem with the pretty work our industry tends to love is that it's rarely efficient at delivering our memes. Small text is usually prettier than large text. Low-contrast text is also a trend that comes and goes in ads. Nonstandard fonts are usually fun ways to express brand personality, but they often reduce the legibility of the content slightly. If you've worked in an agency with a creative team, you've probably witnessed the "wall exercise" where we put all of our creative work up on a wall for a holistic review. In these settings, as we focus specifically on our work in isolation, we might be able to convince ourselves that our swirly white font on our light pink background is plenty legible. We *can* read it. The problem is that we're not talking about *if* someone can read it. We're talking about whether or not someone *will* read it. According to Facebook, people on mobile spend an average of 1.7 seconds per piece of content.[7] So even if that fancy font takes just half a second more to read, that's 30 percent of the overall attention we get from the user spent trying to extract the meme without even processing it. Efficiency of communication is absolutely pivotal to successful meme sharing in social feeds.

Part of the challenge of driving sharing and engagement in social is identifying the most optimal meme machine to carry our memes. Imagine that we're biologists tasked with engineering a glow-in-the-dark frog that has a reasonable chance of surviving in a particular environment. We have two potential paths. In the first, we try to write frog DNA from scratch. Suspending disbelief just a little, let's imagine that we can actually do that. We conduct research on a bunch of different frogs, write our own DNA sequence based on that research, and we embed some glow-in-the-dark genes. The trouble with this path is that exactly how genes interact with one another and their environments isn't always obvious to us in a lab. What may seem like an arbitrary feature could actually be pivotal to some overlooked aspect of our frog's survival, or it may affect other important genes in a way that isn't immediately obvious.

The second path we might pursue is to take a frog out of the environment in which it needs to survive and insert our glow-in-the-dark DNA into its otherwise naturally evolved genetic code. By doing so, we harness the evolutionary process to our advantage rather than trying to re-create it in a lab setting.

The same strategy works for memes. Minus the frogs. Actually, scratch that, frogs included. (This one's for you, Pepe. I'm sorry you got hijacked by white supremacists. You were a good meme.) This is a lesson we need to learn as social advertisers. When we evaluate an eco-system—a social network—and want to find a way for our memes to survive and thrive, it's important for us to understand what content is organically successful at propagating in that environment. While as an industry we pay lip service to the idea that we want our content to feel "native to the channel," our creative reviews rarely compare the content we've made for our brands to the content that organically drives sharing. More often, we compare ourselves to our competitors, and they're usually no more native to the environment than we are.

This isn't to say that every brand should go try to force its latest product messaging into the Drake meme format. It's not uncommon for influencers in advertising and marketing to talk about "hijacking" memes by inserting themselves indelicately into the latest hashtag or Internet meme. Brands that do so without adding value usually show up in communities dedicated to poking fun at them. Internet meme culture is very particular, and not every brand can or should engage with Internet meme culture. Whether or not we aspire to participate in meme culture, we still have much to gain by taking the frog out of its environment and trying to figure out what makes it work. The meme machines that evolve within meme culture are evolutionary products, and regardless of whether we find the memes embedded in them particularly relevant, if a meme machine is effective at propagating, it has a lesson to teach us.

As nonsensical, ludicrous, and even offensive as Internet meme culture can sometimes be, it can teach us valuable principles in creating share-driving content—from the way its meme machines are made, to memes' physical characteristics, to the point of view from which the memes are delivered. Every day, kids with old versions of Photoshop on their parents' computers manage to create content that engages millions of people. And if they can do it, our armies of professional designers, photographers, copywriters, strategists, marketing professionals, communications specialists, and community managers can too. We *can* create engaging content that drives pass-along—or, in the very least, that efficiently delivers our messages.

KEY TAKEAWAYS

- A *meme* in the traditional, biological sense is simply a "unit of idea" or a "unit of culture."

- A *meme machine* is the format used to communicate an idea or meme.

- In order for our brand messages (memes) to effectively drive engagement, we should express them in the lightest, most accessible formats (meme machines).

- Successful meme machines vary widely among different kinds of social networks. Ask yourself, "What types of content and formats are organically successful in this social network?"

THE MEME AND THE MEME MACHINE

The Importance of the Format of a Meme

I f you opened Facebook or Instagram in 2014, the odds were pretty good that you were confronted at some point by a video of one of your friends pouring a bucket of ice water on top of his or her head.[1] In the spring of 2013, a viral sensation called the ALS Ice Bucket Challenge became a massively popular trend in social. The concept was perfectly engineered to social virality. The idea behind the movement was to help raise awareness of ALS, and in order to do so, people dumped buckets of ice water on themselves or their consenting friends. The makeup of each ALS Ice Bucket Challenge video was relatively consistent: the "nominees" tell us who nominated them, they dump ice water on their heads, and then they nominate someone else. Not only does it make for hilarious footage you can't help but watch, but the meme also spreads itself through nominations. *And* it was for a good cause. This triple-pronged approach to virality was immensely successful, with the trend spreading around the world over the course of about a year.

The end of the ALS Ice Bucket Challenge craze happened to coincide with an opportune moment for the Facebook platform. For most of Facebook's early years, image- and text-based content were the most common formats in the News Feed. Most advertising followed suit because these types of posts tended to drive the highest-volume engagement. For Facebook, keeping users engaged and on platform means more ad impressions and better usage statistics. That's why Facebook works so hard at their content algorithm—with the quantity of content uploaded to Facebook every day, ensuring that the most engaging content finds its way to the top of people's feeds is an important and difficult calculation. Before Facebook had a viable native video player, nearly every video on Facebook was actually a link to a YouTube video, and YouTube is owned by Facebook's arch nemesis, Google. Video posts and link posts—the two kinds of posts that sent traffic off-site—were extremely small and poorly formatted in people's feeds. Whether due to user behavior or Facebook's formatting, links and videos didn't demand the attention that images and text posts did.

On an otherwise average day in May 2015, as I opened Facebook for the first of many times during my workday, I noticed something strange. Of the top 10 posts in my News Feed, 7 were video posts, but they were not links to YouTube videos. They were natively hosted Facebook videos, many of which were ALS Ice Bucket Challenge videos. At the time, I was managing a dozen or so brand pages as a social strategist at Energy BBDO in Chicago. For those unfamiliar with BBDO, it was briefly the evil monolithic adversary on the show *Mad Men*—the Goliath to Don Draper's David. The agency is renowned in the advertising world for creating polished, artistic video content. During my tenure, I was the annoying voice in the room questioning that practice in social space. After all, the content that organically drove the greatest amount of sharing was image-based, and I'd proven that to my teams through analyses of hundreds of different Facebook posts across dozens of pages. It was regular practice for me to watch for changes in Facebook's News Feed algorithm because the previous November, Facebook had made a catastrophic change to brand pages, cutting organic reach by over 90 percent for most of my clients. I was perplexed—why was I suddenly receiving so much video content in my Facebook feed?

I was so struck by this change that I published a post to my infrequently updated, now embarrassing blog.[2] I even made a prediction that in the coming weeks, Facebook would begin to tout a new "trend" in video consumption to our teams. Approximately a week after I published the post, I received an email from my Facebook ~~salesperson~~ rep about people suddenly watching more video than ever on the platform, along with a bunch of fun stats about hours watched per day, engagement with different post types, and so on. Attributed to the mass adoption of smartphones and their ever-improving cameras, Facebook began to strongly recommend video as the preferred content format for driving engagement.

It's hard not to speculate that this trend was, at least in part, manufactured. And, yes, I do keep this tinfoil hat on while I sleep, why do you ask? It was no secret to the industry that Facebook had all but exhausted the small pool of budget most brands had allocated to social media, which itself was a small piece of an average brand's larger digital spend. But television budgets? That's where the *real* money was. As much advertising budget as Facebook had captured to date, TV spends dwarfed social and digital spends. In fact, it wasn't until 2019 that digital advertising spend surpassed TV.[3] And, of course, TV ads are exclusively videos. By boosting usage statistics for videos on the platform, touting the trend as an organic insight, and recommending that more advertisers utilize video content, a doorway was opened for brands to take the content they were promoting on TV and adapting it slightly for social media. Add to this the fact that many brands were already struggling with creating good social creative, and it's no surprise that many advertisers were primed to hear this message.

To capitalize on this algorithm change, a new kind of video format started popping up on organic Facebook pages and with influencers. Popular content aggregators started to add text to their videos, almost in the style of the old-school Impact font format popular in Internet meme culture. Sometimes this text was added to dub over what a person in the video was saying, and other times it was used simply to add context to the video. If we were to critique this video content in an advertising creative review, we'd probably have pointed out that dubbing videos was redundant—anyone could just enable sound to hear what was being said. And if the goal was to add context to the video, shouldn't that just have been included in Facebook's text field? While those suggestions may have seemed completely reasonable, the undeniable truth was that a huge number of these seemingly redundant videos accumulated massive amounts of sharing and viewing. Most advertiser content does not.

HARNESS ORGANIC MEME MACHINES TO INTEGRATE INTO DIFFERENT SOCIAL ENVIRONMENTS

If we're trying to understand this from an evolutionary perspective, we look at the content slightly differently. Like our glow-in-the-dark frog from the previous chapter, we can't assume that we understand exactly what's driven a piece of viral content's success in propagating. We need to throw away the critiques that seem to us like common sense and simply acknowledge that this product of evolution has succeeded in propagating. We don't necessarily have to use it, but what can we learn from it? Can we take it apart? What theories might we derive from its success that we can apply to our own approach to content? Regardless of how low quality, mundane, ridiculous, or stupid something might seem to us at first glance, the evolutionary process of content selection has determined this thing a winner. And unless every post we make in social generates hundreds of thousands of engagements, we should probably approach these problems with some humility. Most of us still have plenty to learn about making share-driving content.

When we're viewing these dubbed videos in isolation, many of these qualities inevitably do feel redundant. But from a user perspective, those redundant elements are extremely efficient at delivering the ideas embedded in the videos. A social feed is an extremely competitive environment for content. The instant something seems boring or loses our attention, another piece of content is immediately ready to follow it. When we're scrolling through a competitive social feed, a video requires a drastic change in behavior for us.

Assuming we're on our phones, a video requires us to put on headphones, enable sound, and click to view as full screen, after which, we sit and wait for things to happen. How often do we click "play" on videos only to back out and scroll to the next piece of content when that video doesn't grab us in the first few seconds of viewing? By adding captions to videos, content creators remove the requirement for users to enable sound, meaning anyone viewing the video in a public or quiet space can suddenly access the memes present in the video in ways they couldn't (or wouldn't) with an average video.

In some contexts, and with particular subject matter, videos can be effective. There's a substantial body of research to back that up. In fact, some forms of video propagate extremely well in social feeds. Gifs, which are essentially silent videos, have made a massive comeback in Internet culture. Popular gifs tend to cut immediately to the relevant action and are inserted directly into the conversations or reactions of social network users. The ALS Ice Bucket Challenge is a perfect example of video content that appeals to an audience in much the same way that gifs do. While ALS Ice Bucket Challenges usually do contain sound, they're immediately entertaining (or at least suspense building), and it's entirely possible to enjoy the content without sound. When we're creating particularly animated content or demonstrating something especially visual and motion oriented, videos and gifs can be very efficient at delivering memes that static images can't.

The point here is that video shouldn't be the only type of content we create, and it shouldn't always be our default format. Videos work particularly well on TV and YouTube because they fit naturally into those environments. When we're watching TV, we're generally in a passive state, and in theory, we're already paying captive visual and auditory attention. When a TV commercial airs between whatever we're watching, the flow feels natural—it doesn't require a behavior change to deliver its message. YouTube is a more competitive environment than television, but because people are generally on YouTube to watch videos, video ads feel natural to the environment. However, in most social feeds, video is a cumbersome format when the goal is to efficiently communicate an idea. Video can certainly still be successful in social feeds, but these videos are under different environmental selection pressures. Social feeds are active—people are scrolling manually through posts, not waiting for content to be delivered to them. Text, images, gifs, and gif-like videos are much more active meme machines—they move at the speed of the audience.

TO IDENTIFY WHAT CONTENT IS MOST IMPACTFUL, MAKE SURE YOU'RE MEASURING THE RIGHT SUCCESS METRICS

While both my agency's creative teams and our Facebook contacts pushed our content strategy toward video, I maintained my skepticism and pushed for a test. This test was the pinnacle of an ongoing debate inside the agency, which was in many ways a microcosm of the debate within the advertising industry. How much of the success of a brand in social is dictated by the format of its content? Fortunately, the timing of this test coincided with major content production for one of our most successful brands in social.

This client was a massive household name brand in a situation that was characteristic of much of the consumer packaged goods (CPG) industry. The brand made quality products, innovated new technologies consistently, and was so successful that its brand name became synonymous with its category—in the same way we refer to every bandage as a Band-Aid. Their biggest problem? Store brands and off-label brands were getting better and better at catching up in terms of quality and mimicking innovation while delivering products at nearly half the price. That's not a simple problem to overcome with advertising alone because many CPG brands have the special problem of being primarily bought at shelf, where the price differential is readily apparent. Success meant reaching people deeply enough to affect their decisions at the store.

The previous year, we'd taken this client through a massive rebrand. Often, rebrands happen far too late as last-ditch efforts to revivify long-decayed brand corpses, but that was hardly the case here. The brand's previous content strategy had followed logically from the at-shelf problem. The brand's ads had aimed to highlight the differences in quality and innovation between its products and "bargain" products. Makes sense, right? The problem with that strategy was that it resulted in really, really boring content. As our team reviewed years of content, we saw a consistent formula. Nearly every piece of content was a side-by-side product comparison. If you've ever fallen asleep watching TV and woken up to one of those five-hour-long infomercials, our review of legacy brand content felt a little like that. Something needed to change, but if we weren't leaning into the product superiority, how could we possibly expect people to pick our client over its cheaper competitors? The answer came from a few particularly successful social posts my team managed to sneak through an otherwise ironclad client, legal, and creative approval process. Sometimes, it pays to specialize in an area to which not everyone is paying attention.

Rather than showing people why our client's product was the best, we started to show people how best to use its products. We created content using the product in new and interesting ways. Because the product was relatively ubiquitous—something that almost everyone had in their pantries—life hacks and recipes showing people how to use the product in unexpected ways drove an incredible amount of sharing. The success of this content in our social strategy then informed the larger rebrand, and we started to think about how to adapt this content for TV, print, and other kinds of digital channels. With the rebrand already in practice and general consensus on the subject of the content planned for production, the real test would be about content format—a battle of meme machines.

Having shot both still and motion film for a quarter's worth of content, we designed an elegant test to determine how much the format affected engagement—more specifically, how much it affected engagement and organic reach. Recycling a particularly successful concept from a previous batch of social media creative, we developed four new versions of the content. We created two videos of the concept—a long-form version approximately a minute long and a short-form version approximately 15 seconds long. We posted an article on our brand's website about it. And we took a simple photograph of the content with text superimposed on it. We then fueled each with equal paid support.

You can probably intuit which was most successful. The static image overlaid with instructional text drove 4× more *likes*, 3× more comments, and 2× more clicks of the share button. With *liking*, commenting, and sharing being the primary ways to interact with a post on Facebook, this seems like an open-and-shut case, right? Unfortunately, Facebook's analytics dashboard disagreed with me.

According to Facebook, the short-form video was more engaging than any other piece of content. How? The devil is in the details—or, in this case, the devil is in Facebook's definition of engagement with a video post. For most post types on Facebook—images, status updates, and link posts—Facebook counts engagements as all clicks that happen on a post. Actions like *liking* a post, commenting on it, expanding an image, or clicking a link all count as engagements. But videos get special treatment. When a video auto-plays in a user's feed for two seconds, it also counts as an engagement. So when Facebook claims that video is the most engaging form of content, they're not technically wrong. They're just being misleading about what exactly they mean by "engagement."

Now, there is a fair argument to be made about whether or not we should care about engagement in the first place. After all, a *liked* post isn't exactly a product sold. This is a fundamental problem for brands in social media generally, and it's a complex one. That said, true engagements have real benefits. True engagement means incremental reach. When people engage with a post on Facebook—when they *like*, comment, or share something—they create what's called a "story." A story is a post that has the potential to hit the feeds of that person's connections. If you've ever seen a post on Facebook highlighting "So-and-so commented on this," that's the kind of story we're talking about. Unfortunately, the engagement metric provided by Facebook includes a number of additional actions that don't correlate with incremental earned reach.

To account for this, my team created our own version of engagement that exclusively focused on measuring actions that had the potential to drive earned reach. The formula was the total number of *likes*, comments, and shares divided by total reach. We also weighted sharing as top-tier engagement, commenting as middle-tier engagement, and *liking* as the lowest-tier form of engagement because we found that each action affected incremental reach in that order. This no-frills engagement metric gave our social team a much clearer picture of which content actually drove earned reach. The answer? In this case, static image-based content.

Two years after we changed our social strategy to focus on content that was both product centric and truly engagement focused, we found that our content had earned an additional 10 percent of incremental impressions atop a substantial media buy. With a social spend in the ballpark of millions of dollars per year, earning 10 percent incremental reach has real value to the business. In addition, a third-party partner study demonstrated a return on investment within the top 95th percentile of the other Facebook campaigns they'd measured. The same content approach succeeded in placing us as a top performer in the Pinterest ads alpha and beta programs in terms of engagement and earned reach. A collection of our Pinterest and Facebook posts even made the front page of Reddit when a user collected an album full of our social images and posted them to the r/Lifehacks community. By optimizing our content to be as light and self-contained as possible, we ensured that the memes we wanted to spread stayed intact throughout generations of sharing—within their original social networks and beyond.

KEY TAKEAWAYS

- The meme machine is just as important as the meme. The format of a piece of content is just as important as the subject of that content.

- When creating branded content, look for comparable content that has successfully generated engagement organically, and use that successful organic content as inspiration.

- Be willing to break out of the advertiser comfort zone (that is, video). Test new formats and ways of expressing your messages, and you may well discover new, more efficient ways of sharing those messages.

- Evaluate content performance with metrics that are tied to real value. Social actions and earned reach are both examples of common metrics that help measure how successfully a message spreads.

- Whenever possible, messages should be shared in "complete meme machines" that allow people to derive the value of a piece of content directly in their social feeds.

EVOLVING MEME MACHINES
Five Principles to Maximize Engagement

When social media began to emerge as an advertising channel, it reinvigorated many brands' hope in scalable word-of-mouth marketing. At the time, Facebook's pitch to brands was something along the lines of "Come build up your fan page, and your fans will evangelize your brand to their friends!" The concept of word-of-mouth marketing wasn't exactly new, however. Obviously, word-of-mouth recommendations have been integral parts of our culture that arose organically long before marketing was ever a discipline—they are the natural ways we express what's valuable to us. One popular model of the concept was pioneered in the 1970s by a psychologist named George Silverman, who marketed pharmaceutical products.[1] In focus groups with physicians, Silverman noticed that "one or two physicians who were having good experiences with a drug would sway an entire group of skeptics. They would even sway a dissatisfied group of ex-prescribers who had had negative experiences!" Dystopian medical industry vibes aside, word-of-mouth marketing tantalized marketers for decades. When done right, it appeared more effective than any other form of marketing. But it was almost impossible to predict, let alone generate in a vacuum.

While the Facebook promise of brand fans becoming armies of evangelists hasn't been replicable for every brand at every scale, there is no shortage of brands that have put social media's unique ability to facilitate pass-along to work. While many early "social media gurus" were frustrated by brands' slowness to adopt social media channels for advertising, low prioritization actually came with some benefits. Because most branded posts were reaching only a few thousand people at a time, many marketing organizations were looser with approvals and willing to try things they wouldn't in traditional advertising channels. Social teams weren't handcuffed to overly polished or overly branded creative. The content creation cycle was generally scrappy and low production, which made content feel lighter and more natural to the people who interacted with it. Very few brands had the teams of designers, copywriters, strategists, and analysts that make up social media teams today. Nowadays, it's relatively unthinkable for a major brand to hand a 22-year-old the keys to its social profiles, but that's exactly how my career started.

As social media matured into a viable and scalable advertising channel, budgets grew, production became more polished, and strategy frameworks were put in place. While these new resources greatly increased the scope of what was possible for social campaigns, some of the magic of the scrappy test-and-learn approach was lost. One of the most overlooked opportunities afforded to us by social media is the ability to test content, iterate, and optimize it before we reach a mass audience. Organic social posts are like focus groups full of the people most likely to engage with our brand's content. That means we can test different kinds of messaging and different manifestations of that messaging to understand which will make the most efficient use of our promotion dollars.

Exactly how this test-and-learn process looks is different for each brand. We all face different challenges of brand perception, trends in our categories, competitive brands, and so on. It's up to each of us to discover which memes and meme machines will most effectively propagate our brand. What works for a brand with a massive following will probably not work for the fresh contender brand. What works for the flashy new startup probably won't for the century-old legacy brand. But that doesn't mean we have to start from scratch.

Certain principles of social content creation remain true, regardless of brand, category, or target audience. This chapter provides a high-level overview of some of my teams' most important learnings over a decade of brand building in social media. I've applied these principles to social strategies for brands of all sizes and success levels. They require interpretation through the lens of your particular brand, but these principles should be applicable to any stage of brand development. Consider these principles starting points from which any brand can test, iterate, and improve. Up-and-to-the-right graphs guaranteed.

1. ADD VALUE

Adding value sounds simple, but this is perhaps the most nuanced and important of the five principles we're going to cover. Understanding what adds value means removing our brand-centric lenses and looking critically at what we're making. That's not an easy thing to do when our working lives revolve around forming those branded lenses. We have to ask ourselves these questions: If we weren't in any way invested in the brand for which we're creating content, and this piece of content crossed our social feeds, would we care? Would we stop scrolling? Would we click the share button? Why? Adding value means giving people something with which they have a reason to interact or pass along.

Adding value may seem relatively straightforward, but exactly what is meant by "value" can vary significantly among categories, brands, target audiences, and social networks themselves. Value can mean giving people a useful tool—an infographic with real, applicable information or ideas for new ways of using a product. Value can mean providing something badgeworthy for people to wear in front of their friends—something that helps individuals define themselves in social spaces. Value can mean lighthearted, uplifting, or just plain funny content that makes our audiences laugh enough to want to share that laugh with their friends. Value can even mean creating a shared emotional connection between people. If a brand consistently adds value with each and every post it places in the feeds of its prospective fans, it will continue to build engagement and organic reach. But if adding value were easy, we'd all have massive, engaged fan bases.

We can conceptualize adding value as two perpendicular axes—one axis ranging from "bookmarkable" to "badgeworthy" and another from "commiserative" to "aspirational" (Figure 3.1). Bookmarkable content leverages the chaos of the social feed to its advantage. When we stumble across content we don't want to forget, we often bookmark it to avoid losing it. What and how content shows up in our feeds can be totally unpredictable—we've all had that frustrating moment where we scroll back to find a post that's somehow disappeared. This bookmarking behavior ranges from people clicking the share button on Facebook posts they want to save for later to Redditors commenting on threads to remind themselves of particular content or conversations.

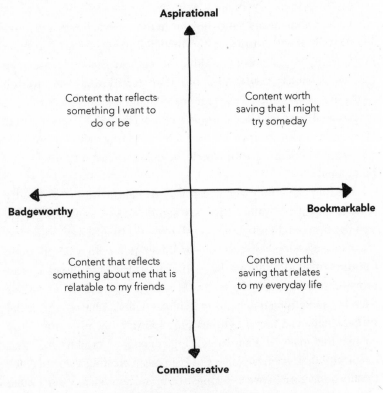

FIGURE 3.1 **Adding Value**

Opposite bookmarkable content on this axis is badgeworthy content. Badgeworthy content allows users to communicate about themselves to their friend groups. Not every brand can create badgeworthy content, but it's not as exclusive a category as it may first seem. In order to find what's badgeworthy about a brand, we need to understand what that brand symbolizes for the people we want to share it. Cleaning products can stand for orderly homes. Shoe brands can symbolize our inner athletes. How we dress, the alcohol we drink (or don't drink), even the brand of water bottle we buy tells the world something about us. Badgeworthy content seeks to harness that expression, and it must be grounded in a realistic evaluation of our brands in the eyes of consumers.

On the intersecting axis, we move from commiserative content to aspirational content. Commiserative content is so relatable or true to us that we use that content to connect with our friends. Share-driving commiserative content is particularly powerful because it places the brand at the point of connection between people. Tongue-in-cheek and lightly self-deprecating humor is extremely effective as commiserative content. The problem with commiserative content is that it requires brands to take risks. As marketers, we're generally trained to stay positive 100 percent of the time, and creating content with which our audience can actually commiserate sometimes requires us to dip down to, say, 60 to 70 percent positivity. That's just a ballpark.

Aspirational content is where we're generally much more comfortable. This is content that helps us represent our ideals, goals, and . . . well . . . our aspirations. Idyllic scenery, lofty ideas, heartfelt values, and inspirational stories are examples of aspirational content.

Each quadrant of this model is equally viable for conceptualizing share-driving content, and exactly which quadrant—or quadrants— any particular brand should use is largely dependent on the brand itself. Higher-end brands, luxury brands, and brands that lean into beautiful photography, use models in their content, or are simply highly desirable to potential customers will likely tend toward the aspirational side of content. Brands that seek to de-position overly serious brands—those that solve relatable problems or have more relatable personalities—try not to take themselves too seriously. They grab attention through wacky or offbeat humor, and they will generally succeed on the commiserative side of the spectrum.

We wouldn't expect Bud Light to use high-fashion outfits on super-models to advertise their new Bud Light cans because the brand is so well known for highly relatable, almost slapstick humor. Similarly, a self-deprecating meme posted by Louis Vuitton will probably feel out of place and tone-deaf because the brand is usually so serious and aspirational. This isn't to say that Louis Vuitton can't use humor, and in subtle ways, the brand actually does. In its spring 2019 campaign that debuted new accessories developed by acclaimed streetwear designer Virgil Abloh, otherwise highly aspirational montages of new pieces were interspersed with candid-feeling moments.[2] One video featured a model dressed in business casual removing his jacket with true model aplomb, tossing his jacket at the camera, accidentally overshooting, and laughing as he realizes his mistake. The overall piece remained aspirational, but the subtle nod to commiseration with the audience made the piece more relatable. For established brands on the far side of the commiserative or aspirational ends of the spectrum, subtle nods to the opposite end of the spectrum often surprise and engage audiences in new ways.

In the scope of bookmarkable to badgeworthy, content becomes more flexible as brands can move through this spectrum more easily while maintaining consistency of personality. Brands that tend toward more badgeworthy content are likely more established—or sit within an established category—because in order to be badgeworthy, people need to wear the content publicly. Clicking share on the aforementioned Louis Vuitton video on Facebook is an example of a badgeworthy piece of content. It represents to their friend connections the sharers' taste in fashion. Louis Vuitton outfits aren't always simply badgeworthy though. Reddit communities like r/MaleFashionAdvice, a community in which men share fashion tips and inspiration, often assemble what are called *lookbooks*, which are collections of photography and illustrations of inspirational fashion. When a Louis Vuitton outfit is shared in a user-created lookbook, that content is used as a reference for assembling new outfits, styling new accessories, or even inspiring poses for photographs. In this context, a Louis Vuitton outfit is more bookmarkable than badgeworthy because it has tangible use as a resource.

Bookmarkable content is particularly well suited to new and contender brands, but it can be broadly leveraged. Content that is bookmarkable can be used to highlight unique differentiators—guides to which ingredients competitors use compared to what our brand uses, which fabrics are best for which types of conditions, how to use (or hack) features of certain products, how to create or improve upon recipes, and so on. This informational strata of content is totally underutilized by most social marketers because we've been taught to cut our messages down into bite-sized pieces. But when we evaluate what types of organic content drive the most sharing, bookmarkable content performs extremely well. Bookmarkable content has the added benefit of lending authenticity and transparency to the brand message, provided that the information is accurate, because it seeks to clarify something.

When a significant portion of the value presented by a brand is the brand itself—like a clothing brand that differentiates by its logo or a drink that serves as an accessory—badgeworthy content is generally a good fit. When a brand faces challenges of complexity for users—like home improvement brands, website hosting platforms, or pest control brands—the demystifying power of bookmarkable content not only helps drive sharing but contributes to the brand image as a simplifier of complex information.

When content is worth bookmarking, it's something our audience wants to save for later use. A life hack is a perfect example of content that is both bookmarkable and commiserative. A life hack is when we take a familiar object and demonstrate a new way of using it—like turning a muffin tin upside down and baking tortillas on it to create taco salad bowls. Life hacks bring a bit of novelty into the world of the familiar. They're commiserative particularly when they solve simple or annoying problems we all face and rarely talk about. Content that's generally useful in our everyday lives fits squarely into this quadrant of the model.

Bookmarkable content can also become aspirational when it moves from the world of the familiar to the world of desire. Aspirational content and bookmarkable content intersect in beautiful DIY projects that we know we'll never *actually* make but seem compelling nonetheless. Who knows, maybe one day I'll actually get around to making that wine cork bath mat. Intricate recipes, beautiful home decor, art and music, behind-the-scenes footage, guides for flashy car modifications, and makeup tutorials are all examples of aspirational, bookmarkable content for different audiences.

Content moves toward badgeworthiness when it contains social value for our audience. Badgeworthy content is content that our audience will wear in front of their network connections. What makes content badgeworthy varies significantly among different kinds of social networks and among different demographics and psychographics—what's badgeworthy on Instagram might be totally different than what's badgeworthy on Twitter, and the content we share on Facebook may be completely different from what we share on LinkedIn. Badgeworthiness also relies heavily on brand perception. When we have the perception of being a bargain brand, we probably won't succeed with aspirational badgeworthy content. But commiserative badgeworthy content is probably fruitful ground for us. Everyone loves to play the contrarian in social media, even if it means pretending to enjoy eating Taco Bell (don't @ me). Similarly, if we're perceived to be a highly polished, upscale brand, it's unlikely that low-polish commiserative content will be badgeworthy to audiences who already know us.

When badgeworthy content is commiserative, it's generally funny and relatable. The r/ReactionGifs community on Reddit is an engine for commiserative, badgeworthy content—particularly for people in anonymous space, but not exclusively. Content from r/ReactionGifs and other Internet meme hubs tends to spread to Twitter and Instagram regularly enough for Redditors to comment on the phenomenon. Usually, this humor is self-deprecating, hyperbolic, and relatable to a broad audience. Fast-food brands like Wendy's and Burger King tend to thrive on commiserative, badgeworthy content.

Wendy's is celebrated by meme culture as part of the club because the brand has so successfully integrated itself into a variety of trends in ways that actually add to the conversation rather than hijacking it. When an Internet meme dubbed "Slaps roof of car" became popular, Wendy's was late to the game, but it still managed to drive 11,000+ retweets and 61,000+ *likes*.[3] The essential Internet meme featured a used-car salesman talking to a potential buyer, and in a voice you can almost hear as you read it, it says, "This baby can fit so much [blank] in it," where "[blank]" was filled by various memes and jokes. Perhaps the original to follow this format featured the car salesman saying, "This baby can fit so much f***in spaghetti in it," a reference to another Internet meme that likens social ineptitude to "having spaghetti in your pocket."[4] Originally coined on 4chan, when a person tells a story of having made a grave social misstep, the mistake may be described as "spaghetti falling out of my pockets." Look, I didn't come up with this stuff. I'm just telling you what it means.

When Wendy's caught on to the car salesman Internet meme and after a wave of popular versions had already come and gone, it created a new one with the Wendy's logo covering the car salesman's face. Wendy's recaptioned it with, "This bad boy can fit so much [dead memes] in it." It's a perfect execution of a *meta-joke*—a meme about the meme—and to cap it off, its tweet copy accompanying the image read "Buy our cheeseburgers." It was a deadpan, self-deprecating joke about its own Twitter activity, as if to say, "Sure, we're part of meme culture, but we're just in it to sell you cheeseburgers." As counterintuitive as it may seem, the Internet appreciates this radical, relatable, somewhat self-deprecating transparency. Generally, when brands lean into Internet meme culture, it's in this quadrant of the model. Succeeding in developing badgeworthy and commiserative content usually requires that we not take our brands too seriously—that we're willing to poke some fun at ourselves.

Ever see those cheesy photos of sunsets superimposed with inspirational quotes that look like something out of an Orlando tourist shop? Those posts your Aunt Merril can't help but share every day on Facebook or that your mom constantly *likes* on Instagram "because they have a good message"? That's badgeworthy content on the aspirational side of the spectrum. It's content we wear not so much in an effort to relate to other social connections but to define our ideal selves to the world. Content often goes too far toward the aspirational side of the spectrum, and that's when we're inspiring more eye rolls than ideal selves. People and brands on nearly every social channel have managed to develop massive followings thanks to aspirational, badgeworthy content. In general, influencer integrations tend toward this space in the model. Quotes from our sports heroes, posts made by professional gamers we follow, outfits we wish we could wear, and events we wish we could attend are examples of aspirational, badgeworthy territory. When we see content that reflects who we want to be—or, more accurately, who we want our friends to think we want to be— we're engaging content that's aspirational and badgeworthy.

To understand what kinds of content are valuable to different audiences, it's helpful to return to the world of organic content once again. Do popular interest-based groups exist about the type of content we're creating? What kinds of content are popular within those communities? How do influencers in that space make content? What are their comment sections like? And if those influencers and communities don't exist, where else might similar content exist? If we're completely unable to find popular content similar to what's being produced for our brands, there's a small chance we've stumbled across a massive opportunity to create an entirely new category of content. But what's much more likely is that the type of content we're thinking about exists and just isn't successful at propagating.

2. DESIGN MEME MACHINES TO REINFORCE THE VALUE OF THE MEME

A common criticism leveled against journalists is that they've written a brilliant article but "buried the lede." Modern journalists face a similar problem to brands in the ultracompetitive content landscape that characterizes social networks. The raw and unpolished "17 Unexpected Foods That Can Kill You (You won't believe #3!)" listicle style often attributed to Buzzfeed is the journalistic equivalent to our observation of Internet meme cultures as brands. And as much as we like to criticize this content we derogatorily label "clickbait," we can't deny its effectiveness at grabbing attention. The format of an article is relatively fixed—it's introduced by a headline and it exists as a web page that is usually separate from the social networks in which it can circulate. Branded content is much more open-ended and diverse in terms of format, but we similarly need to avoid burying our ledes. As brands, we're generally pretty good at finding our hook, but we're often too rigid in the way our hook manifests in our content. The meme machine we choose to carry our brand's memes should help us emphasize our attention-grabbing point of interest.

Tactical as this may seem, one of the most common mistakes in developing branded content is treating the text field of a post as a headline. Imagine we're a food brand sharing a new recipe. The natural inclination for most brands is to shoot highly polished food photography, upload the edited photography to a post, and use the social platform's text field to title the recipe or link to an article about the recipe. When we're evaluating the content in isolation, this approach makes sense. Similar to the way influencers developed the Internet meme style of video optimized toward Facebook's prioritization of video content, adding text or explanation on top of our images and videos can feel redundant when a social network provides an obvious text field. But from the perspective of a user, content that fully contains the valuable information and prioritizes the most compelling memes is much easier to pass along.

When users click the share button on Facebook, for example, they're prompted to write their own text. Simply in terms of visual format, this new text takes priority over the original poster's text, which often falls to the bottom of the post or disappears altogether. This allows people to take a piece of content and make it their own, which is exactly what we want to happen with our branded content if we're interested in engagement. If we're relying on a social network's text field to carry important information about our content—like how to create our hypothetical recipe—it's easy for that information to get lost over generations of sharing. This isn't to say that what we write in a platform's text field isn't important. We just need to reframe how we're thinking about it.

Whatever we upload to a social network—usually an image or a video—is the content. What we write in the social platform's text field is what we're saying *about* that content. A headline, instructions for how to make something, context required to understand a joke or reference, or any other information that is vital to unlocking the value of a post should be present within the content itself. The way we design the content and the formats we use should reinforce the value we're offering. To optimize content toward sharing, that content should be fully encapsulated (Figure 3.2). One way to test whether or not a piece of content fully contains the value being offered is to look at the content itself without social copy attached to it. Does the content make

Incomplete Meme Machine
This post doesn't contain the content's actual value. It requires additional clicks to find the recipe.

Complete Meme Machine
This post demonstrates the content's value directly within a social feed. It is complete because its value is fully contained within the post.

FIGURE 3.2 **Meme Machines**

sense on its own? Can we understand what's being communicated? If someone clicked the share button on this and wrote their own copy in the social platform's text field, would the memes contained within the content remain intact?

There is a delicate balance to strike when it comes to creating fully encapsulated content. While most branded content leans heavily toward content that's visually appealing but lacking in depth, it's certainly possible for content to include too much information and to become crowded and unappealing. It's helpful to conceptualize a visual hierarchy to ensure that content remains appealing but still contains enough context for it to remain independently valuable. At the top of the hierarchy is whatever we think will grab people's attention. Is it the title of the recipe? Is it a visual of the finished product? Is it an image of the ingredients? The second rung on the hierarchy is delivering on that attention grab. The attention grab is a promise, and once we have that attention, we need to fulfill our end of the bargain. What makes the recipe warrant the flashy title? How did we get to the finished product? What will these ingredients do when they're put together?

One helpful way to find this balance of visual appeal and valuable information is to look at organic examples of content that's communicating similar types of memes. With food content, we might look to platforms like Pinterest, where we find that the most successful food bloggers often create visual step-by-steps or even simple recipe cards that merge food photography with recipe instructions. Often, this content is reinforced by longer-form website content that explains details and nuances, which is how these content creators balance lightness and shareability with depth of information. If all the basic information needed to make a recipe, put together an outfit, or laugh at a joke is contained within something simple like an image, that image can be shared, saved, and screenshotted without degrading the memes embedded in it.

While working at a large creative agency, I separated hundreds of social posts from dozens of brands into two categories: encapsulated content and content that required additional context. Much to the dismay of my creative teams, who abhorred the way text polluted their beautiful imagery, when all information was included within the content of a post, it led to 11× more engagement, 35× more earned reach, and 46× more content sharing. Something as simple as tweaking the meme machine to include more information can have profound effects on the performance of social content. Particularly when we're confident that an idea has major potential for driving pass-along, it's worth testing a variety of meme machines to find the right balance of lightness, efficiency, depth, and branding.

3. CREATE SPACE FOR PERSONAL CONNECTION THROUGH NARRATIVE ELEMENTS

There's no denying the power of storytelling, and it's hardly a new concept for advertisers. When information is presented in the form of a story, we remember it better. Some psychologists theorize that we've evolved psychological structures alongside the human tradition of storytelling—that our genes and memes intermingled over the course of our evolutionary history. Storytelling has a demonstrable effect on the appeal and retention of information. In fact, one study conducted by Wharton marketing professor Deborah Small found that when it comes to charitable donations, the kinds of stories charities tell have a dramatic effect on donations.[5] In a series of experiments, researchers gave participants $5 in five $1 bills. Participants were then presented with written charity requests and asked to allocate their $5 to the charities they felt were most deserving. Despite researchers explicitly encouraging participants to think rationally about their decisions, people consistently donated more to charities that told stories about individual people than to those that provided higher-level insight and statistical rationale for how donations would affect large groups of people.

When we hear a story about how young Macy can't afford her books for school, we're likely to donate more money than if we hear about Macy and her little brother, or Macy's cousins, parents, community, city, and country. The term for this phenomenon in academia is the *identifiable victim*. Personal stories tend to generate more empathy in us than statistical ones. It's not always easy for brands—particularly large ones—to find equivalent personal stories that feel authentic and relevant to their messages. But there is still an important lesson here.

Social media presents us with a unique problem when it comes to storytelling. On TV and in print, sequential storytelling is feasible because we generally control the order in which people see our content. In social media, most of our feeds are so personalized to us as individuals that it's extremely difficult to tell sequential stories. In general, we should strive for our content to be more episodic—accessible and valuable in whatever order our audience encounters it. We also face the problem of extremely short windows of attention, which makes storytelling particularly difficult.

Most of the time, we don't have the space to tell long, full stories in social media. However, we can still borrow narrative elements that render our content more memorable. Subtle nods to narrative can make all the difference in driving engagement and content sharing. When we're telling people about a fun new do-it-yourself (DIY) project, showing people an intriguing finished product is an important part of the narrative. An appealing finished product tells the triumphant end to the process of assembly. But we can build an even more compelling narrative by showing the steps toward achieving that final product. By showcasing different steps toward the goal, we allow people to visualize themselves actually using the information.

In a how-to, we want to make something that seems complex feel simple. Or we want to make something that seems simple deliver something that feels complex. If we're working with influencers, we want to highlight the content they produce for us, and we likely want them to popularize our partnership with their fans directly. Providing insight into *why* we decided to work with those influencers and what about their story aligns with our brand ethos, and giving glimpses of the personalities behind the scenes are all ways we can strengthen that narrative. Behind-the-scenes content makes our polished content feel more authentic and human, particularly when it provides genuine insight into the process—bloopers, mistakes, conversations. Narratives humanize our content in powerful ways.

Even details as simple as the title of our projects or the adjectives we use to describe our content can provide subtle narrative elements. When you search for a recipe on Google, say, a chili recipe, have you ever noticed that the results are rarely what you'd find on a restaurant menu? We don't see "Beef Chili" or "Soup of the Day—Turkey Chili." We see top results like "Simple, Perfect Chili Recipe," "The Best Chili Recipe," and "My Chili Recipe." For the record, those actually are the top three results for me when searching for "chili recipe." Adjectives like "simple" and "perfect" tell us that the process of making the recipe won't be too difficult but that the end product is worth pursuing. Superlatives like "best" are also powerful motivators for exploring—no need to analyze too deeply the fact that there are 481,000,000 results for the search "best chili recipe." And having "my" before "chili recipe" is an obvious way of adding personalization. We probably wouldn't use "my" as a descriptor of branded content, but if we'd worked with a blogger to develop a chili recipe, titling our post "[Blogger]'s Secret Family Chili Recipe" would make the content inherently more memorable and interesting.

Subtle nods to narrative go a long way with short-form content in competitive environments. One of the brands whose content I managed was invited to participate in Pinterest's Alpha advertising launch and quickly became a top performer on the platform, thanks to beautifully shot food-related content. In an analysis of the brand's top-performing posts, nearly 60 percent of the most engaging Pins were those that showed process steps. As much as we love our polished, edited, simple photography, showcasing useful, sometimes messy steps to finished products or behind-the-scenes fun brings people closer to the content. Finding ways to humanize our content, to make it feel less produced and processed, gets people invested in the content because they're allowed to be part of its creation.

4. DEVELOP CONTENT FOR A SPECIFIC OBJECTIVE OR ACTION

As much as we like to imagine that our minds are cutting-edge evolutionary technology, our more complex brain structures are built on foundational structures millions of years old. One such relic is deemed the "crocodile" or "reptilian brain" because it so closely resembles the brains of modern crocodiles.[6] This reptilian brain has an extremely fast response time—it's the first system to kick in when we're encountering something new. As prey animals, fast responses to new and surprising experiences were vital to our survival. The reptilian brain makes snap judgments when we encounter new things: Do we want to eat it? Run from it? Kill it? Obviously, we wouldn't want to *mate* with it . . . unless?

This reptilian brain doesn't just kick in for life-or-death situations. It's the first set of processes through which everything we experience is filtered. When we sense that something is attractive, we gravitate toward it. When something appeals to our reptilian brain, it unlocks higher-level thought processes and allows us to explore it more deeply with the social and logic centers of our brains. Likewise, if something feels threatening to the reptilian brain, we run from it. If you've ever exported a Facebook analytics report to see the dozens of tabs and hundreds of data points available to you in spreadsheets, you probably felt a need to run away from it as fast as possible. Unless you're a data scientist or just have a knack for navigating massive amounts of data, raw social media analytics can be completely overwhelming and confusing to navigate. To which data points should we pay attention?

Which can we ignore? What are "engaged users" compared to "users talking about this"? How is the engagement rate calculated? What constitutes a "view"? Do I have any new text messages? What's that notification from Twitter?

One way we can appeal to the reptile brain and avoid getting filtered out is to make things simple for our audience. When we create content, we should have a particular goal in mind, and we should make it as simple as possible for our audience to act in accordance with that goal. Often, we just want engagement—*likes*, shares, and so on. Sometimes, we want people to watch a video or click on an article. Keeping particular actions in mind during the development process simplifies the consumption process. And as we develop content with particular actions in mind, we ought to measure how well that content is accomplishing the goal.

The wealth of data we receive from major social platforms is extremely valuable when used correctly, but often, social creative teams lack the skill sets and resources necessary to extract that value. This problem is compounded by the relatively opaque "simple" versions of analytics provided to us by social platforms' dashboards, which typically lack any actionable insights. In order to make any real use of the data provided to us, we need to isolate a few key measures of success. Once we identify what exactly success means for different kinds of content, we have a much clearer path to measuring it.

Choosing key performance indicators (KPIs) is generally straightforward. What do we want a post to do? It's important to match appropriate KPIs to different kinds of content, rather than simply measuring everything against the canned "engagement rate" metric provided by most social platforms. For most of my teams, we separated three to five KPIs geared toward different kinds of posts. When we posted content intended to drive engagement, we used the alternate engagement rate mentioned in Chapter 2, which we called our "true engagement rate" because it only measured actions that contributed to earned reach. For video content, we looked primarily at viewing metrics and used the same "true engagement" metric as a secondary KPI. For posts meant to popularize deals or offers intended to drive online sales or conversions, we looked to click-through rate (CTR) as a directional success metric. For further down-funnel objectives, most established advertisers have much more robust measurement systems in place than simple CTR metrics, but unless those systems are deeply integrated into our social optimization process, these deeper reports are usually slower than the ones we can see in social media analytics. Likewise, engagement-driven content is often measured by third-party studies to understand effects on brand favorability, affinity, relevance, and so on. These studies are important parts of our broader learning agendas as brands, but they're too slow to help us determine which of our five posts this week we should amplify with paid media.

The KPIs we choose don't have to be perfect. They just need to align our strategy, creative, and community management teams around what success looks like. By isolating one or two key metrics for specific kinds of content, we clarify success for everyone, and we enable deeper learning in our content cycles. Too often, social media creative conversations presume certain goals without stating them explicitly. We generally talk about how much "engagement" posts get without really defining what we mean. Are certain actions more valuable to us than others? If we had to pick one metric in which we'd like to succeed, which would it be? This process may feel totally redundant and obvious, but building these goals into the social creative process and measuring that creative accordingly will lead to more frequent and deeper lightbulb moments for everyone involved.

Key performance indicators corresponding to different types of content should be built directly into a brand's social strategy—the framework in which we do creative work. When reviewing social creative, the type of post and its KPI should be explicitly stated. Is the post meant to drive engagement? Sharing? Clicks to a website? Conversation? Downloads? Views? Not only does this help guide everyone's feedback, it allows us to evaluate content against those goals. Did our post intended to drive sharing succeed in overall engagement but fail at driving pass-along? What kind of engagement did it generate? Which posts actually did succeed in driving pass-along? And if we compare them side by side, what differences do we notice?

Building this analytical thinking into the social creative process is foreign to most traditional ad creatives, but it's a unique benefit only social networks offer. Analytical reviews can be fun too. Traditional advertising has trained creative teams to look toward industry awards rather than actual performance, but when a social post succeeds in surpassing a KPI, it's worth celebrating! The same dopamine rush we receive when our personal posts get *likes* can be applied to the creative process for brands. And when we celebrate those wins, we naturally start to look for what was responsible for driving that success. Create rewards for teams that exceed expectations, get loud when celebrating wins, and try to improve with each content development cycle by analyzing what drove success in the last batch of content.

5. MAINTAIN BRAND CONSISTENCY AND OWNABILITY

Steve Buscemi strolls down the hallway of a high school dressed in a backward cap and band T-shirt with a skateboard slung over his shoulder. He approaches a group of students and asks, "How do you do, fellow kids?" I couldn't get the rights to include a photo of Steve Buscemi here, but if you're not familiar with him, he's perhaps the least teenager-y looking celebrity on the planet. This four-second scene from the show *30 Rock* was deemed by Reddit to be the perfect metaphor for brands participating in social media. An extremely active community on Reddit called r/FellowKids chronicles brands trying desperately to fit into the world of social media.

A traditional r/FellowKids moment is when your bank tweets an update using emojis and hashtags. Or when your neighborhood restaurant puts up a sign with "LOL" and "OMG" written on it. The r/FellowKids community collects evidence of brands having lost their voice in pursuit of engaging young audiences. But r/FellowKids posts aren't all bad—when brands get Internet meme culture really right, they may well find themselves at the top of r/FellowKids. It would be misleading not to mention Wendy's here again because the community regularly celebrates the brand's posts. Wendy's has a knack for being so embedded in Internet culture that its content borders on meta-humor—jokes *about* the Internet's inside jokes.

Perhaps one of the more unexpected brands to show up positively on r/FellowKids is Brita. Yes, the brand of water pitcher you used in college to try to filter vodka because your friend said it would remove the taste. No? Just me? Anyway, Brita created a series of Reddit ads inspired by an Internet meme called "starterpacks." A starterpack is a collection of stock photos, low-resolution Google image results, and/or simple phrases that capture the stereotype of a person or situation. A starterpack for "Every cheap Italian restaurant" features images of a statue of a chubby Italian chef, red-and-white checkered tablecloths, a thin wicker basket full of garlic bread on top of thin wax paper, a red pepper flake shaker, and a parmesan cheese shaker.[7] Brita created a series of starterpacks including the "I'm trying to save money now starterpack,"which featured a person looking miserably at a kitchen stove, an outdated cell phone, a beat up car, a job search with a salary estimate of "a lot" per year, and of course, a Brita pitcher.[8] The headline read, " 'I'm trying to save money now' starterpack from your friends at Brita (r/FellowKids, here we come!)"

Inevitably, the r/FellowKids community screenshotted and discussed the ads, and the community seemed genuinely surprised that Brita even knew about them—"Shit, they've found us," "They're becoming self-aware." Brita wasn't finished, however, and after the initial wave of discussion in the r/FellowKids community, Brita created a new ad on Reddit. But it wasn't another starterpack. Brita collected over 100 screenshots of Redditors' posts in r/FellowKids, put them in an album, and wrote, "Wow. Reddit! 100+ posts in r/Fellowkids and counting, we're flattered. Remember to fill up your Brita, all that salt must be making you thirsty!"[9] This combination of inserting authentically into Internet meme culture, using a slightly self-deprecating tone, and being unfazed by some mildly salty organic posts netted a huge amount of unexpectedly positive attention from one of the most critical communities on Reddit when it comes to branded content.

Not every brand can—or should—try to integrate into Internet meme culture. But as we've explored, every brand can learn lessons in content formatting from what organically becomes popular online. The counterbalance to leveraging popular meme machines is that the finished content needs to be ownable for the brand. Making a popular post on a social network is great, but it's only worthwhile from a marketing perspective if it's attributable to the brand. Our social content should strive to be as engaging as possible within the framework of our broader brand positioning and strategy.

There are simple ways for us to ensure that content remains traceable back to our brands: using consistent brand fonts, staying true to our brand voice, including relatively subtle logos within our content, and ensuring that whatever content we post is actually relevant to our brand. We should ensure that the content itself is fully encapsulated, and that includes attribution to our brand. Our branding should be embedded in the meme machine itself.

KEY TAKEAWAYS

- Content that adds value to users' experience will consistently drive engagement and pass-along.

- The meme machines we use to embody our brand message should aim to deliver their messages as efficiently and frictionlessly as possible.

- Embedding subtle narrative elements in content makes it more memorable and relatable.

- Create content with a particular desired action in mind, and maintain focus on that goal throughout the creative development process.

- Balance optimization toward engagement with a consistent brand perspective to allow innovation while maintaining a strategic foundation.

PART II

SOCIAL MEDIA
AND ITS
DISCONTENTS

WEARING OUR MEMES

The Ideal Self, Managed Self, and True Self

I n 2014, a Dutch graphic design student named Zilla van den Born took a five-week vacation to Southeast Asia.[1] As millennials often did in 2014, Born chronicled her vacation on her Facebook profile. She posted what's become standard issue vacation content—photos of exotic-looking foods, the fancy entrance to her hotel, a photo of herself sitting next to a monk in a Buddhist temple, and an action shot snorkeling with tropical fish. It looked like the kind of vacation to which any college-aged student aspires—a foreign country, new experiences, idyllic photos, and the social capital that follows from posting about each of those. After her vacation was over, Born shared something shocking. She never actually left town.

Her meals were shot in local Thai restaurants. She decorated her bedroom to look like a hotel entrance using some sheets and Christmas lights. The Buddhist temple was actually in Amsterdam where she lived. She snorkeled in the pool at her apartment complex and added some tropical-looking fish to the background—really putting that graphic design degree to use. Born's misadventure caught international attention, and when asked why she went to the trouble of faking a vacation, she said, "I did this to show people that we filter and manipulate what we show on social media and that we create an online world which reality can no longer meet. My goal was to prove how common and easy it is to distort reality. But we often overlook the fact that we manipulate reality also in our own lives."

There is a popular notion that social media brings out the braggarts within each of us—that we're seizing the opportunity to mislead our family, friends, and followers into thinking our lives are better than they are. That's an awfully sinister outlook on humanity, and I don't think it's quite so insidious, even if social media does distort reality. Social networks are structured to give us room to express ourselves in various ways. For many social networks, that means we create a profile that corresponds with our real-life identities—we use our real names, we share actual photos of ourselves and our lives, and we connect with people we know.

When we're presented with such a structure, it's natural that what we gravitate toward posting are highlights of our lives. In lieu of the physical characteristics that define us in our offline lives, we have only the memes we share to define ourselves. The memes we wear in social networks—the things we say, the content we post, the videos we share—are akin to digital clothing. We may not always make an extremely intentional, conscious choice about them, but our memes define us to our social groups. The social media profiles in which we're unabashedly our offline selves act as catalogs of our lives, so it's natural that we curate positive moments, meaningful memories, and other pieces of content and culture that we want to define us.

Even if this highlight reel effect isn't intentional on our parts, there are real psychological consequences to seeing the world through such a filter. Many psychologists believe there is a demonstrable, causal link between heavy social media usage and anxiety and depression.[2] While that may strike us as overly alarmist, it's worth noting that social media is brand new in the human timeline. Evolutionary biologists estimate that modern humans have been around for 260,000 to 350,000 years.[3] Social media has existed for about 20. If the entirety of human existence were a movie, social media would get about half a second of screen time. Our brains—and the mechanisms we evolved to interact socially—are not accustomed to this new phenomenon.

The Internet is overwhelming for the social parts of our brains. For most of human existence, we lived in tribes of 100 to 250 people, and correspondingly, anthropologists estimate that the average number of "stable relationships" we can maintain is about 150—often referred to as Dunbar's number.[4] In studying different primates' social lives, anthropologist Robin Dunbar discovered a correlation between the brain size of a primate and the average size of that primate's social groups—spoiler, humans have the biggest primate brains and maintain the highest number of stable relationships. This isn't to say that the average person can only remember 150 people. As Dunbar put it, this is "the number of people you would not feel embarrassed about joining uninvited for a drink if you happened to bump into them at a bar." If that's really the definition of a stable relationship, my number is more like 2, and one of those is my cat (love you, Matilda).

Compare Dunbar's number to the average Facebook profile in 2016, which had 155 friend connections.[5] The average social media user in 2018 also maintained eight different social media profiles across different sites.[6] It's not hard to see that we're stretching our social cognitive ability far beyond its limits. We have many more "friends" than we have friends. Particularly when we're using a social platform in which we're identified by our driver's license name, we're doing the evolutionary equivalent of peeking through our window at our neighbors. At least, that's how our brains are wired to think. We get glimpses into the lives of our connections, and thanks to the aforementioned tendency for us to use these channels to curate highlights, we find ourselves in a difficult conundrum.

Consciously or not, when we're evaluating ourselves in social media, we're comparing our complex lives full of ups, downs, and in-betweens to other people's highlight reels. Evolutionarily, we're trained to evaluate ourselves against our neighbors because we may learn useful information that way. If our neighbor is much more successful at growing crops than we are, it's useful for us to peek over to see what he or she is doing differently. Or, more accurately in evolutionary terms, the people who peeked over to see how their neighbors were growing crops were more likely to survive than those who didn't.

People with more social awareness are better in tune with their groups, and humans' tendency toward sociability is credited as an important trait for giving us competitive advantage over predators and other primates. Our close evolutionary relatives, the Neanderthals, were stronger than humans, evolved tools earlier than humans, and had larger brains than humans. But a prevailing theory of why the Neanderthals went extinct about 40,000 years ago revolves around the human capacity for sociability and coordination. Some researchers even suggest that human domestication of wolves—arguably an aspect of interspecial sociability—also played an important role in giving them the edge over Neanderthals.[7] We're acutely aware of our broader communities and how we fit into them—it's a fundamental part of how we think.

So when social media gives us this new window into the lives of our neighbors, and those neighbors exclusively post their life highlights, it's easy for us to conclude that we're less successful, less attractive, less happy, and so on. Ironically, being constantly exposed to these highlights has demonstrably negative effects on our mental health. Depression in young people has risen by as much as 70 percent in the past 25 years according to a recent study in the United Kingdom, and some researchers point to social media as the cause.[8, 9] The same study showed that 63 percent of Instagram users reported feeling miserable after using the platform, higher than any other social media site.[10] This study got something right that many social media studies don't—it stratified the effects of different social platforms.

There is a growing body of research about how social media affects mental health, but many of these studies lump every website or app with a feed into the category of "social media." How social media affects our brains is an extremely important territory for research, but nuanced differences in social network structures manifest significant differences in user behaviors and mindsets. In fact, one study conducted by the University of Utah showed that people with serious mental disorders—bipolar, schizophrenia, and depression—improved as they participated in Reddit communities about those topics.[11] By analyzing linguistic dimensions like positive emotion, negative emotion, and sadness, researchers observed that the language subjects used improved significantly in 9 out of 10 categories over a seven-year period. Depressed people who participated in the r/Depression community became less depressed.

How could a community full of depressed people spark such drastic improvements in positive emotion while social networks full of positivity and beauty like Instagram cause users to feel depressed? My theory is that the actual content in a social feed is only a small part of that equation. What's more important is the mindset of the people browsing that feed and their relationship to the memes with which they're interacting. While there is a wide range of variables that differentiates social platforms from one another, two are critical predictors of user mindset: one, how users are identified in a social network, and two, how they're connected to other people. These factors not only determine user mindset but dictate what types of memes resonate with them. In marketing, we tend to talk about how Facebook users are different from Twitter users who are different from LinkedIn users. But we often gloss over the fact that when we talk about a Facebook user, a Twitter user, and a LinkedIn user, we may very well be talking about the same human behind the screen. The differences between these spaces are psychological—they're not often separate populations of people. Most people on 4chan probably have Facebook accounts. They just act very differently on 4chan. Or most of them do, anyway.

IDENTITY AND SOCIAL CONNECTIONS SHAPE ONLINE MINDSETS

Simply by looking at these two variables of user identity and connection, we can create a model that accounts for the broad diversity of user mindsets and behaviors across the Internet. Let's start with online identity. The ways in which we're identified online tend toward one of two categories: either we identify as our offline selves, or we participate anonymously. If we're using our driver's license name, sharing photos of ourselves, and generally behaving in ways that feel—to us—to be consistent with how people know us offline, we're identifying as our offline selves.

Anonymity can be a little more complex because there are different ways in which we can be "anonymous." On 4chan, we're truly anonymous—we have no usernames or identifying information corresponding with our posts. In video games, online forums, and platforms like Reddit, we tend to participate pseudonymously—we create usernames that might be considered alternate personas for ourselves but that we tend to wear for extended periods of time. On platforms like Blind, an app that allows for "anonymous" discourse between people within particular companies or organizations, we again create usernames unrelated to our actual names, but we have an added layer of context that everyone with whom we're interacting is part of our organization. While anonymity does tend to stratify in nuanced different ways, anonymity offers a consistent value to users—freedom.

The second key factor for understanding how mindsets change between social networks is how people are connected to one another. On networks like Facebook and Snapchat, we're generally only connected to the people we know offline. On networks like Instagram and Twitter, we may have many of the same friend connections as we do on Facebook, but with a twist. We also have the ability to connect with a plethora of people we don't know through mechanisms like hashtags and content discovery. Finally, on networks like Reddit, we're not organized around our offline connections at all—rather, we're connected through shared interests, ideas, or passions.

These different ways in which we're connected to people can completely transform our behavior and can determine the types of memes that will resonate with us. The types of memes with which a person might engage in anonymous space may be completely different from the memes that might resonate with them in spaces in which they present their offline selves. As advertisers and communicators, we may be reaching the exact right people in the exact wrong place—or we may find that a little reframing of our message to suit these different spaces drives orders of magnitude better resonance.

IN FREUD'S MODEL, THE MIND IS COMPOSED OF THE ID, EGO, AND SUPEREGO

The intersection between these two fundamental elements of social network structure net a model that's likely to be strangely familiar to students of psychology. In his book *Civilization and Its Discontents*, Sigmund Freud, the father of psychoanalysis, proposed a model of the

mind often represented by an iceberg (Figure 4.1). Just as 90 percent of
an iceberg is submerged beneath the waterline, Freud contended that
90 percent of the workings of a person's mind is unconscious. Before
Freud, most people didn't believe there was such a thing as subcon-
scious thought. In what was then a radical idea, Freud proposed that
a single mind is actually composed of different, sometimes incompatible psychological forces. Freud called our mostly unconscious,
unfiltered, instinctual drives and desires our Ids. As social creatures
living in complex societies, we also internalize our learned cultural
rules, which becomes our conscience and resides in what Freud called
our Superegos. And to mediate between our instinctual desires, our
cultural ideals, and the limitations placed on us by the physical world,
we develop what Freud called our Egos.

While modern psychology isn't particularly kind to Freud, his
ideas changed the world and how we understood ourselves in it. Not

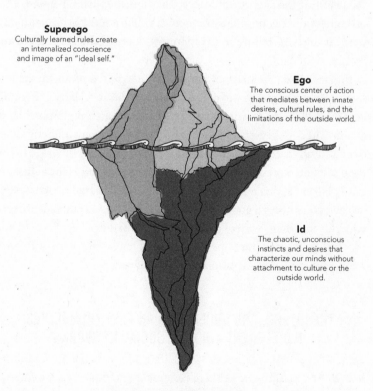

Superego
Culturally learned rules create
an internalized conscience
and image of an "ideal self."

Ego
The conscious center of action
that mediates between innate
desires, cultural rules, and the
limitations of the outside world.

Id
The chaotic, unconscious
instincts and desires that
characterize our minds without
attachment to culture or the
outside world.

FIGURE 4.1 **Freudian Iceberg**

only was the concept of an "unconscious mind" considered ludicrous prior to his writing, but Freud is also credited with pioneering therapy as a practice—"the talking cure," as he called it.[12] Freud was the first to coin the term "Ego," Latin for "I," which we now use to describe the self-conscious aspects of ourselves. In the words of evolutionary psychologist Dr. Jordan B. Peterson: "Freud established the field of psychoanalysis, and with it, rigorous investigation into the contents of the unconscious. Modern psychologists like to denigrate Freud, and I think there's a reason for that. Freud's fundamental insights were so valuable and so profound that they got immediately absorbed into our culture, and now they seem self-evident so all that's left of Freud are his errors."[13]

Freud's model remains unique in that unlike much of modern psychology and neuroanatomy, he intended to represent the mind rather than the brain. The components of Freud's model—the Id, Ego, and Superego—correspond to different phases of mental development and the resulting psychological forces. The Id is the instinct-based, chaotic, generally unconscious mind with which we're born. As infants, we exist solely as Id—we're driven by instincts and desires without any real sense of "self" as being separate from the world. The Ego forms as the desires of the Id meet the limitations placed on us by the real world. As we begin to form a sense of self that is clearly differentiated from the outside world, our Ego becomes our conscious center of action. The Superego is our final layer of development and embodies our culturally learned rules. Within the Superego exists a vision of our ideal self and our conscience. Our conscience measures the actions of our Ego against this embodiment of an ideal self, based on what we've learned constitutes a good person. When we fail to act in accordance with our ideal self, we feel guilt. The instinctual desires of our Id and the cultural rules in our Superego are often in conflict, with our Ego in a constant state of moderation between the two.

THE ID, EGO, AND SUPEREGO MANIFEST THEMSELVES IN DIFFERENT KINDS OF SOCIAL NETWORKS

We tend to occupy one of three essential personas when we interact online, and these personas correlate to this Freudian structure. Which type of persona we wear is closely related to the two factors of social network structure: how we're identified and how we're connected. When we engage as our offline selves and are connected exclusively to the people we know offline, as we do on Facebook and Snapchat, we're manifesting our Egos—managed versions of ourselves (Figure 4.2). We pay close attention to how we communicate about ourselves because anything we say or do has a one-to-one correspondence with how people will think about us offline. We engage with content and interests that we're comfortable wearing publicly for all of our friends to see, and for good reason. Most of us know that even so much as *liking* a post on Facebook has potential to create a story in our friends' feeds, so anything and everything we do in that space is on public display. We know that posting something controversial or offensive in a managed self network is akin to shouting it at a family reunion or at a bar with our friends.

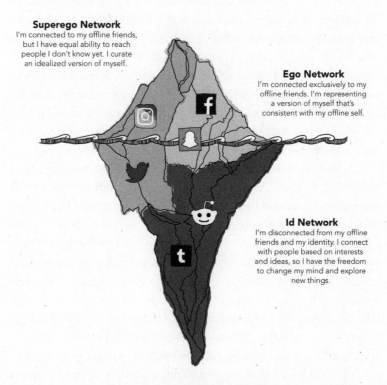

Superego Network
I'm connected to my offline friends, but I have equal ability to reach people I don't know yet. I curate an idealized version of myself.

Ego Network
I'm connected exclusively to my offline friends. I'm representing a version of myself that's consistent with my offline self.

Id Network
I'm disconnected from my offline friends and my identity. I connect with people based on interests and ideas, so I have the freedom to change my mind and explore new things.

FIGURE 4.2 **Social Media Iceberg**

We're also aware that our audiences—the friends with whom we're connected—have particular tastes, ideologies, opinions, and so on. We know which kinds of posts have generated positive feedback in the past and which haven't. We like *likes*. Ego networks also tend to curate feeds that are particular to us—nobody else in the world has the same feed as we do. We're in a mode of self-representation in Ego space, but instead of wearing our favorite bands' T-shirts, we *like* our favorite bands' posts. Instead of a political bumper sticker on our car, we share our candidates' fundraisers. We don't tell our network the story of our vacation. We post pictures and tag our friends. We're solidifying our identity online for the people we know offline.

On platforms like Twitter and Instagram, we're again likely to participate as our offline selves, but there is a significant mindset change that comes from being potentially exposed to millions of people we don't know. It's the difference between recording a silly selfie video you'd send to your friends and a video that might just get broadcast on national television. This is Superego, ideal self space, where we may have the exact same friend connections we did on Facebook, but where we're discoverable by the seemingly infinite number of people we don't know yet. In ideal self space, we filter our selves a little more, we try to be a little quippier, and we tend to curate particularly bright highlights. Our Facebook friends may well know that it rained for five out of six days on our trip to Hawaii, but that won't stop us from posting a glamorous beach photo on Instagram as our vacation recap.

Superego networks are often hierarchical. Social standing means everything. Follower counts, post engagements, trendy profile pictures, and influential retweets are primary markers for where we stand in the social hierarchy. In many Superego, ideal self networks, we don't even have friends—we have followers. These one-way relationships foster a different kind of emergent self-representation. Unlike Ego networks in which we're bound exclusively to the people who know us offline, in Superego space, we owe it to our followers to represent ourselves in ways that are compelling and interesting, even if that means embellishing at times. We're social mercenaries, following the people with whom we want to associate and hoping that those we don't will follow us anyway.

This isn't to say that every account on Twitter or Instagram is a manifestation of someone's ideal self. When we're dealing with such ultracomplex topics as personal identity, we're looking for general similarities among average users. Twitter and Instagram also host significant representations of meme culture, online trolling, interest-based conversations, and other trademarks of the anonymous web. This has to do with individual variability and site functionality. Technically, we *can* be anonymous on Facebook too, but because Facebook requires friend connections to make use of the vast majority of its functionality, anonymous Facebook users just don't have much to do. Anonymous Twitter and Instagram users, however, have plenty of room to join conversations, mobilize trends, stir up drama, and so on. We might even consider trolls on Twitter and Instagram more problematic than trolls in anonymous space because the playing field isn't exactly level. When 4chan users jab back and forth with offensive insults, both parties are anonymous and so have an equal stake in the outcome—very little, if they know what's good for them. Anonymous trolls on Twitter have an endless stream of opportunities to interact with people who have invested some or all of their identity in their handles.

While anonymity has certainly borne the brunt of much of the discourse about online safety, anonymous space can be extremely constructive and healthy for people. Without an offline self to represent, people are free to be expressive and candid. This unfiltered self is an embodiment of the Id. Id networks are those in which users are disconnected from their offline selves and are organized around their interests and passions rather than by their offline connections. Networks like Reddit, Tumblr, Imgur, Twitch, and even 4chan are examples of Id networks wherein people are more free to express themselves, explore new ideas and interests they're not ready to wear in the offline world (yet), and discover communities filled with people of similar interests.

On Id networks, we're looking for content that's funny, compelling, entertaining, or otherwise interesting *to us*—not representative versions of ourselves. We're able to discuss taboo topics without worrying about what our friends and relatives might think. We have the freedom to explore new hobbies and topics that pique our interest but that aren't necessarily things we'd use to represent ourselves to others. We're in a state referred to by some psychologists as *epistemic curiosity*—a pleasurable state of curiosity with anticipation for reward.[14] The "reward" we receive is when we learn something new or stumble across content that's entertaining and novel that we didn't necessarily expect.

Unlike Ego and Superego networks, Id networks tend to prioritize communal feeds over individual ones. On platforms like 4chan, there is no custom feed provided to individual users—individuals simply browse boards that serve the latest posts of fellow community members. Reddit provides users with a Home feed that is customized based on the communities of which a user is part. While that feed is customized to particular users, its contents are dependent on community voting, not individual profiles. Reddit's fundamental structure lies in its communities, which display the same content to all members.

These shared experiences generate a sense of community that truly differentiates Id networks from other social media platforms. Counterintuitive as it may seem, anonymous Reddit users feel deeply connected to one another and the platform they share in ways that users in identity-based networks usually don't. People on Reddit describe themselves as "Redditors" in a way that Facebook users never identify themselves as "Facebookers." This community sensibility enables constructive, nuanced conversations among people of very different perspectives, and because users are disconnected from their offline identities, they are generally more open-minded to new ideas and information. It's easier to change your mind when no one is looking.

For those unfamiliar with Reddit, it is truly a marvel of online community structure. Not only does the broader Reddit platform identify as a community, but Reddit can also be characterized as a network of individual communities called "subreddits," which fly under the Reddit flag. Each community on Reddit is staffed by a team of volunteer moderators, and those moderators create and enforce rules specific to each community, such as what can and cannot be posted, how to title posts, how to behave, and what kinds of information are off limits. As one Redditor put it, "I add 'reddit' after every question I search on Google because I trust you all more than other strangers."[15] That post generated over 35,000 net upvotes and remains a top post in the r/ShowerThoughts community. For reference, a "shower thought" is described by the community as "those miniature epiphanies you have that highlight the oddities within the familiar."

Granted, the anonymous Internet has its thorns too. Like communities offline, online communities can be problematic. Questionable behavior in anonymous, community-based Id networks often manifests in very different ways than in identity-based Ego or Superego networks. While fake news stories now plague identity-based social networks, anonymous communities tend to be more resilient, thanks to the communal nature of Id network conversations. However, when an undesirable idea catches on in an Id network community, it also has the potential to mobilize at a broader scale and with more velocity than in identity-based networks. When a number of celebrities' private, nude photos were leaked in 2014, an event dubbed by the Internet as "The Fappening," people posted about the leaks on Twitter, Instagram, Facebook, and just about every other identity-based social network.[16] But it was 4chan that originally popularized the images, and a Reddit community called r/TheFappening soon became a hub of activity, conversation, and content sharing about the event. The r/TheFappening community has since been banned, but the coordination of Id networks enabled these leaked photos to trend at a much broader scale than if they'd been limited to identity-based networks alone.

The social media ecosystem is vast and complex. The rallying cry leveled against social media users' "mindless consumption" has become a caricature of itself. Social media isn't simple, and neither are the driving forces that compel us to participate. While it can certainly be addictive, social media is driven by our deeply rooted nature as social creatures. The average social media user maintained 8.5 different profiles across different websites in 2018, and that number rose from 8 in 2017 and 7.6 in 2016.[17] Were social media simply a vehicle for mindless consumption, we'd expect social media profiles to consolidate, but the opposite is happening. Why? Different social network structures satisfy different social and psychological needs for us. Ego networks allow us to solidify our connections to our tribes and define ourselves to the group of people who know our offline selves. Superego networks allow us to express the selves we one day hope to be—the selves we most want to represent to the world—and to peer into the ideal selves of others. Id networks give us license to explore new territory, try on new ideas and interests, and form bonds with those who share our passions.

In the following chapters, we'll dig further into Id, Ego, and Superego network structures, what makes them tick, and how brands are leaning strategically into the value people derive from participating in each. In Part I, I noted that adding value should be our top concern as marketers building brands in social media. I also mentioned that, while simple, the problem with adding value for people in social media is that different social networks provide different kinds of value. By examining these different essential mindsets for social media users, we'll begin to understand exactly how we can add true value to these vastly different online spaces. We'll be better equipped to find our niche and build scalable, strategic campaigns that generate engagement with our audiences in ways that feel natural and native to the space. We'll explore examples of brand engagement, campaigns ranging from the iconic Wendy's Twitter account to Charles Schwab on Reddit to how Squatty Potty got people on Facebook to talk about pooping.

KEY TAKEAWAYS

- How we're identified and how we're connected to people characterize two of the most important factors for determining the structure of a social network.

- In *managed self networks*, which correlate to Freud's Ego, we're connected to our offline friends, and we are identified as our offline selves. We represent a version of ourselves consistent with the persona we wear offline.

- In *ideal self networks*, we manifest our Superegos. We're connected to some of our offline friends, but we're also discoverable to a network of people who don't know us. We represent an idealized version of ourselves.

- In *true self networks*, we're disconnected from our offline selves and our offline friends. In this Id space, we have the ability to explore new interests and express ourselves in ways that we may not be comfortable with in Ego and Superego spaces.

ONLINE REPRESENTATION OF THE OFFLINE SELF

The Ego and the Conscious Center of Action

The piece opens with a profile shot of a man with a stern face and a soft, present voice.[1] He tells us that he once worked as a forensic artist in the San Jose police department. Then we're introduced to a woman who describes her experience of not quite meeting this forensic artist. He's now seated at a drafting table in a bright, airy loft with high ceilings and more windows than walls. Pencil in hand, he sketches something we can't quite see. On his right, a luxurious drapery of translucent cloth obstructs his view of an empty white seat. The video cuts to another woman who's presumably had the same experience as she walks toward the white chair. "I couldn't see them, and they could see us," she says. "Tell me about your hair," he inquires.

"I didn't know what he was doing, but then I could tell after several questions that he was drawing me," the first woman says. What has been alluded to in earlier scenes is eventually made explicit by the artist, "Once I get a sketch I say, 'Thank you very much,' and then they leave. I don't see them." The forensic artist has been depicting these women's faces purely based on their self-descriptions. We learn that the handful of women from whom we've heard also return to the studio a second time—but rather than describing themselves, they're asked to describe one of the other women.

Approximately halfway through the three-minute video, both drawings are revealed to the women they depict. The artist explains, "This is the sketch you helped me create. And that's the sketch somebody described of you." When revealed, the self-described sketch highlights minute flaws and areas of self-consciousness, while the version described by another participant appears more accurate and beautiful. Following closeup shots of the women's reactions to their drawing reveals, one says, "I should be more grateful for my natural beauty." The artist then asks the question at the very heart of the campaign, "Do you think you're more beautiful than you say?" Through near tears, the same woman responds, "Yeah . . . ," but her eyes shift, and she seems to pause as if some qualification should follow. She resolves, however, to punctuate with a more decisive, "Yeah." The spot ends with a simple line: "You are more beautiful than you think."

If you're not crying yet, I simply haven't done it justice—the campaign plucks masterfully at the heartstrings. The Dove brand has a legacy of championing "real beauty" in campaigns for over a decade, with its first campaign of the series launching in 2004.[2] From a marketing perspective, the positioning is as brilliant as it is wholesome—in a competitive industry filled with overly stylized, modified, and generally unattainable beauty standards, the Dove brand made a bold decision to embrace real people with real bodies. But the reason we're looking at this campaign isn't simply to highlight Dove's brand identity work—Real Beauty Sketches generated more than 630,000 shares on Facebook in its first 10 days.[3]

The video is three minutes long—about two minutes and 53 seconds longer than what Facebook recommends for its ads. And that's including a solid minute and a half of setup—it's not obvious what the video is about until the storyteller establishes the relatively complex framework. We need to understand that these women are being sketched by a forensic artist, that there are actually two sketches being produced—one based on self-description and another based on a description from someone else—then we need the emotional foundation of how women described themselves as compared to how they described each other, and so on. It's not a quick get. It breaks just about every "best practice" I can find about creating successful digital campaigns, but it managed to drive an astronomical amount of earned reach based on organic sharing. So why did it work?

As brands, we often lose sight of one of the most important principles for driving engagement in social space—and particularly in Ego networks like Facebook. When people engage a piece of branded content, they have no intention whatsoever to communicate with us as the brand. What they're really telling us is this: "Something about this brand and its content represents a part of myself, and I'm using this content to express myself to my friends." When someone shared the Dove Real Beauty Sketches campaign, they weren't thinking about what the video meant to the Dove marketing team. They were thinking about what it would mean to their friend connections—and, more specifically, what it would mean for their friend connections to see that the video came from them.

The Dove brand understood well that its target demographic, presumably young to middle-aged women, felt a certain way about the beauty industry—namely, that it was fake and unhealthy. By creating an emotional video with a message that both aligned with a prevailing ideal among its target audience and simultaneously progressed the Dove brand identity, this ad found a true sweet spot of share-driving creative. The people who engaged with this campaign were saying, "Hey, I think this is an important message, and I am championing that message to my friends!" Through consistent execution and strong brand identity work over time, engaging with the Dove brand has become synonymous with standing against unrealistic beauty standards and embracing real bodies.

In Ego space online, we're connected almost exclusively to the people we know offline, and we're clearly identifiable as our offline selves. Facebook, Snapchat, and any network that remains closed around your curated group of friends while identifying as your offline self qualifies as an Ego network. The word *Ego* gets a bad wrap—in the Freudian model, the Ego isn't the vain, shallow, narcissistic scapegoat pop culture has made it out to be. *Ego* comes from the Latin word meaning "I." In the Freudian model, the Ego is our conscious center of action. It's the part of the mind that forms when a person realizes their separateness from the outside world, that begins to control the drives of the Id, and that starts to face the limitations the outside world imposes on us. The Ego deals with three primary forces: the outside world, the Id, and the Superego. The Id characterizes our most basic selves and desires, while our Superego is the accumulation of our learned cultural rules. The Ego works within the confines of these three forces to act in the world—to get food when we're hungry, to move when we touch something hot, and to temper ourselves when we're in a heated argument.

When we participate in Ego networks like Facebook and Snapchat, we're more bound to our real-life selves than we are in Superego and Id networks because the only people with whom we're connected are the people who know our offline selves (Figure 5.1). The things we do and say in Ego networks have a greater sense of realism attached to them, not just because we're connected to our offline friends but because our identity is also strongly reinforced. Our real name accompanies every post we make, every article we *like*, and every comment we express. Being digitally connected with people we know offline makes for an interesting social dynamic. Offline, we communicate through our physical appearance—the way we groom ourselves, the fashion we wear, the expressions on our faces. Online, we wear content as a kind of digital clothing. We engage and share content that we deem simultaneously worth our friends seeing and defining of ourselves.

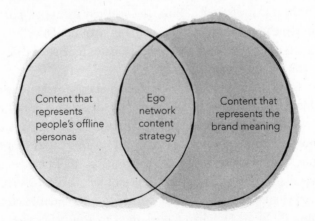

FIGURE 5.1 **Ego Content Strategy**

In 2017, the *New York Times* conducted a study to understand why people share content. The researchers wrote that 68 percent said they share "to give people a better sense of who they are and what they care about," and 84 percent said they share "because it is a way to support causes or issues they care about."[4] It's all about self-representation.

ADDING VALUE IN EGO NETWORKS MEANS HELPING PEOPLE REPRESENT THEMSELVES

As brands, if we ask ourselves how we can add value for users in Ego networks, our answer must relate to the self-expression of our audiences. Too often, we set out to create campaigns that "generate engagement," but we fail to ask ourselves a simple question: What would it mean for a person to engage with this content? I don't mean "What would it mean *to us*?" I mean, if people engage with our content, what are they expressing about themselves socially? What would their friends think about their engagement with that content? Will that content help them receive positive social feedback? Every piece of content a person engages with in Ego space is run through the unconscious social filter of, "What does this say about me?" In order to drive meaningful engagement within Ego networks, it's not enough to position ourselves to our audiences. We need to help our audience define themselves to *their* audience.

Finding ways to help our audience brand themselves to their friends doesn't always mean long, deep, emotional content. When executed perfectly, as was the case with Dove, that type of content has strong sharing incentive because it's natural for many of us to share (some of) our emotions socially. But there are plenty of other ways people brand themselves in Ego networks. Video is often too heavy and slow to grab attention consistently in social media generally, and Ego networks are no exception. The Ziploc brand is another example of a consumer packaged goods (CPG) brand that managed to drive massive amounts of sharing by equipping its audience with shareable, attention-grabbing creative that helped people represent themselves.

While many of Ziploc's ads historically have focused on product attributes, the brand made a strategic pivot in social creative that led to a great deal of earned reach through sharing. Creative ranged from cake decoration ideas to portioning tips to life hacks and simple recipes—all using various Ziploc products. Top posts such as "Cheese-cake Stuffed Strawberries,"[5] "DIY Tie-Dye Crayons," (crayons made in an oven),[6] and "Pecan Pie Chocolate Bark"[7] generated hundreds of thousands of clicks on the share button. The team wasn't light on the branding, either—not only was product featured in every photo but a logo lockup also appeared in the bottom corner of each post. The Ziploc team understood well that people aren't hesitant to engage with branded content—the content just needs to be valuable enough to engage.

The strategy was simple and consistent—provide new and interesting ways for people to use the product. Each post was product centric, but it's clear that its purpose was first and foremost to add value to the feeds of the Ziploc audience. The incentive for the audience to share the content was twofold. First, the content was useful and interesting, and by the simple limitation of platform functionality, the easiest way to save a post on Facebook is to share it. It's bookmark-worthy. Second, these posts helped users build social equity among their friends. The moment I click the share button on Ziploc's content, the content is no longer Ziploc's. It's mine. And when I can give my friends novel, fun, unique ideas to change up recipes, organize the house, and so on, I'm letting my friends know who I am. I'm crafty in the kitchen, I'm the one who finds and shares creative ideas, I know the best life hacks, and here's the content to prove it.

Once a post is shared, it almost doesn't matter who originally posted it because the post takes on a life of its own within the sharer's social network. That's why the memeology principle of ensuring that our meme machines are complete is so important. When generation after generation of people share our content, what page posted it and with what copy are lost—only the content remains. It'd better be traceable back to the brand.

Ziploc's social creative followed many of the best practices the Dove brand broke. Each piece of content was consumable right within the feed with very little technological resistance. The brand used the immediacy and efficiency of static imagery to convey many of its ideas. That meant a very low barrier to entry for each person reached. The brand also created a broad editorial calendar of content and shared each post organically, likely to gauge the initial reception to determine which were best candidates for paid promotion. The meme machines Ziploc used to house its life hacks and recipes also felt familiar—particularly to those who've engaged with mom bloggers and at-home foodie influencers. Step-by-step imagery, multipaneled shots, well-shot-but-rustic food photography, bright colors, airy spaces, and a multitude of other aspects of Ziploc's content felt natural within the popular food space. But they also felt distinctly Ziploc.

Ego networks aren't often where trends start, but both Ziploc and Dove were able to generate significant amounts of organic reach within Facebook. Both brands were able to swim successfully upstream because their content tapped into the preexisting mindsets of their audiences. The majority of online trends require incubation in a common group or community, and Ego networks are organized around more fluid, personal connections that are particular to each individual user. When a new video game becomes popular, or a new sneaker takes over the fashion scene, or a wacky meme becomes the new vogue format, we can usually trace the trend back to a group of people connected to each other through common content. But there are exceptions to that rule.

In Ego space, trends can form when a particular idea or piece of content harnesses a preexisting, widespread belief—especially when that belief is relatively dormant. The Dove brand created a trend within an Ego network by articulating an idea that was held by a wide number of people but that was otherwise difficult to express in a compelling way. Dove didn't change people's minds about the beauty industry—most of their audience already felt ostracized and unrepresented by popular beauty brands. Dove helped those people express that belief in a way that was powerful and easily shareable. Ziploc tapped into the less charged but still potent sense that people love novelty, and novelty is a fun way to connect. Maybe you'll never actually gather pomegranate seeds into a plastic bag, cut off the corner over a glass, and squeeze it for juice, but now you know you could. (It actually doesn't work that well, but it still managed to drive strong engagement.[8])

In Ego networks, the branded content that succeeds at driving sharing is the content that helps people connect with each other.

It's easy to imagine how a heartfelt video about embracing our real beauty accomplishes that. It's also easy to imagine how life hacks and novel recipes spark conversations between people—"Let's try this next time!" or, "Wouldn't this be fun?!" Content that speaks to us personally, be it emotional, applicable to our real lives, or a joke among our friends, will drive engagement because our connections in Ego networks are the ones in which we have the most personal and emotional investment. These are the people we know offline and who know us. The facade of a separate Internet self is thinner in Ego space. As brands participating in these ecosystems, we need to think of ourselves less as destinations—very few people actually visit brand pages—and more as the connective tissue between our audiences and their friends.

WORD-OF-MOUTH IS DRIVEN BY CONTENT-LEVEL CONVERSATIONS, NOT BRAND-LEVEL CONVERSATIONS

I've already poked a little fun at Facebook's initial pitch to advertisers—"Build your fan page, grow your *likes*, and they'll become your endorsement engine to their friends!" Initially, the marketing world bought into the idea that Facebook had created an engine for word-of-mouth marketing. Unfortunately, that model failed miserably, but there is an important truth to be extracted from it. The problem with Facebook's fan page model was that people continued to subscribe to more and more pages, so their feeds became inundated with branded content. That meant people saw less and less of the actual content they came to see on Facebook—stuff posted by their friends. To ensure that user feeds rebalanced themselves, Facebook began to limit branded pages' organic reach. Seemingly overnight, brands' pages went from reaching most of the people who subscribed to them to reaching less than 1 percent of their audience with each post. Let me tell you, that was not a fun call to my clients. It was an even less fun day for our Facebook reps.

The strategic model here still works, but the relationship between brands and fans is less permanent than Facebook had assumed. If our content is compelling enough in Ego networks, we have the opportunity to reach not only our direct audience but also the friend connections of that audience. This opportunity exists at the level of individual pieces of content, however, and not between brands and actual human beings. People don't have the Hebrew National logo tattooed on their chests, but many like Hebrew National franks. Very few are big enough fans of your brand to share every piece of your content—we still have to earn that engagement. When we're able to deliver a piece of content that successfully helps our audience express something about themselves, we also receive that meaningful recommendation from our fan to their friends. That's the initial promise of social media, and while it's elusive, it's powerful. The challenge is complex, but it's laid out in front of us: how can we help our fans define themselves to their friends within the context of our brand identity?

There remains an ongoing debate within the marketing world of the value of reaching loyal brand fans. From one perspective, solidifying connections with brand fans increases the likelihood that they'll drive word-of-mouth recommendations for us. Reaching brand loyalists may also help shorten the sales cycle among already high intent customers. But from another perspective, reaching brand fans is redundant. These are the people who are already going to buy our product. Social media—and Ego networks in particular—complicate that conversation because fans and nonfans are intermingled. Maximizing the utility of an Ego network isn't just about reaching the right person with the right message. It's about finding a way to leverage our fans' appreciation of us into personalized endorsements through engagement. The path to creating this relationship remains mutually beneficial: find a way to help people express themselves to their audiences.

Perhaps having benefited from watching the evolution of Facebook's advertising model, the Snapchat platform managed to productize people's natural tendency toward self-expression in Ego networks brilliantly. Among Snapchat's available advertising formats are *filters*, which brands can create as optional overlays for user videos and photos, and *AR lenses*, which use augmented-reality technology to interact with user videos in real time.[9] If you haven't used them yourself, it's probably how your kids made a video of themselves looking like anime characters or conjuring a dancing hot dog. Not only are lenses feats of technology—I honestly never thought I'd see my own face open up to reveal a Westworld cyborg—but they also lean naturally into the way users derive value from the platform. That makes the job of advertisers much more straightforward—adding value means giving people new ways to express themselves visually in short-form videos and photos. Executing a successful lens isn't necessarily simple because Snapchat has become a relatively crowded space for advertisers, but the platform's products offer a strong combination of deep engagement and friend endorsement.

The creative canvas afforded by formats like AR lenses is seemingly limitless, and again, the best examples aren't just interesting to engage as individual users but aid those users in their pursuit of self-representation. People in Ego networks tend not to be quite as precious about heavily curating a self-representation as they are on Superego networks like Instagram or TikTok because they're generally confined to the safety of a curated friend group. And who doesn't love when a brand lets out their weird? Taco Bell never really hides its weird, but for Cinco de Mayo in 2016, Taco Bell created a wacky "taco shell lens" that quickly became the top-performing branded filter at the time.[10] The concept was too strange not to be shareable—the lens superimposed a person's eyes and mouth onto a taco shell with signature Taco Bell fixin's. For a brand with a cult following, the taco filter was a brilliant way to drive earned reach. First, it ignited brand fans, creating meaningful engagement with loyalists who readily shared their taco lensed faces. Then, it reached the friends of those fans, perhaps encouraging them to engage with the lens too.

American Express also executed this strategy. The half-baked "What if we made a holiday . . . ?" concept has shown up in just about every advertising brainstorm ever, but American Express actually made it happen for Small Business Saturday.[11, 12] The brand registered a national holiday that happens the Saturday between Black Friday and Cyber Monday, and American Express promoted it with a "Shop small" campaign tagline. It's a nice, altruistic positioning for the brand—who could get mad about a credit card company spending its marketing dollars to support small businesses? Part of the campaign involved a simple Snapchat filter, which framed a user photo with a heart-shaped Small Business Saturday wordmark, encouraging small business owners to talk about their companies. Not only did

American Express reach the small business owners to whom they were marketing, but they also provided a platform for business owners to talk about their businesses to their friends. When small business owners shared inspirational stories and photos with their friends using the Small Business Saturday branding, the American Express brand appeared as a friend and champion.

There's no shortage of brilliant, however formulaic, uses for Snapchat filters and AR lenses promoting movies, video games, and any other narrative-driven products. Sony Pictures was able to attribute more than a million ticket sales for the movie *Venom* to their interactive Snapchat virtual reality (VR) lens, which "consumed" engaged users with special effects seen in the movie.[13] Mildly creepy, heavily shareable. Deadpool, X-Men, Alien, and a laundry list of other film franchises with iconic characters and distinctive worlds leverage Snapchat ads to similar effect.[14] In Ego space, when we give people something with which they can communicate about themselves to their friends, we're maximizing our media dollars and the utility of the network.

Given that Ego space is where our identity is most closely associated with our offline selves, these networks are also the ones in which people are most strongly attached to their preconceptions about our brands. Brand building in Ego space happens piece by piece through the content we share, meaning it's very difficult for us to get people to change their minds about us. Returning to our Dove campaign example, imagine if the same video had been produced by a different brand—say, *Cosmopolitan* or *Glamour* or *Vogue* or any other beauty brand known for manipulating model photography. The message would have felt inconsistent with our preconceptions of these brands. Even in the case of thoughtful rebranding, it's a slow, gradual process of changing brand perceptions in spaces based on identity. Had Dove not been so consistent in its brand identity work, it's unlikely that the video would have generated the earned reach it did. Dove has remained consistent about this real-beauty message for more than a decade, and while not every brand requires a decade of brand building to succeed, consistency of identity is absolutely critical.

This is where the world of traditional marketing excellence and brand building still have much to teach us as social advertisers. It's not enough for an individual piece of content to grab attention and add value if our goal is meaningful engagement. Part of the meaning is itself rooted in our brand: What do we stand for? What does our brand represent to people? What do people think of the kinds of people who support our brand?

BRANDS ARE BUILT IN SOCIAL MEDIA ONE POST AT A TIME

The types of content we create and our brand identity are entangled—we can't change one without affecting the other. Individual posts we create in social media contribute to the perception of who we are as a brand. Our brand identity (usually) has more gravity than each individual post, but over time and repetition, the two forces pull at one another. While content can—and often does—change rapidly, brand perception and identity change much more slowly. In order to maintain a strong, long-term strategy that maximizes the utility of Ego networks, we need to think beyond the level of engagement with individual pieces of content and consider our brands more holistically. We need to constantly evaluate what engagement with our brand represents to ensure that we're optimizing toward the right kind of engagement. After all, as one of my strategist friends used to say, if we optimize too far into engagement, we'll always end up at cats and porn. The Internet loves cats and porn.

Regardless of consistency, some brands and categories will inherently struggle to drive engagement within Ego networks, and that should be expected. We don't share everything with our Facebook friends, and for good reason. That doesn't mean that (nearly) every brand won't find utility in the marketing opportunities within these channels. Some brands represent categories people just don't like to socialize. Brands that are synonymous with embarrassing problems like dandruff shampoos, cockroach killers, weight-loss products, financial aids, feminine products, gaming brands, and plenty of other personally revealing categories will face an uphill battle in Ego networks. That doesn't mean there aren't paths to engagement, even for the most unlikely brands. We just have to get a little more creative.

According to its Facebook page, the Squatty Potty has a very specific mission: "Squatty Potty toilet stool elevates your feet for better elimination. End constipation, hemorrhoids, irritable bowel syndrome (IBS), pelvic floor issues, straining, and bloating."[15] Can't wait to tell my friends! If you've never seen one, a Squatty Potty is an accessory for a toilet that elevates the user's feet, placing them in a squat position, which is apparently a more natural angle for pooping. I know this because I saw their viral ad about it on Facebook. Squatty Potty is a small, family-owned brand run out of Saint George, Utah. It's not owned by P&G, it isn't hooked into a massive marketing machine, and it doesn't have a dedicated social marketing team to develop optimal channel strategies. But an ad for the Squatty Potty generated over 1.6 million shares, 480,000 comments, and about 700,000 *likes* on Facebook alone.[16]

The ad is titled, "This Unicorn Changed the Way I Poop," which is the perfect combination of clickbait and absurdism for driving the initial view. The video features a man dressed in a fancy medieval-looking getup narrating while a unicorn—well, a guy in a unicorn mascot suit—poops rainbow soft serve swirls onto an ice cream cone. "This is where your ice cream comes from—the creamy poop of a mystic unicorn," he begins, as he grabs the cone. "Totally clean, totally cool, and soft-served straight from a sphincter. Mm, they're good at pooping," he says as he savors an overly indulgent lick. "But you know who sucks at pooping? You do." The narrator goes on to explain the basic mechanics of how in a traditional seated position on a toilet, certain muscles impede the pushing process, but how in a squatting position, those muscles are relaxed, making pooping easier. It's equal parts hilarious, disturbing, and educational.

By taking an unpleasant topic, applying an absurdist creative direction, and explaining in plain-but-entertaining terms exactly how the product helps solve a common problem, Squatty Potty was able to make its ad totally shareable and friendly for conversation. Not only was it brilliant and hilarious, the ad was entirely self-aware about how real people might think about and use the product. The video focused first on entertainment, second on the problem being solved, and third on how the product solved the problem that flowed naturally from the first two—almost like a kind of soft serve. (Sorry, it just came out.)

The problem was also established as universal. The problems Squatty Potty set out to solve—constipation, hemorrhoids, IBS, pelvic floor issues, straining, and bloating—all seem like very personal and embarrassing issues in isolation. But Squatty Potty used the ad to make those problems universal—this is just how we're built! Also this guy is licking poop, gross! Had the brand focused on any of those individual problems, the spot would likely have struggled to drive sharing because doing so would feel to the person sharing the spot that he or she was revealing an embarrassing problem. By approaching the conversation from the standpoint of human anatomy, Squatty Potty removed the personal stigma. Nobody wants to admit to sometimes being constipated, even if it happens to all of us.

To drive meaningful engagement within Ego networks, we need to understand the implications of engagement for our audience. When people posts content on a platform in which they're connected to their offline identity and to their offline friends, they're in a vulnerable state of representing a version of themselves that's consistent with the one they wear offline. As brands looking to drive engagement with our audiences, our role in Ego networks must be to help our audience connect with their friends and define themselves.

For some brands, our identity already carries that meaning in the world, and we simply need to find that point of intersection between our brand meaning and what our audience wants to express about themselves. For new and challenger brands, we can take up meaningful causes, stand up for important issues, or just find unexpected and interesting ways to spark conversations between people. In Ego space, we need to go beyond thinking about what our campaign means from the perspective of our brand and consider what it will mean to our audiences. Remember, our audience is asking: What would it mean for me to engage with this content? In what context would it make sense for me to share this? With whom might it connect? How might they use it? And most importantly, what does it say about me?

KEY TAKEAWAYS

- Ego networks are those in which we're connected to the people we know offline and are identified as our offline selves. We're most tangibly connected to people who know the "real" us, and we're simultaneously in a mode of self-representation and social connection.

- To drive meaningful engagement in Ego networks, we not only need to brand ourselves but help our audience represent themselves to their friends.

- We can help our audience represent themselves by championing shared perspectives, sparking conversations between connections, or otherwise creating content that allows our audience to build their identity through our brand meaning.

- Brands that represent embarrassing or personally revealing information may struggle in Ego space, but there are paths to success through humor and commiseration.

THE GUIDING INFLUENCE OF CULTURAL IDEALS

Superego Networks and the Expression of the Ideal Self

'm going to tell you a story about a friend of mine. You don't have to believe that this happened, but it did, and it was really, really weird. It was a lightbulb moment for me in understanding the relationship between Instagram and reality. My friend runs a relatively successful leatherworking and denim shop. She makes her clothes by hand because that's the type of person she is—a maker. She runs her shop mostly online, and Instagram is a natural part of her marketing mix. Her shop's Instagram profile is polished and well curated. She uses consistent colors, textures, filters, and so on to create a unique ambiance not just within individual posts but throughout the explorable album on her user page.

Her Instagram account represents more than a fabricated, calculated, brainstormed, and strategized brand image. The brand is a part of her natural expression of self. While the account is filled with information about her products, latest concepts, and updates on stock and pricing, she also uses this Instagram profile to talk about her life, marriage, thoughts, and opinions. She takes photos of her blue-dyed hands after long days of working with denim. She posts goofy pictures with her friends. She shares her life in such a way that the people who follow her don't feel like it's transactional when she posts about an upcoming sale. It just feels like an extension of her life—this just happens to be who she is. At least, part of her.

Not long after I'd met her, I invited her and her husband to see a band play a show in downtown San Francisco. I didn't know much about the lineup, and as far as I knew, neither did they. After a small handful of unexciting openers, coupled with growing embarrassment about how they represented my taste in music, the headliner went on stage. This caused a small commotion at our table, and I looked inquisitively at my designer friend who seemed to be the source. She'd recognized the bass player, who had purchased a belt from her online shop, and he was wearing it! She was beyond flattered. We joked about her newfound celebrity and the long list of accomplished musicians who would go on to wear her belts. She recounted a few of the conversations they'd had on Instagram and mentioned what a down-to-earth, nice guy he was.

After the show, I noticed the bassist hanging out by the bar, and I introduced myself to him. I told him about my designer friend who'd made his belt, and I reminded him of the name of her shop. He laughed about the coincidence. He remembered the shop, and when I asked if he'd come back to our table to meet her, he happily obliged. When we were approximately three feet from the table, my designer friend looked up at me, over to the bassist, back at me with a look of pure horror on her face, and bolted. Poof. Gone. I don't mean that she was in the process of getting up, caught my eye, and just failed to stop her own momentum. I mean she shot away from the table so fast she nearly knocked it over. We agreed that she must have . . . uh . . . gone to the restroom. He headed back to the bar.

When she returned a few minutes later, she didn't skip a beat, "Why would you do that?!" Stunned, I explained that I figured she'd want to meet the guy in person since she'd designed his belt and they'd chatted on Instagram. She'd want to say hi, right? Wrong. She explained to me that she didn't really want to *talk* to him. She didn't want to meet him in person. She wanted to send him a photo from the show via Instagram to let him know that she loved hearing his band play. She had created a representation of herself, and that representation was too separate from her offline self for the two to merge in an actual conversation. She identified more with—and was more proud of—the representation of self she'd curated on Instagram than the flesh-skin-and-bones she wore around in real life.

Instagram elevates each of us to the level of influencer, even if our audience is small. We don't have friends on Instagram; we have followers. We share content that isn't as much about starting conversations or connecting with our friends as it is about emergent self-representation. We curate our feeds a little more than we do on Facebook, we're a little more selective of the photos we post, and we filter those photos a little bit more. We may be connected to many of the same friends we have on Facebook or Snapchat, but we also have the potential to be discovered by an entire world of people we don't know. We apply hashtags and tag locations to our content that encourage discovery—after all, we're only one good post away from the Internet fame we deserve!

Superego networks are ones in which we're usually identifiable as our offline selves, have some connection to the people we know offline, and simultaneously have the potential to reach an entire network of people we don't know yet. Instagram, Twitter, TikTok, VSCO, and even LinkedIn are examples of Superego networks. Each of these platforms employs mechanics like hashtags to connect otherwise disparate users and content (Figure 6.1). In response to these connections of self-expression, we tend to manifest idealized versions of ourselves. Most of us do so naturally and without intent to deceive—it's not that we're trying to dupe anyone into thinking that our Instagram profile reflects our whole life. It's that when we're invited to express ourselves in space that connects our self-representation with the representations of others, it's natural for us to curate highlights, positive moments, idealistic beliefs, and pictures that make us feel really, really, ridiculously good-looking.

In the Freudian model, the Superego is the last part of the mind to form, following the development of the Id and the Ego. As you may remember, the Id characterizes the basic, essential drives with which we're born, and the Ego forms as the desires of the Id face the

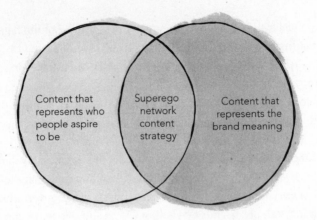

FIGURE 6.1 **Superego Content Strategy**

limitations of the real world—the conscious center of action. The Superego, then, is the combination of our learned rules—the cultural norms that characterize what it means to be a good person, how we ought to relate to the people around us, and who we ought to be. "Don't hurt other people" and "Don't take what isn't yours" are simple examples of early Superego inputs. The Superego continues to grow in complexity, however, as social interactions provide us with feedback. Because the Id deals with unfiltered desires and the Superego imposes cultural rules about what is acceptable, the two are often in conflict with one another, and it's up to the Ego to mediate between them.

Within the Id, Freud notes that there are a great many drives and impulses that simply aren't compatible with a large-scale, civilized society. While problematic drives aren't the only characteristics of the Id, they're the drives that tend to be repressed and buried deepest in the unconscious, while drives deemed acceptable by the Ego and Superego flow more freely. Inevitably, these repressed drives eventually "sublimate" and find expression in different ways. The process of repression and sublimation is akin to air being trapped underwater. When an idea or drive is deemed unacceptable by the conscious mind, it is "repressed"—that is, it is pushed down beneath the surface into unconsciousness. But like an air bubble trapped underwater, the repressed drive will eventually find a way to surface, even if not via the same path through which it was repressed. That is to say, if a sexual drive is repressed, it may sublimate as something entirely different—something more palatable for the Ego and Superego. For Freud, dreams were windows into the cycle of repression and sublimation and provided important insight for analysis into psychological life.

Freud focused most on aggressiveness and sexuality as the primary forces repressed by culture and its Superegos. In order to deal with these drives that are incompatible with peaceful coexistence, society imposes rules to limit those expressions. Monogamy is a culturally enforced method of limiting sexual expression so that, at least in theory, no one's sexual expression impedes anyone else's. And our rules for the expression of physical aggression are even more strict—generally that such behavior is only acceptable in self-defense. Freud contended that when people repressed their sexual or violent drives, those drives might transform through this process of sublimation into more socially useful achievements, like art and academic pursuit.

Repression, however, comes with a cost in Freud's model: "If civilization imposes such great sacrifices not only on man's sexuality but on his aggressivity, we can understand better why it is hard for him to be happy in that civilization."[1] In fact, the tyrannical nature of the Superego—and, perhaps, of strict cultural rules—inspired the title of Freud's *Civilization and Its Discontents*. The book describes in detail not only Freud's Id, Ego, Superego model but the inherent conflict between the Id and the Superego—the basic desires that emerge from within us and the rules we've learned about what constitutes "good" behavior.

On one side of human development is our innate sense to survive, reproduce, and freely express ourselves. On the other are the rules that keep our societies peaceful, functioning, fair, and equal. For most of human development—and for most of the history of life on Earth—the world has been dominated by the former, in which cultural rules have often given way to forcible grabs for power and resources. Freud's critique in *Civilization and Its Discontents* could be imagined as the proverbial pendulum having overcorrected from one dominated by Id to one dominated by Superego. Given the cultural Victorianism of nineteenth-century Austria in which Freud lived, that certainly would have been the case.[2] In a very different way, we might say that platforms like Instagram and Twitter are once again inflating (some of) our Superegos to tyrannical, unhealthy scales.

IF LEFT UNCHECKED, THE SUPEREGO CAN BECOME A TYRANNICAL DICTATOR

Erring toward the Id devolves the world into chaos, while erring toward the Superego traps us in a tyrannical, totalitarian nightmare. The same metaphor plays out in our online lives. Superego networks can become psychologically tyrannical if we invest too much of ourselves in them. If we allow our fuller offline self to be guided purely by the types of behaviors for which we get positive Superego feedback, we risk putting our happiness and sanity in the hands of people who might not even know us.

We see this imbalance of Superego when people feel a need to film an entire musical performance on Snapchat rather than enjoy the performance themselves. Or when people line up to witness a natural wonder or feat of architecture, only to view the experience exclusively through their phone's camera. Or when people order a dish at a restaurant purely to photograph it. And especially when the value of our experience is defined by the amount of social media engagement our post about that experience generates. When working properly, the Superego is a force for good, but when we start to lose touch with the anchor of our natural, mostly unconscious self, we start to fracture ourselves in problematic ways. Freud cited this incompatibility of the Id and Superego as the source of many neuroses, or psychological ailments.

Remember the aforementioned research finding that 63 percent of Instagram users reportedly felt miserable after having used the platform? And that Instagram was the platform that showed the most dramatic depressive effects? Those users who reported feeling miserable after using Instagram spent an average of 60 minutes per day browsing the app. The same study noted that 37 percent of responders described feeling happy after using Instagram.[3] However, the "happy" camp of people only used Instagram an average of 30 minutes per day.

A 30-minute difference may not seem like a lot, but 30 minutes per day can have dramatic psychological consequences. Research studies about meditation have found that 30 minutes per day of mindfulness can help ward off anxiety, depression, and even more physical ailments like heart disease and chronic pain.[4] If 30 minutes per day of meditation can have such profound positive effects, it shouldn't surprise us that the same amount of time spent browsing social networks could also affect our psyches. The problem isn't the Superego—or even Superego networks. The problem starts when the Superego goes unchecked and unbalanced. Browsing highlights from our friends' lives isn't a problem. Rather, it's when we become servants to those highlights that we lose touch with our fuller selves.

Instagram started as a photo editing app, and the social network that grew on top of that app reveals its origins. Photography, fashion, modeling, and visual stylings of all kinds thrive naturally on Instagram. These highly visual industries tend toward idealism, often to the point of distortion. These idealistic categories conspire to pull Instagram into Superego space. But there are plenty of photo editing apps and image-centric social networks that haven't generated the same culture and user mindset as Instagram. We might conclude, then, that Instagram's culture has as much to do with its structure as with its visual nature.

Different Superego networks also manage to pull ideal representations out of us, but they're often different idealized versions of ourselves. Instagram's origin as a photo editor guided the culture toward an idealism of aesthetic, but Twitter culture is very different. While Twitter is very similar in structure to Instagram, its culture is less visual, and it remains squarely in Superego space. Both Instagram and Twitter are organized primarily around user profiles, they rely on one-way "follow" mechanics, and they encourage discovery through hashtags and trending content. Twitter, however, tends to prioritize short-form text as its primary medium while Instagram prioritizes photos and videos. The Superego manifestations of Twitter, therefore, are less based on creating a visual Superego identity and center more around wit, accomplishment, connection, and clout. According to self-admitted Twitter addict and *Atlantic* writer Laura Turner, "Twitter is a megaphone for achievements and a magnifying glass for insecurities, and when you start comparing your insecurities with another person's achievements, it's a recipe for anxiety."[5]

In her article "How Twitter Fuels Anxiety," Turner explains how the platform perpetuates a self-reinforcing cycle of anxiety and self-evaluation. Turner tells us that Twitter provides an endless stream of comparisons against which we can measure ourselves, but at the same time, Twitter culture is generally open to the expression of feelings like anxiety. Brains are tricky though. Turner cites a Harvard study that found that disclosing information about oneself—such as one's emotional state—activates the same pleasure center of the brain that responds to food, money, and sex. In Freudian terms, it's a kind of sublimation—we feel anxious, we repress those feelings of anxiety, and then we find a way to express that anxiety in a way that changes our experience into something more consciously palatable. In fact, the same study also noted a relationship between people who spent more time on social media and elevated anxiety levels. Pamela Rutledge, director of the Media Psychology Research Center, draws an evolutionary correlation between the two: "When we're anxious, we feel compelled to be continually scanning the environment. That's how we make ourselves feel safe." The cycle feeds itself.

ENGAGING AUDIENCES IN SUPEREGO SPACE MEANS HELPING THEM MANIFEST ASPECTS OF THEIR IDEAL SELVES

As brands in Superego space, we're in delicate territory. The content with which people are willing to engage is much more tightly curated. Our audiences' expressions in Superego space are not only filtered through their selves as known by their offline personal connections but through the representations of their ideal selves. And to complicate the matter, there are many different kinds of ideal self-identities that might manifest in these spaces—some identities are created around looks; some about travel and lifestyle; others about food and exclusive social lives, occupations, political ideologies, philosophies, and other ideals. One person's ideal self may be the same self another represses, and vice versa. For some brands, this Superego mindset actually helps drive engagement, particularly when the brand represents some part of users' ideal selves. Remember, when we're identifiable as our offline selves, the content we engage with becomes our digital clothing. When I engage with a Nike post on Instagram, I'm defining myself as an athlete, just as when I engage with a small, local clothing brand, I'm defining myself as fashionable and offbeat.

In Superego networks, we return to the problem of adding value with a unique set of constraints. How can we provide people with content that speaks to their ideal selves? Or satisfies their need for social approval and acceptance? Or reduces their anxiety as they compare themselves to others? The reason we ought to pose these questions for ourselves is because our audience will judge us much more harshly—"If you don't add value to my experience, I will not interact with you in any public way." And "public" is important here because that's how brands demonstrate their social status in Superego spaces. The principles for adding value remain consistent, although badgeworthy content tends to outweigh bookmarkable content because self-representation is our primary aim in Superego space.

Perhaps the best example of a badgeworthy campaign in Superego space is the Beats By Dre "Straight Outta Somewhere" campaign. Having partnered with Universal Pictures on the launch of the film *Straight Outta Compton,* the Beats brand drew on a simple but powerful insight—that, like Dre, everyone is proud to represent their hometown.[6] The brand created a site called www.StraightOuttaSomewhere.com, which allowed visitors to represent their hometowns within the iconic "Straight Outta Compton" lockup. The tool was simple and very similar to many popular "meme maker" apps online. Users could upload their own background images and replace "Compton" in the logo with their own custom text. Inevitably, people got more creative with the tool than simply following the formula of "Straight Outta [wherever you were born]." One featured an empty egg carton and read "Straight Outta Eggs," while another used a painting of Jesus in the background with a lockup that read "Straight Outta Jerusalem."

The campaign successfully walked the razor wire between campaigns that are too customizable, leading to brand safety issues, and campaigns that are too static and rigid to be infusible with anything meaningful by the audience. Campaigns like these take bravery to launch. I can just about guarantee that the Beats By Dre brand manager responsible for approving this campaign was up the night before imagining all of the awful things people *could* do with their site.

This was the right kind of bravery. Too often, brands shy away from flexible social media strategies that allow their message to be absorbed and co-opted by their audiences for fear of bad actors. When someone used the Straight Outta Somewhere site to create something lewd or offensive—which they absolutely did—the final content was more reflective of the person posting than it was of the Beats By Dre brand. The Internet allows for a scary amount of sharing and editing, but that doesn't mean we just keep our brand under glass.

The Straight Outta Somewhere campaign afforded its engaged audience a truly unique mode of self-expression. How often do we get to talk about our hometowns? And how many of us have parts of our identity rooted in the places from which we come? It's also worth noting that the output of engaging with the campaign was itself badgeworthy—the content created by the www.StraightOuttaSomewhere.com generator was cool and worthy of posting. It's easy to imagine a similar brand insight resulting in a hashtag-based photo campaign that prompted people to "Share a photo of your hometown!" Had Beats gone that route, this campaign would have been dead before it started. These low-effort stabs at driving user-generated content are all too common in social strategies and lack a basic understanding of why people engage with brands in the first place.

At least part of the success of Straight Outta Somewhere is in its meme machine—the flexible Straight Outta Somewhere lockup was consistent enough to be recognizable while flexible enough to become different and interesting for each iteration. If the brand had executed our hypothetical alternate strategy and asked people to share photos of their hometown, we'd be asking them to create a new meme machine with every submission. What copy should I include? Should the photo be personal or reflective of the town? Should I say something about myself or the place? Straight Outta Somewhere simplified the process of self-expression by providing the meme machine shell in which many different memes could live.

"Where are you from?" is the type of question that we're generally very comfortable asking as normal humans but that is terrifying for many brands. What if someone is from a poor area? What if the person had a tough childhood and used this branded prompt as a place to vent? What kinds of things might we be attaching to our brand image by asking such a question? But part of the success of the Straight Outta Somewhere campaign is exactly that—the question had weight to it. It gave people a real avenue to tell stories about themselves, or at least to represent parts of themselves they don't often get to represent. Where are you from? How do you represent that? And how do *you* represent that? These are questions with actual connections to culture. They're questions that, when answered, tell us something important about a person.

Too often, brands pay lip service to the idea of wanting to "become culturally relevant" without being willing to engage a topic with cultural weight. We need to allow conversations to flow into space where people actually care to engage. When we do, the results speak for themselves. The Straight Outta Somewhere campaign became the first number 1 trend across Instagram, Twitter, and Facebook simultaneously. The site drove more than 11 million visits, 8 million downloads, and 700,000 shares in social.

Self-expression in Superego networks isn't always heavy or serious. Humor plays a major role, and not always in straightforward ways. Often in Superego networks, we make light of what bothers us most or tease ourselves about our insecurities. It's a way of bolstering our ideal selves. As full, complex humans, we might be insecure about our weight, appearance, how a tweet went over, getting drunk at a Christmas party, and so on. But in Superego space, we may well hide these fears in plain sight by making self-deprecating jokes and pretending we're impervious. One way self-deprecation manifests in social media is through over-the-top fast-food fandoms. Part of the reason brands like Taco Bell, Wendy's, and McDonald's drive massive amounts of engagement in social media is what they represent—light-heartedness, pleasure in the moment, contrarianism to health culture, etc.

The Heinz brand leaned into this tendency for people to rally around their favorite foods in a controversial campaign about a new product called "mayochup."[7] Mayochup, a combination of Heinz mayonnaise and ketchup, wasn't actually a product the brand was trying to sell. The campaign was designed to drive awareness of the new Heinz mayonnaise. Sounds ludicrous, right? To announce an actual product, they created a fake product and produced a campaign around it . . . ? Strange as it may sound, the campaign far overdelivered on its goals—Heinz generated over a billion impressions in 48 hours and saw a 28 percent lift in awareness for their mayonnaise product. The brand could easily have taken the straightforward path to launching a product—just post a product shot with a white background sweep across owned social channels and wait for the dozens of engagements to roll in. By creating a fake, divisive product, the brand stirred up a tongue-in-cheek debate that drove massive amounts of engagement and earned reach.

At launch, Heinz shared a mocked up photo of mayochup and posted it on Twitter—"Want #mayochup in stores? 500,000 votes for 'yes' and we'll release it to you saucy Americans." The tweet generated more than 25,000 *likes*, 14,000 retweets, and nearly a million votes. The "yes" crowd won by a narrow margin—55 percent and just enough to get the product on shelves. In true Twitter fashion, the debate between mayochup proponents and naysayers raged for months afterward, often leveraging the #mayochup hashtag. Heinz was able to harness the often disagreeable but ultimately good-humored nature of Twitter culture by putting forth a debate too absurd to take seriously. Is it fry sauce? Is it fancy sauce? Is it Russian dressing? Is it disgusting? Twitter couldn't decide, and that's exactly what you need if you're a brand launching a new kind of mayonnaise.

In a followup phase to the #mayochup campaign, Heinz took to Twitter once again to determine which city should receive the first shipments of product.[8] The brand encouraged people to tweet using #Mayochup[YourCity], which was a brilliant mechanism to create local relevance in a large-scale campaign. By pitting different cities against one another, the brand was able to respark the debate, and people filled their cities' hashtags with gifs representing their excitement, memes in anticipation, and even videos of people chanting their cities' mayochup hashtags. Like the Beats By Dre campaign, the Heinz brand provided a platform to infuse the campaign with their own self-expression.

When executing a campaign across a large geography, many brands default to localization strategies—adapting content and targeting it only to particularly relevant regions. When the goal is to spark discussion and engagement, we need to rethink that instinct.

Heinz may well have targeted people in Chicago with creative touting #MayochupChicago, but the structure of the campaign allowed these local conversations to intertwine and affect the broader mayochup debate. What happened in #MayochupChicago meant something to people in #MayochupDetroit, and vice versa. Allowing these local conversations to meet each other helped spark new organic conversations and kept the debate alive.

Both the Straight Outta Somewhere and Mayochup campaigns played on how people define themselves in social media to gain relevance. Both campaigns acted as platforms for the self-representation and expression of engaged users. By definition, Superego networks tend toward badgeworthy content because self-representation is a fundamental part of the value we derive from participating in them. But bookmarkable content also thrives, especially within categories that are inherently badgeworthy.

Bookmarkable content simply needs to pass through the ideal self test: "Would I be glad that people know I saved this?" Food and recipe content is a good example of the principle. Food photography is an organically popular, badgeworthy stream of content that's well represented in Superego networks. But bookmarkable recipe and kitchen hack content also thrives in Superego space. This content isn't only about showing a badge. It helps viewers understand how to break down complex recipes, learn to do something new, or dress up something ordinary. Many of us aspire to be great home chefs and would love to demonstrate to the outside world how crafty and creative we are in the kitchen.

The content that demonstrates the steps in a new recipe, then, isn't just about helping us learn. It's also about representing the depth of our interest. We aren't just consuming the final products, we're learning how to create them. The @buzzfeedtasty account boasts more than 34 million followers on Instagram and exclusively features recipe hacks and how-tos.[9] It's not uncommon for their short-form videos to generate a few million views each. Fitness, niche hobbies, photography, and really any informational content that helps people understand an interest they're proud to share with the world has strong potential to succeed in driving Superego engagement.

CONTENT CAN BE BOTH USEFUL AND EVOCATIVE OF PEOPLE'S SUPEREGOS

The Lowe's brand developed a particularly strong series of book-markable content that spread naturally around Superego space with its #LowesFixInSix campaign.[10] Executed on Twitter and Vine (aw, remember Vine?), the concept was simple, and the execution was polished but relatable. The Lowe's creative team at BBDO developed a series of six-second videos that demonstrated simple life hacks, DIY projects, and home improvement tips. The creative team cited the low-cost production as a major driver of success because it allowed them to create over 100 pieces of content over the course of the campaign. When it comes to developing content with strong organic success, it's almost impossible to predetermine a winner, especially from the concepting phase, so investing in a higher volume of creative output is generally a good strategy. Production value usually has very little to do with what drives organic sharing.

The campaign creative was executed brilliantly and leveraged low-barrier, easily shareable meme machines to deliver ideas. The Vine platform proved particularly beneficial in constraining the brand's meme machines to be light and efficient in their communication. Not only was Vine a trending platform at the time, but its format was also conducive to social sharing generally. The platform required every post to be a six-second, looping video—essentially, a short gif with sound. These short-form gifs were well optimized for every social channel because they required such efficiency of communication. Videos featured life hacks like using rubber bands to remove stripped screws, using a rubber mallet and cookie cutters to make the perfect jack-o-lantern, and using painter's tape to hang level shelves.[11, 12, 13]

The #LowesFixInSix content was both useful and representative. Hopefully, the usefulness of the videos is obvious—that was their primary purpose. But the videos were also representative in that engaging this content communicated something about the sharer. Sharing these videos might say something like, "I'm new to home maintenance, and these are the kinds of problems I face now," or, "I'm a proud homeowner, and here's a video of something *even I* stood to learn," or, "I'm a very handy person, so I already knew how to do this, but it's been so helpful to me that I think you should know it too."

By creating content that is both informative for its audience and lends itself to self-expression, the Lowe's creative managed to spread naturally throughout social media platforms and earn significant reach. The #LowesFixInSix videos generated millions of views on Vine alone—and no, Vine didn't have an advertising platform to help pay for reach. Its video showing how to use a rubber band to remove a stripped screw alone drove 7.4 million plays. Because Lowe's was an early adopter, it was able to carve a new niche within the Vine platform, and because the Vine platform itself was still up and coming, the brand was able to ride a wave of organic popularity. Much of the copy in the videos would be considered out of place by today's standards— "Lighten up! DEWALT 2-PC 20V Combo Kit was $199, will be $149 on Black Friday."[14] Many posts had similar down-funnel, sales-centric copy. But because the content added value, the sales messaging wasn't a problem. That's another big mistake many brands make throughout their social media strategies—we're advertising things to sell. We know. They know. We know they know. And besides, they know we know they know. We don't need to hide it. We just need to add value while we're doing it.

Would the #LowesFixInSix creative work in Ego space? Absolutely. The brand shared some of these videos on Facebook where many of them generated hundreds of thousands of views.[15] As frequently happens with organic content, it's not unusual for stellar social media creative to find audiences across platforms. Given that both are generally spaces for self-representation, many of the best practices that work on Facebook also work on Instagram, but they succeed for different reasons.

One of the main differentiators between Ego and Superego spaces is that in Superego space, we're less bound to our offline sense of reality and identity. While our ideal self is a factor when participating in Ego space, it's embodied in Superego space. We often express ourselves vicariously through people who represent aspects of our ideal selves. If we identify with a particular kind of fashion, we might follow and engage a celebrity designer. If we identify with a particular sports team, we might follow the franchise or our favorite players.

If we identify with adrenaline rushes and extreme sports, we might follow GoPro.

GoPro shares the epitome of aspirational content: professional extreme athletes performing ludicrous stunts. Most of us, and I apologize if I'm projecting here, probably don't ride our bikes down jagged mountain outcrops, skydive in formation, surf waves as tall as buildings, or scuba dive in underwater caves. But that doesn't mean we don't identify with what those represent—daring, adrenaline, conquering death, nerves of steel. It also doesn't mean we don't want a camera that *could* capture all of those extreme activities. Subscribing to GoPro and engaging with its content is a way of communicating that we're adventurous, that we're energetic about life, and that we're willing to confront our fears. With more than 16 million followers on Instagram and over 2.2 million followers on Twitter, GoPro is a brand that has embraced the natural Superego niche cut out for it.[16, 17]

The same phenomenon is true of the fitness category in general. The most-followed fitness influencers on Instagram aren't those with the most practical knowledge or the people who went from being reasonably out of shape to being reasonably in shape. They're the most ludicrously fit (or at least ludicrously fit-looking) people on the planet. Stars like fitness model Michelle Lewin with over 13 million followers, professional bodybuilders like Kai Greene with over 5 million followers, and celebrity trainers with abs-popping-out-of-their-abs like Simeon Panda with over 5 million followers win the eyeball contest.[18, 19, 20] Is that because people like to follow their training routines? Or is it that they offer the best inspiration for our fitness goals? Not even close.

We enjoy seeing and engaging people who've reached beyond their limits—or maybe *our* limits—because these are the people who express our visions of our ideal selves. Nike's advertising has anchored itself squarely on this very insight—we're all athletes. When we wear Nike shoes, when we're at the gym ready to quit, when we're debating whether or not to get out of bed for a workout, a part of us imagines ourselves as the superathletes we see Nike represent, and we feel empowered. The brand places us in that same class of athletes.

Elevating a brand to the level of Superego aspiration is no easy feat, but for some categories, the fit is reasonably natural. Fashion, food, fitness, music, and any category that represents an aspirational hobby or interest is usually able to find a way to align with people's ideal selves. One way brands have evolved to leverage this tendency for people in Superego space to admire their idols is to hire those idols as influencers.

Superego networks go hand-in-hand with influencers in part because they tend to relate to some aspect of our ideal selves. Superego network structures also allow influencers to find and grow their followers relatively naturally. When influencer campaigns are done right, brands are able to borrow the credibility influencers have built, offer something useful to those influencers' audiences, and convert a swath of new customers. Unfortunately, it's easy to take an influencer campaign down the wrong path—overpriced, ineffective creative lacking any viable reach, or worse yet, embarrassing ourselves in front of the audience we want to convert.

INFLUENCER CAMPAIGNS REQUIRE THAT WE PUT OUR BRAND MEANING IN THE HANDS OF OUR PARTNERS

Influencer integrations are more art than science. Too much brand touch, and the partnership feels forced and inauthentic. Too little, and the partnership will fail to propagate the advertising message and generally confuse the influencer's audience. The Madewell brand is a best-in-class example of how to run influencer campaigns. The brand is well known for its ongoing influencer marketing, and that makes particular sense for them as a relatively young fashion brand.[21] Instagram has created an entire class of amateur-bordering-on-professional models, and Madewell curates a range of aspirational-but-relatable influencers who fit the style of their clothing. The brand successfully balances partnerships so that they feel like natural parts of the influencers' lives and are clearly tied back to the Madewell brand and products.

Madewell doesn't fall into the trap of the forced "key message," which is a cardinal sin of influencer marketing. When a brand provides copy or requests that influencers use a particular key phrase in their caption, the content almost always feels inauthentic and contrived. Probably because it is. "But we're paying them to post it!" says your client. And yes, that's a totally fair point. We just need to be a little more creative with how we integrate our brand's message. Influencers can spend near full-time working hours creating, maintaining, and growing their channels—their audiences know them very, very well. Even if our brandspeak caption passes our own sniff test, it probably won't pass the audience's.

Madewell utilizes a particularly brilliant tactic to bridge the gap between key messaging and the influencers' natural editorial voice. The brand often provides influencers a prompt rather than suggested copy. In a campaign around Valentine's Day, Instagram user @citysage created a post for Madewell denim.[22] In her photo, she's sitting with a red coffee mug in Madewell jeans with her legs kicked up on some Instagrammy pink chairs. She tells her fans, "In honor of Valentine's Day @madewell1937 asked me to share some things I love . . . like the first cup of morning coffee, the comfiest goes-with-everything jeans, the cheeky romance of pink + red . . . happy ♥💜🧡🌹 everyone! #denimmadewell #flashtagram (Photo: @teamwoodnote)."

The post managed to hide the ickiness of an influencer integration right in plain sight—"Madewell asked me to do this." Madewell often employs multiple influencers for any given campaign, and the prompt also helps to address this problem of scalability in a strategic way. A prompt allows each individual influencer to interpret things slightly differently. Even if we were able to sneak a brand phrase naturally into an influencer's post, if the phrase is repeated across multiple influencers, it's easy to recognize exactly from where the inauthenticity comes. (Hint: it's us.) Had Madewell asked influencers to post the line, "I love my @madewell1937 jeans because they're comfy and go with everything!", the campaign would have fallen into that uncanny valley of social copy and felt completely contrived. But the broader prompt of "Share some things you love" is adaptable and scalable enough to generate a wide diversity of on-brand content from influencer partners.

Madewell also leverages consistent hashtags when working with influencers, not just for particular campaigns but throughout their social activity. Not only does this help tie a long history of branded influencer content together but it also encourages user-generated submissions and organic sharing. When influencers share updates with their Madewell hashtags, a particular aesthetic is created in the accumulation of those posts. And because in Superego space we're all mini-influencers, it's natural for us as followers of those influencers or lovers of the Madewell brand to also share our photos with the same hashtags. Rather than creating a new line of jeans and writing cringe-inducing copy that asks people to, "Share photos of why you love Madewell denim!", the brand has created an engine of user-generated submissions by remaining understated in its calls to action and allowing the social network's mechanics to work naturally. In fact, the brand has a dedicated "Community" section on its website, which features photos from their various hashtags, recognizing their fans for contributing.[23] Madewell uses Instagram to empower fans to post their outfit of the day right alongside their influencer idols', making particularly strategic use of Superego space.

In Superego networks, our social standing means everything, especially as brands. High follower counts, strong engagement with our photos, tags and retweets from influential accounts are all ways we build credibility in Superego space. As brands, we tend to default to an apologetic demeanor in social media. At the slightest sign of resistance, we're quick to back down, remove the post, delete the video, scrap the campaign, fall to our knees, and beg the social media gods for forgiveness. As brands in Superego space, we need to build up a thicker skin than may seem immediately comfortable. Among a handful of other things they get absolutely right, the Wendy's brand is a prime example of taking criticism in stride and staying on course toward a strategic, thoughtful, and entertaining outcome.

Perhaps more than any other brand, Wendy's has managed to become part of meme culture. And not in a killed-by-the-locals-and-cooked-in-the-communal-stew kind of way, either. The brand has genuinely been accepted by the tribe. Meme culture and Superego networks have an interesting relationship, and in some counterintuitive ways, much of the humor that thrives within Id networks also succeeds at propagating in Superego networks. Sometimes that's because self-deprecating humor is an aspect of many people's Superegos, sometimes it's because being in the know about cutting-edge meme culture is an ideal for some people, and sometimes it's because Superego networks tend to have a significant representation of anonymous profiles.

Regardless, Wendy's succeeds in driving massive amounts of engagement by understanding and contributing to meme culture.

One of the easiest places for brands to fail in meme culture is incorrectly using a meme machine. Whether it's messing with the cadence of the text, using the wrong font, or misusing the sentiment of the original meme altogether, getting the meme machine right requires patience and attention to detail. When Wendy's demonstrates that it has mastered a meme by successfully adapting a new format, the people who engage with the branded meme are expressing two things. First, Wendy's has made an entertaining meme that's relevant to meme culture. And second, I'm in on the joke too. Because meme culture uses ideas and meme machines to define boundaries, and because those memes are constantly evolving, people identified with meme culture have an incentive to continue to demonstrate their membership in the tribe. Wendy's has learned to speak the language fluently.

Meme culture truly does represent a new language, and learning to speak a new language isn't easy. When we're learning something new, we're bound to make missteps. Inevitably, as Wendy's has honed its brand voice and meme culture-related content, the brand has made mistakes. And undoubtedly, the Wendy's team has received messages along the lines of, "Get out of meme culture—you don't belong here." There are plenty of social media teams who hear that feedback a couple times and scrap the strategy. But not Wendy's. Wendy's doesn't back down when its content is critiqued, and that's absolutely vital to maintaining a respectable demeanor in Superego space. That's not to say that Wendy's doesn't take care of customers who've had bad orders. When something goes wrong, the brand responds with a sincere message along the lines of, "This isn't the service we expect. Please DM us with the location and your contact info so we can look into this further." But Wendy's is known for its Twitter roasts.

When one user provoked the Wendy's account with, "If you reply I will buy the whole Wendy's menu right now," the brand responded, "Prove it."[24] The original poster retorted with a photo of a trash bag and the caption, "Here's your proof 👌." Wendy's clapped back with, "Thanks for sharing your baby pictures." That response alone generated over 3,000 retweets and over 15,000 *likes*. While the tactic is hilarious and engaging in its execution, the mindset is actually deeply important in Superego space. It says, "We're confident in our brand. We won't be bullied." And let there be no doubt—brands get bullied on Twitter all the time.

Unfortunately, most brands are so apologetic in social media that they seem guilty just for occupying space. Some people respond negatively to the memes Wendy's posts, but it takes that feedback in stride, and when appropriate, isn't afraid to jab back. As brands, we need to understand the difference between genuine, widespread backlash and a handful of negative comments. To demand respect within the culture, we need to stand steadfastly behind what we say, and we need to exhibit brand behaviors that align with what we say our brand is.

When we're organized around profiles that facilitate self-representation, we are connected to our offline identities and to many of our offline friends, and we have the potential to reach a world of people we don't yet know, it's natural for us to manifest an ideal version of ourselves. We're not dishonest in Superego space. We just tend to embody a more curated persona than we do in networks based on mutual connection and anonymous exploration. As brands looking to engage audiences in Superego space, we need to find ways to align with people's ideal selves—or find a way to allow our brand to represent something related to our audience's ideal selves.

Superego space puts us in a mode of emergent self-representation. The photos we share, the content we engage, and the friends with whom we interact are the ways we define ourselves to the broader network. As brands, we must not only find ways to add value for our audiences' ideal selves, we must also maintain our authenticity and consistency. Finding ways to add value in Superego space requires a strategic understanding not only of who the audience is but who they aspire to be. If we can find a way to help our audience express their aspirational selves, engagement will follow naturally.

KEY TAKEAWAYS

- Superego networks are ones in which we're usually identifiable as our offline selves, have some connection to the people we know offline, and simultaneously have the potential to reach an entire network of people we don't know yet. We're representing idealized versions of ourselves.

- To drive engagement in Superego networks, we have to create content that aligns with some aspect of people's ideal selves. That requires an honest, self-aware understanding of what our brand represents.

- Nearly every piece of content with which a person engages in Superego space is in some way badgeworthy.

- Social status is extremely important in Superego networks, and we can demonstrate our status through high levels of engagement, growing our following, and partnering with other reputable influencers and brands.

- Influencer integrations can be strong tactics for building relevance and lifting social status, but they must feel organic in order to meaningfully sway opinions.

THE UNREALIZED POWER OF TRUE SELF NETWORKS
The Id and the Unconscious Self

"Anonymity has poisoned online life," reads the subtitle of a 2016 *Atlantic* article titled, "How to Fix the Internet."[1] The article begins:

> We have to fix the internet. After 40 years, it has begun to corrode, both itself and us. It is still a marvelous and miraculous invention, but now there are bugs in the foundation, bats in the belfry, and trolls in the basement. . . .
>
> I love the internet and all of its digital offshoots. What I bemoan is its decline.

This article captures the prevailing attitude of the media toward online anonymity. The logic seems to be that if only we could strip the Internet of anonymity, we could solve the problems of online trolling, bullying, and general bad acting. There is no shortage of rhetoric scapegoating anonymity as the source of problematic online behavior. In 2012, New York State lawmakers went so far as to propose a bill that would require New York–based websites to remove any and all content that wasn't directly attached to an offline identity.[2]

Worse yet, most of these arguments fail to cite any real research on the effect of anonymity on online behavior, and when they do, the connections between the research and the conclusion are tenuous at best. Take a BBC article titled, "The Dangers of Online Anonymity," for example. The article states that "studies show people are more likely to behave in a dishonest or morally questionable way when they can hide behind it."[3] The citation for that claim? A 2012 research paper about how students tend to cheat more often when technology makes cheating possible.

Rarely, if ever, do we hear arguments in favor of online anonymity, despite the popularity of anonymous networks. Reddit ranks among the top 10 most trafficked sites in the United States according to Amazon's Alexa Rank, and there is a massive long tail of similarly structured anonymous communities based around interests.[4] When we do hear a defense of online anonymity, it's usually with regard to relatively fringe, though compelling, cases like whistleblowing and breaking otherwise suppressed news. In "Disruptions: A Digital Underworld Cloaked in Anonymity," the *New York Times* credits anonymity with enabling government document leaks for dissidents in Iran and Egypt, which seems ... well ... pretty important.[5] But that positive note is quickly undone by the next line, "drug dealers and gunrunners prefer anonymity, too."

Anonymity is a strange thing. It's not something we're afforded naturally. Throughout history, we humans have made use of objects like masks to obscure our faces for a variety of reasons—protection, artistic expression, ritual, entertainment, and yes, to avoid being caught. Anonymity online is very similar. The ways in which people use anonymity online are varied, and anonymity comes with some built-in risk. It provides us with protection for our selves—mental breathing space that's safely separated from our curated identities. Anonymity allows for creative vulnerability and expression without social ramifications. It gives us space to explore new interests and ideas we haven't yet integrated into our social identities. It's the freedom to learn about something without announcing "this is what I believe."

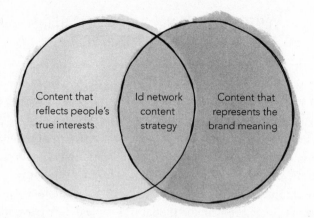

FIGURE 7.1 **Id Content Strategy**

When we participate in anonymous networks, we tend to be organized around our common interests and ideas because . . . well, what else are we going to organize around in lieu of our offline iden-tities? Because people are organized around topics, Id networks also tend to facilitate shared experiences among users (Figure 7.1). No two Facebook feeds are the same, but everyone who browses Reddit's r/Sneakers community sees the same shoes. The combination of peo-ple's shared experiences in networks organized around common ideas generates a sense of community that's distinctly different from how people relate to one another in identity-based networks. From this identification with online community comes a deep sense of trust—something of which marketers are in short supply.

Trust online is a strange thing too. It's probably no surprise that when it comes to getting trustworthy information about brands and products, Google and Amazon reviews rank near the top. A 2018 sur-vey showed that 88 percent and 89 percent of users of the respective platforms trust the information they receive.[6] It probably isn't surpris-ing that platforms like Facebook, Twitter, and Instagram lag behind: 58 percent, 64 percent, and 66 percent, respectively. What might sur-prise you, though, is that 86 percent of Reddit users trust the brand and product recommendations of other Redditors. Anonymity aside, online communities foster a deeper sense of trust than identity-based social networks.

CONTENT ONLINE MAY HAVE IMPLICATIONS
FOR REAL-WORLD BEHAVIOR

Today, our identities follow us everywhere. Most websites allow us to log in with our Facebook or Google identity. It's easy to forget that anonymity characterized the majority of Internet life for much of its early evolution. Had anonymity been such a destructive force, the Internet would never have succeeded in becoming the cultural and economic power we know today. Most critiques of anonymity also fail to grapple with an important piece of the equation. Anonymity doesn't create problematic thoughts. People do. It's naïve to think that ridding the Internet of anonymity would erase otherwise harmful ideas. The real question we ought to ask is, What is the relationship between these harmful ideas, anonymous expression, and their real-world implications?

One macro-level study about the effect of online anonymity happened mostly without us noticing that it was a study at all. In 2006, Clemson professor Todd Kendall produced a research paper describing the United States as a set of 50 individual case studies about what happens when people gain access to the Internet.[7] (Trigger warning: The following paragraph discusses a study about violent crime, specifically rape. I take this subject very seriously and do not go into detail about any specific cases, but if this is too sensitive for you personally, you may pick up reading with the paragraph that begins "*Slate* author . . .")

While controversial, what Kendall found was striking. As each state gained Internet access, the number of rape crimes in those areas decreased. According to Kendall, a 10 percent increase in Internet access was associated with a 7.3 percent decrease in reported rape crimes. Kendall's hypothesis was that, "Internet access appears to be a substitute for rape." More specifically, the Internet provides free access to pornography. This finding drew criticism from the sociology and psychology communities. Karen Cimini, a psychologist who specializes in sexual issues, noted that rape "has more to do with control and power."[8] This idea is also controversial among psychologists, with some scholars suggesting that some portion of rape crimes are indeed sexual in nature. Others theorize that even the act of viewing pornography may itself fulfill a craving for power and may therefore be consistent with both Cimini's and Kendall's propositions. Regardless, this increase in Internet access was found to have no effect on other types of crime, and Kendall noted that the decrease in rape reports was most prominent among 15- to 19-year-old men, for whom pre-Internet pornography was particularly difficult to attain.

Slate author Steve E. Landsburg noted a connection between Kendall's research and a study conducted by University of California professors Gordon Dahl and Stefano DellaVigna.[9] In this study, researchers looked at the effects of movie releases on violent crimes. They found that when violent movies are released, violent crimes tend to decrease. The researchers compared two movies with similar levels of in-theater viewership—*Hannibal* and *Wallace and Gromit: The Curse of the Were-Rabbit*—which both drew about 12 million attendees in theaters and were released on different weekends. Dahl and DellaVigna noted a 2 percent drop in violent crimes for every million people watching violent movies, and even weeks later, the study found no evidence of a resurgence to compensate for the initial decrease in violent crimes.

"You're taking a lot of violent people off the streets and putting them inside movie theaters," explained Dahl in a *New York Times* article. That strikes me as a particularly shallow analysis of what is more likely to be a deep psychological phenomenon. It also happens to be something about which Freud and the psychoanalysts theorized at length.

Carl Jung, a student of Freud, offers what I find to be a much more compelling explanation for the phenomena described by these studies. Jung conceptualized a part of the mind, often equated with Freud's Id, which he called "the shadow"—the unconscious, unexplored parts of our psyches. For Jung, the practice of becoming a conscious, fully integrated person involved voluntary confrontation with this shadow: "Everyone carries a shadow, and the less it is embodied in the individual's conscious life, the blacker and denser it is."[10]

Perhaps it's a confrontation with—or outlet for—the shadow that's happening at broad scale with online anonymity. Rather than repugnant, taboo ideas being repressed en masse, the anonymous Internet provides an outlet for the expression of these ideas without offline incident. When we allow space for the expression of the repressed parts of our selves, we're able to release some of that pent-up tension. If we simply continue to repress these parts, we risk them growing and festering. Like the aforementioned Freudian model of repressed ideas acting like air bubbles held underwater, anonymity online allows for the sublimation of these repressed parts without physical manifestation.

This is not to say that all violent crimes and undesirable behaviors can be solved with access to anonymous online conversations. Rather, if violent movies can reduce some amount of violence and access to the Internet can reduce some amount of sexual crimes, then perhaps some portion of other problematic behaviors can also be avoided if we allow for their expression in simulated containers, like anonymous online communities. We may feel a moral aversion to pornography and violent films, but if there are indeed demonstrable negative correlations between online expressions and their real-world correlates, we ought in the very least to investigate.

To say that the shadow and unconscious are characterized only by dark desires is deeply incorrect—both in the psychological reading and in this metaphor for online anonymity. Platforms like 4chan, which are inherently less strict about enforcing platform-level rules, do indeed foster offensive, disgusting, and otherwise problematic conversations, but even in the darker parts of the Internet, users with malicious intent are the exception more than the norm. As an authority on marketing to Redditors, I'm often asked by people unfamiliar with the platform, "If people are anonymous, aren't they just hateful, racist, misogynist, disgusting, and so on?" I'm always tempted to respond with another question: "Is that who you would be?" For most of us, the answer is an emphatic "No!" Anonymity simply provides us with a fresh lens through which to view the world and one that is significantly more flexible than the Ego- and Superego-driven personas we build on other social platforms. Anonymous platforms allow space for exploration—both of the world and of the self.

ANONYMITY ALLOWS PEOPLE TO CHANGE THEIR MINDS WITHOUT A COST TO THEIR EGOS

This space without Ego is important to users and vital to us as brands— people have room to change their minds. When we participate in social networks like Facebook and Instagram, it's rare to see nuanced discussion, especially about charged or taboo subjects like politics or religion. In Ego and Superego space, we're more interested in defending our beliefs (and the sense of self our beliefs uphold) than we are curious about exploring new ideas. Our posture is, by default, a defensive one. Content that challenges our sense of self feels like a threat. If our opponent outmaneuvers us in a political conversation, we're more likely to disengage than to turn our critical analysis inward.

In Id space, conversation about the taboo thrives, including the political. A political debate isn't on public display—at least not between selves. Political conversation in anonymous space is more a battle between disembodied ideas than between the people who believe them. So while we may find some rhetoric infuriating, frustrating, or appalling, when the discussion happens in anonymous space, the focus remains on the ideas being discussed. Perhaps the best illustration of this sentiment in action is a Reddit community called r/ChangeMyView. As the name suggests, the community is built for users to check their deeply held beliefs in constructive debate. Debates tend to remain civil and live within intellectual confines, rarely devolving into the name-calling, ad hominem attacks we see in more Ego-centric spaces.

The r/ChangeMyView community uses a particular structure for facilitating conversation. First, original posters (OPs) write headlines describing the beliefs they'd like to debate; then they expand on the title with a few paragraphs explaining why they've come to that conclusion. Provided that fellow community members upvote the post and affirm that there is fertile ground for conversation, the other community members chime in to provide different perspectives. Sometimes that means starting from a place of total disagreement, but more often, the divergence of perspective happens in more nuanced parts of the OP's initial statement. Posts in r/ChangeMyView tend to be long, as do the comments, which is a testament to the community's health. Not only are people willing to read long blocks of text but they're willing to do so with the full knowledge that those posts are being written by their intellectual opponents. When a responder offers a perspective that changes an OP's view or gets him or her to think about the problem differently, the OP awards the comment a "delta." The Greek symbol for delta (Δ), synonymous in physics and mathematics with change, is worn as a badge by r/ChangeMyView participants.

Topics in r/ChangeMyView range from politics to corporate policy, religion, ethics, morality, and so on. The community boasts nearly a million members, but the spirit of the community is felt much more broadly throughout the Reddit platform. Often, communities with opposing views develop middle-ground territory with similar mechanics to r/ChangeMyView. Atheist communities created the r/DebateAnAtheist community to facilitate skeptical discussion, and likewise, Christian communities developed r/DebateAChristian. Libertarians created a community called r/AskLibertarians, LGBTQ+ Redditors host a community called r/AskLGBTQ, and vegan Redditors run a community called r/DebateAVegan. Similar communities exist at the fault lines between deeply held beliefs throughout Reddit.

ENGAGING PEOPLE IN ANONYMOUS SPACE REQUIRES THAT WE ADD VALUE AT THE LEVEL OF COMMUNITY

As brands, we're in the business of changing minds. Changing minds is at the heart of everything we do—advertising, marketing, public relations, packaging, positioning, and so on. We're trying to get people to think about our brand as being relevant to them, or recognize that our product solves a problem they have, or agree that our product is better than another product, or that we represent something different from their preconception. Changing minds is central to brand building. And our Egos and Superegos don't like change. By strategically engaging Id networks, we're able to move our messaging upstream to the points at which the broader Internet is actively forming opinions.

As a result of this freedom of expression and more fluid sense of identity, people tend to be more candid in Id networks. They also expect brands to be more genuine. Content that goes behind the scenes, makes people feel involved in something larger, and that sparks genuine discussion will be highly effective at driving meaningful engagement in Id space. Succeeding in Id space also requires a flexibility of persona that's often uncomfortable for traditional brands. UNIQLO is a prime example of the value of candor and flexibility when engaging in conversation as a brand. In 2015, organic posts on Reddit drove more traffic to UNIQLO's online store than any other social channel, with individual posts accounting for upward of 20 percent of all online sales.[11] And not just once—the brand reported that when it posted offers or special sales, individual posts on Reddit regularly accounted for one-fifth of all online purchases.

But that's not where UNIQLO started. Like many brands, UNIQLO noticed some organic chatter about itself in Reddit's fashion communities. A few influential posters advocated for UNIQLO's affordability, good quality, and fashionable aesthetic, and they included the brand in lookbooks and inspiration albums. In 2012, UNIQLO saw some organic traffic spikes directed by Reddit, and the brand began to foster relationships with relevant Reddit communities, like r/MaleFashionAdvice, a community dedicated to sharing fashion inspiration to help men dress better. Actually, it may be a little misleading to say that "the brand" took notice because what followed wasn't a polished suite of new ad creative and an ironclad strategy for capitalizing on this initial signal. Instead, UNIQLO dedicated one e-commerce manager to simply post on Reddit as herself. Arielle Dyda built a relationship with Reddit's fashion communities so strong that the name UNIQLO is as likely to show up in satire about Reddit fashion as it is to appear when the brand is having a sale. And when Redditors start to satirize how much other Redditors love your brand, you'll know you've made it.

Dyda's Reddit account was the antithesis of traditional brand social media presences. Her responses weren't canned—they were prepared fresh. They weren't uniform and preapproved, either. The rough edges and candid approach were features of her interactions. When someone asked a question and Dyda wasn't able to provide the ideal answer, she explained, "I'm on my phone, so I can't access the one from last year (still doesn't load on mobile). If you google UNIQLO linen shirt, the one from last year should still show and load."[12] Can you imagine most major brands acknowledging a flaw on their website *before* people were upset about it? Me neither. Dyda also participated on Reddit in more places than just the fashion communities. She answered questions in r/AskReddit, shared cute pictures of her pets to r/Aww, and posted her wedding video to a frugal wedding planning community to demonstrate why she felt video wasn't the place to cut budget.[13] People on Reddit noticed this, and they loved her for it. She became part of the community, as did UNIQLO.

When UNIQLO gave out vouchers for free apparel from their latest line of HEATTECH and promptly ran out, Redditors weren't happy with the brand. In a thread titled, "PSA: Uniqlo on 5th Ave claim the free heattech vouchers are no longer accepted," designed to alert (and maybe incite) other Redditors to the brand's misleading marketing, Dyda's username was quickly mentioned in the comment thread.[14] In stark contrast to the typical brand social response of "We're sorry to hear that, thanks for letting us know. Please contact us at wedontreallyreadthisinbox@brand.com or give us a call at 1-800-idklmao," Dyda was immediately forthcoming about the situation. She posted, "The fine print says 'while supplies last.' Folks who pulled the 'incognito let me get 5 free t-shirts' ruined it for the rest of you guys." Her comment received over 170 upvotes, more than the initial post itself. The original poster of the thread responded, "I had a shirt in hand, so did [another user]. There was plenty of stock." Dyda explained:

> Of course we have plenty of stock in store to *sell,* but we had a set number of quantity that we were able to give away for free.
>
> You can't honestly think we were going to give away every single unit of Heattech we have on the shop floor, right?
>
> I know it's incredibly frustrating to be one of the ones that were there and suddenly it runs out, but we hit the limit on how many we could give away.
>
> Thanks for the thanks <3 This weekend is going to be a nightmare on Twitter because of this /cry
>
> Let me see what I can do for you guys on here.

Note: For reference, the "<3" is meant to represent a heart, a relic from the pre-emoji Internet. And to "/cry" is to invoke an action as one might in a video game—typing "/cry" into a dialogue box would cause one's character to cry in many online games.

Her response received 196 upvotes, more than any other comment in the thread—and still more than the post itself. Through candor, honesty, and a little bit of snark, Dyda's posts turned what could have been a community uproar into yet another win for UNIQLO. But it's not just the writing style that won the day for Dyda. This response is punchy. It doesn't pull the same "apologize and move communications to private messages" rabbit-out-of-a-hat trick that most community managers are taught. Because she was dealing with a community, she responded to the community. And she did so in a respectful, common-sensical way that explained and defended the brand position. Would Reddit have loved for Dyda to provide everyone with free HEATTECH shirts? Sure. But that type of over-the-top generosity is a combination of PR and marketing strategy and comes with a cost. Dyda's approach to heading off outrage by simply providing a reasonable brand per-spective—something many brands are afraid to do publicly in social media—changed people's minds about the debacle and prevented a potential media frenzy.

This isn't to say that the surprise-and-delight strategy wasn't part of UNIQLO's presence on Reddit. But the brand had the sense to sep-arate moments of genuine brand generosity from PR crisis aversion. In r/AskReddit, a community designed to allow Redditors to ask open-ended questions to the broader community, one poster asked, "Teachers of Reddit, what's the saddest thing you've ever found out about a student?"[15] Inevitably, the comment section filled with gut-wrenching stories from teachers, parents, and fellow students. Among the most popular was this one:

> I just discovered this today, actually.
>
> One of my brightest anatomy students (we'll call her Molly) is going on our school's spring break trip to France. While chat-ting with the teacher chaperone for that trip today, the French teacher mentioned that she bought Molly some clothes and was wondering if Molly was wearing any of them today. When we asked why the teacher had bought Molly clothes, we got this tale:
>
> Molly's mom died while she was in middle school. Molly's dad is a drug addict or alcoholic. Molly, her 2 siblings, and her

dad were all living with Grandpa (who splits his year between IN and FL). Last year, grandpa and dad had a falling out, grandpa kicked dad out of the house, and called CPS for the kids. Since then, Molly and her two siblings have been placed in foster care.

The only reason Molly is able to afford the trip to France is because Grandpa is feeling guilty and is assuaging his guilt by financing the trip.

Back to the clothes: Molly has about 3 outfits that she rotates through. And going on a 10 day trip to France, she simply needs more than that.

On top of the crappy home life, Molly had saved up money to take on the trip with her—about 300 euro. Her dad visited last weekend and stole it. So, she's now using her social security check for the month.

The teacher has bought her clothing, is buying her travel size toiletries, and is covering her "tip" for the tour guide. . . ."

And when the teacher gives Molly all of these things, Molly doesn't even know how to react or accept them. Her exact words were, "Why? You didn't have to do this."

Molly is such a bright student, she has so much potential, she is so sweet and motivated and just an amazing person. Learning this about her past broke my heart today and has been weighing on me ever since . . .

I tried to see if my publisher could print this on waterproof pages, but no dice. Our beloved Dyda, whose username appeared in the r/FrugalMaleFashion subreddit with the flair "Our Lord and Savior" but who is just another Redditor on most other corners of the site, posted a response, "I work for a major clothing retailer. Can you send me Molly's clothing sizes? I'd like to send you some clothing for her." Soon after, Redditors from fashion communities noticed who made the offer and posted a new thread within the r/MaleFashionAdvice community to thank Dyda, "Shoutout to u/midnight1214 (our friendly Uniqlo rep) for this kind gesture on AskReddit," linking to her comment and offer to send clothing to Molly.[16] The poster of Molly's original story soon updated the comment:

EDIT: The outpouring of love and support for Molly has moved
me to tears tonight! Thank you all for your generosity and kind-
ness! I wish I could continue replying to each comment, but this
teacher needs some sleep! I WILL POST UPDATES TOMOR-
ROW AND PM ANYONE THAT HAS SENT A REQUEST.

THANK YOU, FELLOW REDDITORS!! You have restored my
faith in humanity after such a heartbreaking story!

Following suit, Dyda updated her response too:

EDIT did not expect this to blow up. Reddit you are incredi-
bly kind. Your words made me tear up. I need to go to bed. OP
is planning on messaging me with details. Not sure where I'd
post a follow up, but we should try to respect Molly's privacy
as she's in an impossible situation. This isn't about karma, it's
about making sure a young lady has a kick ass trip to France
where she can focus on learning and experiencing and not
worry about what she's going to wear the next day.

Hundreds of Redditors replied to Molly's story and Dyda's offer to
donate clothing. The original poster of Molly's story followed up with
a new post after being encouraged to retell the story in the r/Donate
community. The post was titled, "Molly's Trip to France":

Hello, r/donate!

I posted a comment in r/AskReddit yesterday and received
an overwhelming number of responses for people wanting to
donate money, clothing, and other resources to a student in
need. Here's the link.

For all of you that offered to donate, that offered advice,
and that offered your own stories in light of Molly's, thank you.
Words cannot express how grateful I am to each and every one
of you. This money will be used to fund Molly's trip to France,
provide her and her siblings with clothing, and let her experience the overwhelming generosity of mankind. Thank you will
never be enough!

. . .

Your support of this student and so many like her is what makes teaching just a little bit easier. The community that we have built is so important on so many levels and I am truly awe-struck at the generosity of the reddit community.

Thank you, thank you, thank you!

EDIT Please remain patient with me for updated amounts. . . . Right now, our Community Relations Chair is for-warding me every email she receives (one per donation) and I'm personally adding them up for a total. Our poor Community Service Chair's inbox. . . . Reddit Hug of Death . . .

UPDATED AMOUNT $2,093.98 !!!!

Because the scholarship was set up for this France trip, we have decided to use the funds in the following ways:

(1) The teacher was able to add and pay for a morning trip to Versailles for all the students attending.

(2) All students' tip to the tour guide will be covered.

(3) All students' lunches will be purchased with the money.

(4) A nice souvenir for each student traveling will be purchased.

Because of your generosity, Molly gets to keep her social security check and we are recommending that she sets up a bank account this summer, as soon as she turns 16 (and no longer needs the guardian signature, to our knowledge). This will help her be able to better care for her savings and keep it from the unfortunate circumstances that befell her first savings.

Boxes of donations are beginning to arrive and we are beyond amazed at your generosity!

Clothing from Uniqlo!

Instax Camera and Film![17]

If that's not one of the most genuine, human, authentic, insert-whatever-buzzword-you-want-here interactions between a brand and community, I don't know what is. Again, the windfall and posi-tive reception were in large part thanks to Dyda's approach. She didn't swoop in with a response crafted by PR professionals or try to insert buzzy brand language. She was just being a nice fellow Reddit com-munity member who represented UNIQLO. Dyda's simple one-line response and offer to donate a few articles of clothing generated over 13,000 upvotes from Redditors, attracting orders of magnitude more eyeballs than that.

Over time and thoughtful moments like these, Dyda created a genuine connection between the UNIQLO brand and Reddit's fashion communities. Years later, long since Dyda left her role with UNIQLO, Redditors continue to post favorably about the brand and are often mentioned in user-created guides like "The Basic Bastard: British Budget Edition," which became a top post among r/MaleFashionAdvice's 2.2 million subscribers.[18] UNIQLO is so commonly recommended by Redditors that those new to Reddit's fashion communities often spark threads like "Best of Uniqlo," a post in r/FemaleFashionAdvice which reads:

> Is there a best-of-Uniqlo thread that I can't find? Please tell me your faves, if not! I'm heading to a brick and mortar store for the first time this week, and I'm eyeing the merino wool sweaters, the heattech turtleneck and the leggings pants. Any other best pieces I need to try?[19]

The post generated over 300 upvotes and over 150 comments.

As you may surmise from many of these posts, Redditors talk about Reddit in a way that's distinctly different from how people on Facebook talk about Facebook. Reddit users feel like "Redditors" in a way that Facebook users will never be "Facebookers." The sense of community within Reddit is thanks in large part to the way the platform organizes people. Because Reddit is by default anonymous, it organizes people around interests and ideas rather than offline connections, which generates more shared experiences among members. The same principle is true for a huge number of other interest-based forums, anonymous networks like 4chan and Tumblr, and in rare instances even extends to some interest-based groups in Ego and Superego networks. When organized around interests and ideas, people tend naturally to form a sense of community. They're exposed to the same content, they engage in group conversations, and their borders are drawn around their commonalities. They form customs and inside jokes—shared memes—that differentiate the locals from the tourists.

PEOPLE ARE MORE AUTHENTIC WHEN THEY'RE ANONYMOUS, AND THEY EXPECT BRANDS TO BE MORE CANDID TOO

In Id networks, people are willing to discuss problems and questions they can't begin to address in identity-based networks. The r/Relationships_Advice community is brimming with threads like, "My friend is about to ask his girlfriend to marry [him] and I'm the only one who knows how unfaithful she is. Do I say anything?"[20] The r/AskWomen community is filled with men asking women candid questions like, "What are some things that guys misinterpret from women as 'she's interested in me'?", and the r/AskMen community facilitates an inverse set of similar conversations.[21] The r/PersonalFinance community allows people to discuss everything from loans to debt to figuring out what to do with lottery winnings. Seriously, one infamous thread from 2015 was titled, "Serious—won lottery, paid of all debts, terrified of financial advisors and investing. Advice?"[22] In case you're curious, the user was pointed to a community called r/FinancialIndependence, which contains resources to help people calculate a "safe withdrawal rate" that will allow them to retire early and comfortably.

For financial brands, communities like r/PersonalFinance offer unique kinds of engagements given Redditors' comfort in discussing intimate details of their financial lives. The Charles Schwab brand took an interesting approach to adding value to these conversational financial communities by opening lanes of dialogue with challenging questions. With its brand creative platform being, "Own your tomorrow," Charles Schwab prompted Redditors with an open-ended question: "What's something you're doing today to set yourself up for success tomorrow?"[23]

Encouraging Redditors to answer from all aspects of their lives, the brand generated an engaging thread of constructive life choices. Redditors talked about doing yoga, putting more money into savings, starting investment portfolios, contributing toward future children's college funds, and so on. But as these open-ended threads tend to go, the top comment wasn't a straightforward response to the prompt. The comment the Reddit community upvoted most was this one from u/esotericendeavor:

I just want to take this opportunity to thank you guys for being such a great bank. With my history of travel, simply making use of my Schwab checking account has been unbelievably helpful. I have never had to worry about finding an acceptable atm and even when I have had issues, while it may sound cliché, your customer service has always gone above and beyond. One time I was stuck in a foreign country for a minute and I forgot to add a travel alert beforehand. Luckily the "Live-Chat" team saved the day and was able to get my card working again without the trouble of an international call. So to be honest, "what [I'm] doing today to make [my] tomorrow better" is by sticking with Schwab. Because you have proven that you have my back, once I am out of college, I will not think twice of investing with you too.

It's the kind of response you wouldn't fault the Charles Schwab marketing team for having conjured up in a group daydream. But here it was, and this comment greeted every new user who entered the thread. The Charles Schwab brand developed an editorial series of similar prompts designed to generate interesting discussion, ranging from lofty, engagement-focused questions like this one to more specific and informational prompts like, "What does 'wealthy' mean to you? Here's where some of the top US cities draw the line between 'financial comfort' and 'wealth'" and "What's your approach to tracking gains and losses in your trading history and learning from your past?"[24, 25]

Inevitably, Charles Schwab has answers for many of the questions that arise naturally in these threads, but they wield their authority carefully because the brand recognizes the communal nature of Reddit. Redditors trust the opinions of other Redditors, and when relevant, Charles Schwab's team interjects with helpful information, content from the Charles Schwab site, or the team directs people to the company's customer service channels. By utilizing their marketing dollars to add value by providing a platform for financial discussion, the Charles Schwab brand continues to earn its place in Reddit's finance communities.

Reddit isn't the only example of this sense of community mani-festing in Id networks. Even the edgy and controversial 4chan boards foster a sense of community among members. Sometimes that man-ifests in strange ways, such as the time 4chan hijacked a Walmart Facebook contest to send Pitbull to one of the smallest towns in the United States.[26, 27] Pitbull took the trolling in stride, though, and delighted the residents of Kodiak, Alaska, with a performance. All 6,000 of them.[28] Then there's the time that Mountain Dew hosted a contest to name their new apple flavor, and 4chan voted en masse for names like, "Hitler did nothing wrong," and, "Diabeetus," putting an end to the myth that all PR is good PR.[29] Or there was the time Tay-lor Swift offered to perform for the top-voted school in a Facebook contest, and 4chan managed to place the Horace Mann School for the Deaf and Hard of Hearing at the top of the list.[30] Swift ended up donating $50,000 to the school anyway, turning the stunt into a happy ending while still making for some darkly hilarious news headlines. Most of the time, 4chan pranks aren't meant to be overly malicious. In 4chan terms, trolling is done "for the lulz"—the pranks are what happens when a dedicated army follows through on one person's half-baked "Wouldn't it be funny if . . ." showerthought.

When 4chan does find a cause to care about, the community mobilizes. One of my favorite examples of 4chan for good started on September 1, 2010, when a poster shared a photo of a flier he or she found at a grocery store in Ashburnham, Massachusetts. It was an invitation to the birthday party of a man named William J. Lashua, a 90-year-old World War II veteran.[31, 32] "Wanted," read the top of the flier, below which sat a deadpan photo of Lashua sitting in a kitchen chair. "People for Birthday Party. Date: September 4, 2010. Time: 1pm to 4pm. Ashburn American Legion." Whether the sudden outburst of empathy was sparked by the idea of a senior vet spending a birthday alone or the fact that Lashua bore a striking resemblance to the old man in the Disney movie *Up*, the movement gained traction overnight.

"Awesome! Everybody send him nice cards, it will be pretty cool, not to mention 4chan could use some pure honest good publicity," one commenter pointed out. As a brief aside, that's an interesting way for an anonymous user to think about the platform on which he or she is posting. In my entire career of observing social media activity, I've never witnessed someone strategize to drive good publicity for Facebook or Twitter or Instagram or Pinterest or Google. This comment alludes to a very different relationship between user and platform than what we traditionally think of as social media. 4chan users, problematic as they can be, consider themselves a community.

Hundreds of handwritten notes and thousands of posts later, 4chan and the other communities they managed to recruit followed through on their promise. Video recaps of Lashua's birthday generated hundreds of thousands of views and featured group cards signed by people from all around the world.[33] Well wishes flooded in from Australia, Ireland, all around the United States, and everywhere in between. Heartwarming photos surfaced of Lashua kneeling beside massive piles of cards, a look of mild confusion ultimately overwhelmed by the joy of the surprise; Lashua saluting next to an American flag; and even a photo of Lashua deadpan flipping off the camera.

4chan isn't likely to show up in many brands' marketing mixes, and it'll probably never be an important connection point between brands and their audiences, but the sense of community 4chan fosters and the relationships between the 4chan platform and its users are indicative of how Id networks differ from traditional social media platforms. However we feel about 4chan and its antics, the community has a point of view and culture shared by its members. They embrace their status as outcasts, feeling as if their moral compass is better honed thanks to their "outside" perspective. It's the same sentiment shared by groups of outcasts throughout history—the Internet simply provides this community with unique ways to organize and express that identity.

For many brands, entering into community-driven space sounds nice in theory but difficult (or impossible) in practice. Few social marketers will discount the power of a platform like Reddit when its community coordinates to do something. The problem most brands face is in finding a way to harness that energy into something constructive, intentional, and mutually beneficial. Entering anonymous Internet space and trying to drive users toward a goal can feel like jumping into a pool and trying to put some water in your pocket for later. When we enter community space, we need to understand that we can't command every part of the conversation surrounding our brand

and category. When someone splashes you in the pool, the correct response is to laugh and splash back. The more we struggle to bend communities to our will, the more energy we waste and the more frustrated we become. That's why we need to channel our thinking into organic behaviors that we can amplify rather than trying to define behaviors ourselves.

When I joined Reddit in 2016 to build the brand strategy team, the question underlying my conversations with nearly every large brand was, "Why take the risk?" If we can't control the entirety of our narrative in community space, why bother? The answer has two parts. First, the community will talk about your brand, regardless of whether or not you're there. Second, these are the places people are making decisions about your brand. For some brands, that happens to work out nicely—the community simply loves your products. But for most brands, the conversation is mixed. Some people have great experiences, and a few people don't. Unfortunately, the Internet tends to be more interested in the latter than the former, and as consumers, we tend to be more vocal about the latter anyway. At the very least, we ought to be listening for what these candid conversations are saying about our brand, and we ought to find a constructive way to participate in this space too.

Earlier in this chapter, we discussed some statistics about online trust. Amazon and Google ranked at the top, Reddit fell a few percentage points behind, and the cluster of traditional social media networks fell 20 to 30 percentage points behind Reddit. The trust built up within Reddit is in part due to the community culture of valuing truth over influence. On Reddit, you're judged more by what you say than who you are offline or what your profile picture looks like. Reddit not only surfaces content democratically but it also ensures that its conversation hierarchy is dictated by a parallel democratic process. That means users collectively choose what content gets seen and what conversation happens around that content. This attitude is something of which Redditors are consciously aware, and they're often vocal about their trust in the community. In theory, all opinions are weighed equally on Reddit.

As we peer down the road toward the future of online trust, riddled with potholes like deep fakes, fake news, political scandals, media bias, opaque algorithms, and the rest, it seems only natural for trust to return to online spaces that are user driven, meritocratic, and community centric. Compounded by the natural flow of content from Id networks to Superego and Ego networks, building positive relations between these communities and our brands must be a priority for our broader digital strategies. As brands, we need to recognize that we have a footprint within these anonymous communities and that people are trusting the impression they form within them. Shouldn't we be there to participate, express ourselves, and course correct when necessary? In doing so, we're able to affect brand sentiment upstream where positive impressions are likely to flow through the rest of the social ecosystem.

As with all engagement marketing, our primary focus in Id networks should be to add value. What adds value in anonymous, community-centric space is often very different from what adds value in identity-based social networks. UNIQLO's approach to adding value involved a combination of customer service, surprise and delights, and value-based offerings like sales and discounts, Where UNIQLO chose to deliver that value through an engaging organic presence, Charles Schwab delivered its series of editorial prompts through paid promotion. Both strategies come with trade-offs. An organic-first strategy stands to deliver more evergreen, ongoing results that build over time. Participating organically in communities like Reddit also requires manpower and process to keep the brand presence streamlined and consistent. Advertising in Id networks requires much the same mindset as maintaining an organic presence, but it provides a clearer path to scale with more flexibility of moderation, which is particularly helpful for those marketers with brand safety concerns.

ADDING VALUE IN ANONYMOUS SPACE MEANS PIQUING GENUINE INTEREST, THEN DELIVERING

Whether we're approaching these channels from the perspective of paid media or organic presence, we're always aiming to add value. One way we can do that is simply by being entertaining. We can usually predict what will be entertaining to a community by observing what they do organically, and finding a way to improve or polish that experience. The Audi brand did exactly that with its Think Faster series on Reddit.[34] The brand noted a highly engaged community called r/iama, in which celebrities and people with generally interesting experiences offer to conduct what's called an Ask Me Anything (AMA). In an AMA, a person dedicates a few hours to answer any and all questions upvoted by the Reddit community. Barack Obama, Bill Gates, Edward Snowden, Jane Goodall, and a vacuum repairman rank among Reddit's most prominent AMAs over the years.[35, 36, 37, 38, 39, 40] Yes, the vacuum repairman is worth reading—he's hilarious. Just Google "iama vacuum repair technician."

The Audi brand decided to run the AMA through its brand filter. The result was Think Faster, a series of livestreamed AMAs conducted from performance cars on actual racetracks. Celebrity partners were brought to the track, strapped into an Audi TT RS, and driven around by professional racecar drivers at over 130 miles per hour—all while trying to answer the Internet's wacky questions. The first two episodes of Think Faster featured Adam Scott and Elizabeth Banks, two celebrities with major fan communities throughout Reddit. The two AMAs drew over 1,000 comments during their three-hour stream. The campaign generated 75.6 million media impressions and 10.4 million social impressions. Audi went on to host four more episodes of Think Faster, which continued to draw massive viewership and engagement among Reddit communities.

When working with an organic trend with as much popularity and rigor as the AMAs, it's vital to follow the organic formula, except in cases where we have very good reasons to diverge. Audi balanced this perfectly in its attention to detail about the culture surrounding the AMAs. Organically, in the dozens of AMAs that happen every day on Reddit, the hosts provide a "proof photo" to clarify who they are. Audi created similar proof photos for promotion of the AMAs, while dressing talent in white Audi-branded racing suits. And where it may have been functionally easier to separate the question-gathering phase from the actual livestream, the brand understood how important the real-time feel was. As with the traditional AMAs, the Think Faster comment threads opened for questions a few hours before the AMAs actually started, infusing this campaign with the excitement of a live event. Preserving the essential AMA structure allowed Audi to step naturally into the Reddit community, even though the entire experience was delivered through advertising.

In Id networks, it's especially important to demonstrate that the brand understands the local culture. Because these spaces are more community minded and because they develop their own customs, memes, vernacular, and so on, as brands in this space, we need to proceed with some humility and start with listening. Once we understand the culture and how people participate organically, it becomes easier to understand what types of brand behaviors we can exhibit to add value to people's experiences in ways that are mutually beneficial. While that might sound like a lot of work, the truth is that cultural relevance—something to which most brands aspire according to their social strategies—takes work. Humans are complex. Communities are even more complex. Succeeding in this Internet ecosystem requires thoughtfulness and observation. We wouldn't extend our brand into a new country without carefully considering how our brand name, visuals, taglines, and ads might translate into the local language. The same considerations ought to apply to how we think about online cultures.

Perhaps the best example of a brand truly listening and reacting to the Reddit culture came from Wieden+Kennedy's The Lodge team on behalf of a robotics company called Anki. The Lodge set out to introduce the Reddit community to a little toy robot with a big personality named Cozmo. Cozmo could recognize faces and play a couple games, and he acted like a tiny digital pet with a little extra attitude. Cozmo didn't serve much of a functional purpose, but once his personality was on display, it was obvious how much fun he could be.

So one day, Cozmo got lost in Reddit. That was the narrative behind the campaign—the creative team worked with professional set designers and stop motion artists to construct an elaborate series of escape rooms themed after subreddits.[41] Cozmo was placed in the first room and broadcast via livestream to the Reddit community—but with a twist. The livestream was an interactive choose-your-own-adventure experience in which Redditors had to band together to solve puzzles, navigate the escape rooms, and help Cozmo find his way to the front page. Cozmo started his journey in a room themed after r/HailCorporate, a dark and dingy, post-apocalyptic downtown

New York–feeling set, which represented a community of Redditors dedicated to calling out seedy advertising. Immediately, this self-deprecating note set the right tone with Redditors. The only thing Reddit likes more than making fun of advertisers is when advertisers make fun of advertisers.

What room should he enter next? What should he do when he gets there? How can he solve the puzzle? Which block should he move where? The livestream's comment thread lit up with debate about where to take Cozmo. In a room themed after the r/RarePuppers community, Cozmo navigated around actual puppies to unlock treats for the doggos. In the comments, one skeptical Redditor mentioned, "I only believe this is live, when a dog makes a shit," and as fate would have it, another quickly responded, "There's one there!"[42] In the r/WhatCouldGoWrong room, Redditors had to adjust a trebuchet that would fling Cozmo across the set and (hopefully) into the safety of a hammock. Disclaimer: a number of Cozmos were hurt during the process of filming. The r/WhatCouldGoWrong community is an accumulation of videos that prompt watchers to rhetorically ask themselves, "What could go wrong . . . ?", and the room delivered on the community ethos. The trebuchet itself was actually a nod to another inside joke among Redditors. The r/TrebuchetMemes community is an odd slice of meme culture in which subscribers rally around the fact that trebuchets were more effective siege weapons than catapults. A word of advice, don't mention catapults on Reddit. Don't ask why. (Because I don't really know.)

Cozmo, himself being a high-quality robot, navigated through the r/ShittyRobots room, where he dealt with some less capable robo-brethren. Cozmo activated and deactivated parts of an unpredictable shark-with-hands robot to avoid destruction and unlock the next room. After a lengthy six hours of solving eight escape rooms, Redditors finally solved each of the puzzles. It was the first time anyone—let alone an *advertiser*—had reflected back to Redditors with such production value and cultural awareness an experience based on the communities they'd built. It was, at the time, the most engaging Reddit campaign to ever launch, and Redditors were vocal about their love.

"This is the best use of obvious advertising on the Internet!!! Prior to this, I had no use for a tiny robot, but now I want one so bad!!!!"

wrote one player.[43] Inevitably, some commenters had mean things to say about advertising, but the majority of Redditors wanted to make sure the Cozmo team knew they'd done a great job: "Commenters— you are doing an awesome job, this is all in all a pretty impressive effort to make this thing happen. I know it's marketing, but it really shows you spent a lot of thought and effort into this, don't let nasty comments spoil it. Can't wait for the gag reel."[44] Cozmo successfully won over Redditors by immersing in the culture and reflecting that culture back with some surprises and an overall fun experience. The livestream was so compelling that some Redditors, unable to access the content, started to share instructions on how to disable ad blockers so they could view the experience and participate.

The paths to engaging Id network communities are truly limitless, with best-in-class examples ranging from the ultrapolished and productionized Cozmo Gets Lost in Reddit and Audi's Think Faster series to simply asking interesting questions the way Charles Schwab did. For some brands, the ability to interact with these deeply engaged and influential communities without polished brand assets is a major opportunity. When we observe spaces like Reddit, Twitch, 4chan, 9gag, Tumblr, and the rest of the anonymous Internet, these communities tend to organically create and circulate low-polish, no-frills content. As advertisers, we should feel confident following suit. In contrast, for brands that pride themselves on polish and flash, this norm of amateur-created content can provide a perfect foil for creating high-production experiences that surprise and impress our audiences, when done in culturally relevant ways. The most important rule for engaging anonymous online communities is to start from a place of observation aimed at cultural understanding. Online communities can be double-edged swords for brands. When done right, building relationships with online communities means creating an ongoing endorsement engine, a passionate and vocal group of fans, and a built-in focus group. When mishandled, communities can organize to cause problems that people in social media platforms generally don't.

When people enter online space anonymously, they're more open, honest, candid, creative, expressive, and truthful. As brands, truthfulness sometimes hurts our feelings. However, this prioritization of truth above influence will only continue to foster this elusive sense of community built up in anonymous networks. And with community comes trust. If we're truly invested in making our brand relevant in digital culture, receiving actionable feedback from people, and becoming more trustworthy, Id space is exactly where we need to look. Anonymous communities capture the most creative, altruistic, weird, and wacky parts of people. They're far from the hellish pits the popular media make them out to be. They're not perfect, but they're among the most candid and truthful modes of expression yet available to us as humans. Whether or not we choose to engage in these spaces directly, maintaining cultural relevance online depends on understanding these communities.

KEY TAKEAWAYS

- Id networks are those in which we're disconnected from our offline identities and organized around common interests and ideas. We're more expressive and more willing to explore new ideas.

- Because we're organized around common interests and exposed to more shared experiences, Id networks foster a sense of community that's distinctly different from identity-based social platforms.

- To drive meaningful engagement in Id networks, we must appeal to the community rather than to the individual, which means fostering group conversation and creating content with depth.

- Members of Id network communities trust the opinions and information uplifted by the group. In order to change brand perception, we should address the community, not just individual members.

- Because users are their most transparent, candid selves in Id networks, we should aspire to be our most transparent, candid selves as brands too. PR and marketing-speak almost always backfire in Id network community relations.

PART III

SOCIAL MEDIA'S RIGHT AND LEFT BRAINS

LEFT AND RIGHT BRAIN NETWORKS

The Known and the Unknown

I t's your first day on vacation. You're somewhere new. And it's not like, "Oh, the license plates are a little different here." You can't even read the street signs let alone recognize the alphabet. You sit down in a restaurant that serves a cuisine you've never tried. The menu isn't much help, but at least there are a few pictures for reference. Your server comes over to ask if you're ready to order, the two of you discuss specific dishes and the proper amount, and you place your order. The smells of the restaurant are new and unfamiliar—even the bread they've placed on your table tastes like nothing you've had before. You're excited to try something new, even if part of you wonders if you'll like any of the food you've just ordered. Maybe part of you is even wondering how late the fast-food place by your hotel is open . . . you know, just in case. But that's not the part of you that brought you here.

Your food comes, and you realize you've ordered twice as much as you can actually eat. But that was all part of the plan, really. Each dish is a new cliff for you to jump off, and you willingly dive into uncharted waters. What is it made from? Would you eat these ingredients if you knew what they were? Your brain is acutely tuned to the influx of novelty you're experiencing in the present moment. You like most of it just fine. You absolutely love one of the dishes, and you've hardly touched a couple others. Just as you've resolved to put down your utensil, the waiter comes back to your table carrying a small bowl of vanilla ice cream.

What are your emotions? Surprise? Gratitude? Happiness? Maybe tinges of homesickness and nostalgia? Assuming that vanilla ice cream is a food with which you're well accustomed, this little taste of the familiar in an unfamiliar territory is a welcome respite. It carries some powerful positive emotions. Had you been in your favorite ice cream shop back home, you might not have batted an eye at "plain vanilla," but here among exotic, new flavors, this little dish of ice cream feels anything but plain. It's a little taste of order among the chaos.

Now imagine that you've returned home. After having traveled abroad and experienced more new things than you can count, you visit your favorite casual lunch spot. You order a dish you've had dozens of times before. If you'd starred in a 1990s TV sitcom and had just requested, "The usual!", it's the dish that would show up. It's a dish you can picture with near total clarity through your mind's tongue. When it arrives, you take a bite and notice something different. Maybe it's made with a different ingredient, or it's accompanied by an unfamiliar side dish. You ask the waiter to confirm your order, and he does—they've just made some tweaks to the menu.

What are your emotions this time? Surprise again? Some disappointment? Frustration? *Betrayal?!* You're a dramatic one, aren't you? You haven't even really decided whether or not you like this new version of your old dish, but one thing is certain—you didn't get what you expected. And that's jarring, even in cases where change turns out to be good.

In neither case have we made an explicit value judgment about the experience of novelty. In the first example, we're immersed in the unknown. We're in an unfamiliar place eating unfamiliar food, and our brains are tuned into these raw, new experiences. Even if we're a little apprehensive about all of this unfamiliarity, we have no prior knowledge with which to compare, so we have no choice but to be present in the experience of something new and to process things as they're presented to us. When we're in this mode of exploration, what's usual becomes exotic, and even something simple like a bowl of vanilla ice cream can become a welcome refuge of familiarity.

When we're surrounded by the world of the known, our world-view changes. When we feel familiar with a place, situation, or person, our brains have created internal representations of them by processing our past experiences. We've placed our familiar subjects into categories and frameworks that allow us to make sense of the world around us. Otherwise, we'd have to treat every experience as new and unique, meaning we couldn't really learn anything useful about the world. When our internal simulation fails to match up with the way reality unfolds, we're forced to rethink our model. When we're immersed in what we know, even a hint of the unexpected can feel jarring. A new set of mental processes is thrown into gear.

How our brains deal with what is familiar and what is novel has much to do with the context in which we experience them. The way we interact with things that are familiar to us is fundamentally different from how we interact with something new. In fact, some psychologists theorize that our brains are structured around this divide. We know, for example, that in patients who've had their corpus callosum severed, the band of nerves that connect the left and right hemispheres, the two hemispheres begin to operate almost independently of one another.[1] We also find that the corpus callosum seems to inhibit information as much as it transfers information between the hemispheres, as it appears that both sides of the brain are capable of performing overlapping tasks.[2] We're equipped with two fully functioning minds with drastically different worldviews.

OUR RIGHT HEMISPHERES DEAL WITH THE CHAOTIC UNKNOWN, FROM WHICH OUR LEFT HEMISPHERES CREATE A SENSE OF KNOWN ORDER

Throughout our evolutionary struggle, it was crucial that our ancestors maintained two separate perspectives about the world. And not just our ancestors either—the hemispheric structure of the brain is found in most vertebrates.[3] In his book *The Master and His Emissary*, psychiatrist Dr. Iain McGilchrist offers an explanation as to how the two consciousnesses evolved. Even in simpler creatures like birds, two separate consciousnesses are necessary for survival. First, a bird needs a broad, big-picture awareness of its surroundings to avoid danger. Danger can come from anywhere at any time, and it can present itself in many different forms. Second, a bird requires a focused beam of attention to hone in on food, land on branches, and peck accurately. The former is the responsibility of the right hemisphere, while the latter is the responsibility of the left. McGilchrist identifies these as the primordial conditions from which humans' more complex left and right hemispheres emerged.

Our right hemisphere is the domain of raw experience with the world, while our left hemisphere creates a workable representation of the world based on the right's experience. Our right hemispheres evolved to deal with the abstract, omnipresent concept of danger. The right brain experiences the world directly through sensory inputs, and each of its experiences is treated as new and unique. We also find more white matter in our right hemispheres, which is associated with coordinating communication between brain regions. Because danger presents itself in many forms, our right hemisphere tends toward broader but low-resolution awareness of the world. It sees the big picture and is able to connect seemingly disparate ideas into concepts like metaphors.

The right hemisphere tends to see the world as a complex, fluid, living experience. It's in the right hemisphere that we recognize other living things as more than parts of an environment. Research has shown that between 70 and 80 percent of mothers tend to favor carrying their children on their left side, making eye contact with the left eye controlled by the right hemisphere.[5] And it's not only true of humans either—walruses, orca whales, kangaroos, and a number of other animals have demonstrated the same preference. The right hemisphere's emotional processing is associated with our ability to empathize—to understand the experience of something we recognize as a fellow living being.

In contrast, the left hemisphere takes on a more mechanistic view of the world. It tends to see the world as an accumulation of small, dissectible parts, and focuses on specifics. The left hemisphere relies on experiential inputs from the right hemisphere to develop its re-presented worldview. The left brain is the domain of categorization, analysis, and manipulation. It's the left hemisphere that recognizes objects as tools, allowing us to manipulate the world to our benefit. Where the right brain experiences the world as a set of unique instances, the left categorizes each instance into a working model of the world—something we can examine, and from which we can abstract broader truths. By creating this re-presented model of the world, the left hemisphere creates a domain of familiarity—after all, if every experience were completely new and unique, we could never predict what might happen next. The left brain categorizes the experiences of the right so that we can put those learnings to use in the future.

Much of what we've learned about the functions of the right and left hemispheres comes from studying the effects of damage to either side. Patients with damage to their right hemispheres, for example, sometimes develop what is called the *Capgras delusion*, wherein they believe someone close to them, often a spouse or family member, has been replaced by an identical imposter.[6] The afflicted patient is unable to connect the person they knew previously—an internal representation—with the person standing in front of them. Some forms of right hemispheric damage even cause patients to be unable to recognize faces because the individual parts that make up our faces are constantly distorting as we communicate.[7] We squint our eyes, raise our eyebrows, flare our nostrils, and distort the shapes of our mouths to express particular emotions. While the left brain's focused beam of attention sees each part, it is the right brain that recognizes that these individual parts belong to a single living whole.

THE RIGHT HEMISPHERE IS EXPRESSIVE, WHILE THE LEFT HEMISPHERE IS REPRESENTATIVE

True to its pop culture caricature, the right hemisphere does indeed deal more with emotion than the left, and the left's abilities to categorize and analyze are often equated to its function as the logic center—although the relationship isn't quite that simple. Because the left hemisphere is the domain of representation, it's better able to categorize and analyze the world. The left brain's ability to perform high-level logical processing caused early neuroanatomists to identify it as the dominant hemisphere. However, McGilchrist is wary of that designation. In reality, even seemingly cold, logical processing first passes through the emotional center in the right brain and returns to the right brain after that logical processing occurs. Everything is processed by the right hemisphere, while the left is limited to particular functions. Given the purposes of each hemisphere, this structure should make intuitive sense. The world is, by default, unknown to us. There is a lot more of the unknown than there is of us.

One way to understand the distinction between right and left hemispheres is to think of the right hemisphere as expressive and the left as representative. While language was long thought to be contained exclusively within the left hemisphere, different kinds of language are stored in both hemispheres. The left brain is responsible for understanding grammar, storing our broader vocabulary, and generally maintaining representations of higher-order learned rules, while the right contains essential expressive and metaphorical language connected directly to our emotional processing and experience of the world.

While both hemispheres represent vastly different, perhaps even incompatible, worldviews, the relationship between them is deeply nuanced. Rarely, if ever, do we use one side or the other exclusively. We're constantly passing information back and forth—and inhibiting certain information from being transmitted—between our left and right hemispheres. I emphasize the nuances here because as we discuss these characteristics, it's tempting to conceptualize them as separate, closed systems. In reality, the hemispheres are in constant communication. One will always affect the other.

The right hemisphere also tends to be associated with unconscious thought processes, while the left controls what we often consider to be higher orders of conscious expression, like speaking and writing. As we review these qualities of the right and left hemispheres, we'll start to recognize overlapping characteristics with the Id, Ego, and Superego—and the social network structures with which they correspond.

The Id, containing our unfiltered, unconscious self, seems to share many of its characteristics with the right brain—expressive, experiential, and explorative. The Ego, being a representation of the self in the context of the outside world, and the Superego, being a representation of our learned social rules, seem to fit comfortably in the left brain's domain of categorization and analysis of the represented world.

In Ego and Superego networks, we're creating literal representations of ourselves in simulated social worlds, and we're connected to people in an environment we've curated—a world of familiarity. When we're scrolling through a feed filled with content from the people we know, we're generally in known, left brain territory. When we're searching for new information or are exploring a new topic as we might in Id networks, we're wading into the unfamiliar—right brain territory. We're not concerned with creating a representation of our offline selves because we tend to be anonymous and engaged directly with information as we encounter it.

Intuitively, Ego and Superego networks may seem to be the more likely candidates for genuine personal connection because these are spaces in which we're connected to the people we know offline. But again, we're most often dealing with public representations of our friends, not our friends directly. When something tragic happens to us, our friends may make public posts offering condolences in an Ego network, but our close friends likely (hopefully) also reach out to us through a more direct medium like calling, texting, or emailing. The public post is a representation of their support and friendship, while the direct communication is a raw emotional expression between living beings. With empathy being a function of the right brain's emotional processing, it follows that communities tend to form more naturally within Id networks suited to right brain expression.

We may even think about Ego and Superego networks as tools of a kind. We use them to create and maintain representations of our social selves. As social creatures, we're constantly building our "personal brands," whether consciously or unconsciously. When we participate in left brain, identity-based networks in which we're connected to our friends, we generally know what to expect—or at least we like to think we do.

ID NETWORKS ARE EXPRESSIVE, WHILE EGO AND SUPEREGO NETWORKS ARE REPRESENTATIVE

When we participate in social media, we create representations of ourselves that are informed both by our inner selves and the complex social ecosystems into which we're entering. These personal brands we build to represent ourselves aren't expressions of vanity or narcissism. They serve real utility in complex social environments. If you can expect me to behave in a way that's consistent with how I've represented myself to you, and if I can expect the same from you, we have a shared foundation for interaction. While the right brain is responsible for recognizing consistency of personhood—understanding that you are the same person you were yesterday despite your new haircut, those new nose piercings, and that sick new face tattoo (is that

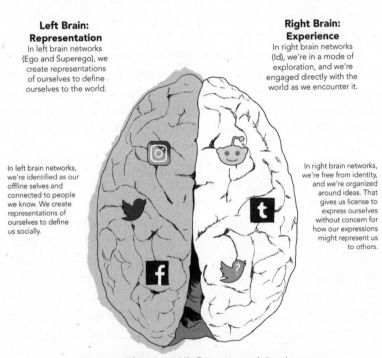

Left Brain: Representation
In left brain networks (Ego and Superego), we create representations of ourselves to define ourselves to the world.

Right Brain: Experience
In right brain networks (Id), we're in a mode of exploration, and we're engaged directly with the world as we encounter it.

In left brain networks, we're identified as our offline selves and connected to people we know. We create representations of ourselves to define us socially.

In right brain networks, we're free from identity, and we're organized around ideas. That gives us license to express ourselves without concern for how our expressions might represent us to others.

When we use a left brain network like Twitter anonymously, it can become a right brain network for us as individuals. Likewise, if we engage a platform like Reddit as our offline persona, it can become a left brain network.

FIGURE 8.1 **Left Versus Right Brain**

Gonzo from the Muppets?)—it's likely a left brain function to navigate self-representation. In doing so, we create "known" territory about ourselves for others. In left brain Ego and Superego networks, our connections expect us to maintain a consistent represented version of ourselves (Figure 8.1).

While we can conceptualize Ego and Superego networks as known space, it doesn't take much to submerge us in chaos. You know that feeling when you find a spider in your bedroom and suddenly you're *absolutely positive* you just felt something crawling on your back? The same thing happens when we see an unexpected political rant on Facebook, or when someone airs dirty laundry about their ex on Instagram. The unknown rears its ugly head. When we're in left brain territory, the unknown and unexpected threaten to tear down our represented structures, so whenever possible, we try to ignore it. We don't want to change our minds in left brain space because that means throwing out a set of presumptions that we're actively using to navigate the world.

Only when the unknown presents itself in manageable, positive ways are we able to embrace it as harmless novelty—like a friend popping up in our feed doing the ALS Ice Bucket Challenge or a D-list celebrity responding to a tweet (because, let's be honest, Jeff Goldblum isn't going to get back to ~~me~~ you about naming ~~my~~ your Roomba "Jeff Goldblum"). Because the left brain deals with a world characterized by representation and categorization, something that doesn't fit into the framework automatically registers as a threat. We expect our connections to act in ways that are consistent with the versions of them stored in our heads, and we resist new information that doesn't fit neatly into our representation of the world.

When we're freed from our represented selves and disconnected from our friends, and we're in a mode of exploration, we're immersed in the unknown—Id, right brain networks. Even when we're familiar with a particular Id network space, like a community we frequent, we're never sure who is posting, how other community members will react, or what might emerge next. Our right brains are in constant search of anomaly. While sequential reasoning is generally a function of the left brain, insights that occur when we're not consciously focused on a problem happen within the right. There is a relationship between the familiar, pleasurable "Aha!" moment of realization and activity in our right amygdala, which helps to process emotions.[8] Emotions appear to be an important factor even in logical processing, just as the left brain's perspective is rooted in the right's. Our participation in Id networks is less about representing an image to the world and more about an interaction between our essential selves and a world of unknown things.

So far in this book, we've covered how individual pieces of content act like replicators—memes—and the characteristics of memes that successfully propagate through the Internet. We've also explored how different structures of social networks affect how we represent ourselves and the types of memes with which we're most likely to engage. In this final section (Part III), we'll begin to fit these pieces together in a more holistic context to understand the relationship among these psychological spaces, expression of different aspects of our selves, and the essential bits through which we express those selves.

As brands, we spend a lot of energy representing ourselves—not just to the outside world but even within our organizations. We create "brand strategies" and "style guides" to articulate who our brand is, how it behaves in the world, what characteristics are most important, and so on—in other words, what people should expect of our brand. We create "known" territory so that we're predictable and easy to navigate for our audiences. The unknown emerges from our brand when the unexpected happens. In negative manifestation, that can mean a bad customer experience, brand behavior that's inconsistent with our positioning, a tone-deaf ad, or a product recall. Novelty can also manifest in positive ways from our brand when we leverage surprise-and-delight tactics, go above and beyond in customer service, altruistically support a meaningful cause, or when we demonstrate fluency in a particular culture or trend.

To reach people effectively in different social networks, we need to understand the mode in which they're interacting: Which space are they occupying? Known or unknown? By understanding how these psychological contexts affect our audience, we can be more strategic about which messages we direct to which channels and how we embody them. When we want to seed a new idea or change people's minds about our brand, we need to reach people where they'll be open to receiving new information. Likewise, when we want to reinforce our identity or build our brand consistency, we want to reach people in represented space where they're forming and reinforcing the categories into which we fit. In right brain Id networks, we want to create content that stokes their natural curiosity, appetite for exploration, and genuine self-expression. In left brain Ego or Superego networks, we want to provide content that lends itself to self-representation and expression of identity.

In left brain space, the right amount of novelty can help us stand out and grab attention—which also happens to be what our audience wants to do. To create the right kind of novelty, we not only need to engage people in known space but we ourselves also need to *be* known space. And if we're a relatively unknown brand, we need to surround ourselves with enough attachment to the known to be credible. That's why logo walls, "as seen on TV," and celebrity endorsements are particularly helpful for new companies—they lend known credibility to an unknown brand. For established brands, our "known territory" is an accumulation of what we've done and said in the world, and while packaging, logos, website copy, and other traditional marketer concerns aren't usually enough to grab attention on their own, they're an important backdrop to our engagement as a known entity.

INTRODUCING NOVELTY INTO KNOWN, LEFT BRAIN TERRITORY HELPS GRAB ATTENTION

Once we're steeped in the known, we can start to introduce the unknown in fun, novel ways to keep our brand alive and dynamic. The Target brand is a prime example of strong, traditional brand building that has successfully differentiated itself from Walmart, Kmart, Lowe's, and other home goods retailers by introducing just the right amount of novelty. When Target creates an ad, even when it comes from a brand-new campaign, it's distinctly Target. Leveraging its iconic white and red logo, clean aesthetics, and upbeat music, Target's ads are textbook case studies in brand consistency. From its marketing materials to the actual look and feel of stores, Target has created a brand that is familiar for most Americans. This is the foundational known territory for which most brands strive.

Target also adds strategic novelty to its shopping experiences, particularly in retail clothing. Following in the footsteps of more clothing-specific retailers like H&M and UNIQLO, Target started partnering with high-end designers in 1999.[9, 10] Thanks to notable integrations with designers like Missoni, Jason Wu, Alexander McQueen, Michael Graves, Jacques McAllister, and a laundry list of recognizable names, Target inserted itself into high-end fashion conversations that would previously have been completely unattainable for the average home goods retailer. (Oh, by the way, I made up the name Jacques McAllister to see if you were paying attention. He doesn't exist. Well, I mean he might, he's just not a high-end designer. See how a little something unexpected catches your attention?)

According to Target CMO Rick Gomez, "Design has always been a part of Target's DNA. From our stores and the products we create to the partnerships we cultivate, our focus on accessible design sets Target apart and is one of the reasons guests love to shop with us." For a retailer known for affordability, partnerships with high-end designers are a perfect complement—especially when design is part of the differentiation strategy. Suddenly, design blogs, fashion communities, and the followings of these high-end designers have a reason to talk about Target. Creating that association with high-end design and reaching the upstream, influential tastemakers in home decor and fashion elevate the Target brand in a way that's also familiar and consistent.

The strategy of high-low collaborations is perfectly suited to engaging the left hemisphere and left brain territory. A *high-low collaboration* is when a brand known for its mass production or affordability partners with a more artisanal brand, usually known for craft, quality, and industry prestige. It's essentially a borrowing of credibility, like an influencer integration but deeper. Target's high-low collaborations challenge our internal category of the brand just enough to elevate it without forcing us to rebuild our perception altogether.

High-low collaborations have the added benefit of driving conversation in right brain networks where people gather around their interests, passions, and favorite designers. If Jacques McAllister actually existed and had an engaged following of fashion enthusiasts, they'd inevitably discuss his partnership with Target, and again, the context matters. A spike in organic conversation about Target among coupon clippers doesn't do much to elevate the Target brand, but an uptick in conversation about Target among fashion tastemakers elevates the entire Target retail clothing section, creating impact that extends far beyond the pieces from the partnership with Jacques. And having pieces from high-end designers—or even just *talking about wanting* pieces from high-end designers—is a form of badge in and of itself. Doing so creates a seamless bridge between right brain conversation and badgeworthy left brain representation. When we say we "can't wait for McAllister's fall/winter line," we're communicating first, that we know who Jacques McAllister is (and no, you don't) and second, that his style is representative of our style.

Nike leverages a similar strategy through its SNKRS app in the United States and SNEAKRS app in the United Kingdom. For years, sneakerheads worldwide have idolized limited-edition sneaker releases to the point of absurdity. Fanatical sneaker lovers are infamous for waking up at ungodly hours, queueing around city blocks, and even camping out in front of stores for particularly hyped releases. Some of the rarer pairs of Nike sneakers fetch prices in the tens of thousands of dollars at resale. And although the love for sneakers within the sneakerhead community runs deep, sneakerheads make up a very small proportion of Nike's revenue. Nike hasn't tried to capitalize on the booming sneaker resale market. Instead, in its SNRKS app Nike has made sneakerhead culture more inclusive by creating experiences tailored to sneaker lovers.

Plenty of retail brands have apps. And frankly, most of them simply shouldn't. Very few people are loyal enough to a particular clothing brand to proactively download its app, let alone open that app regularly. Plus, most retail brand apps simply contain their clothing lines— the same ones available on their website. Nike takes a very different approach. On Nike.com, dozens if not hundreds of shoes, clothing items, and other kinds of gear are available any day at any time. But the SNKRS app revolves around "drops"—limited-edition releases of sought-after shoes available only at specific times. These drops are often developed in collaboration with designers, athletes, artists, and other brands, extending their reach and word-of-mouth potential.

In order to capitalize on a drop, a SNKRS user has to log in at a precise time for a chance to purchase the shoe. This mechanic does a few strategic things for Nike. First, it creates demand around particular moments in time, which drives a massive amount of organic conversation among sneakerheads. On platforms like Reddit, it's natural for particularly sought-after releases to spill conversation over into streetwear, fashion, sports, and other communities that might be relevant to the collaboration.

Second, the app creates scarcity. Highly anticipated collaborations are often produced in runs of 50,000 to 100,000 pairs, and sneakerhead back-of-the-napkin math predicts a less than 1 percent shot at winning a competitive SNKRS raffle. In response, people create bots and fake accounts to up their chances, engaging in an evolutionary arms race with Nike's account verification system. Did I mention that you still have to pay for the sneakers if you win . . . ?

Third, the SNKRS app allows people on the outskirts of sneakerhead culture to fully convert. Waiting in a line wrapped around the block at 6 a.m. is a high barrier to entry for becoming a sneakerhead. Logging in to an app to try your luck at a drop is much, much lower. It's an ideal tactic for allowing current superfans to influence peers and bring them into a community that's badgeworthy and that elevates the entirety of Nike's line.

Like Target, Nike curates collaborations that help move the brand into new categories. Its collaborations with high-end streetwear labels like Off-White and hip-hop artists like Travis Scott keep Nike on the bleeding edge of popular culture. For a brand that's over 50 years old, staying cool to generation after generation is no small feat (no pun intended). Fresh collaborations keep younger generations from categorizing Nike as their parents' brand of footwear—even though that's exactly what Nike is. I mean, except for that whole "dad shoe" trend in 2018—that time Nike did want to seem like their parents' generation of shoe. But ironically. I think.

Creating moments of novelty for our audience can be simple. We don't always have to collaborate with the world's top designers and influencers to do so. Sometimes, taking a small creative risk to enhance an otherwise normal part of our audience's experience with us pays off in dividends. This point is well-illustrated by authors Dan and Chip Heath in their book *The Power of Moments: Why Certain Experiences Have Extraordinary Impact.*[11] The authors emphasize the importance of considering the customer journey from the perspective of the customer. Doing so allows us to identify places where small changes might make big impacts.

The authors use the Magic Castle Hotel in LA as an example—it was the top-rated hotel in LA in 2017. The Magic Castle Hotel generated 94 percent positive feedback from over 3,000 reviews on TripAdvisor, despite looking like "a respectable budget motel," according to the authors. The Magic Castle Hotel delights patrons with moments of novelty—like a bright red phone next to the hotel pool called the Popsicle Hotline. When guests pick up the phone, an employee asks if the guest would like a cherry, orange, or grape Popsicle, which is then promptly delivered on a silver tray by a waiter wearing white gloves—for free.

Could the hotel charge $2 per Popsicle and still tout it as a fun offering? Could it place a freezer by the pool and allow guests to serve themselves to cut down on staff time spent delivering orders? Could it skip these services altogether and still function as a hotel? Of course. But what happens to that absurdly wonderful moment of novelty when the waiter appears? What happens to the customer experience? It melts all over that unused silver tray.

By creating these delightfully novel experiences for its guests, the Magic Castle Hotel actually exceeded ratings for the posh Four Seasons in Beverly Hills and renowned Hotel Bel-Air. Our experiences with small, thoughtful moments of novelty outweigh the experiences we expect to happen, however grand. When our audiences believe they know what to expect from us—when their internal voices pipe up, "Here we go again"—creating fun, bite-sized moments of the unexpected disrupt the left brain's framework to form a lasting impression.

WHEN BRANDS FAIL TO MAINTAIN THEIR KNOWN TERRITORY, CHAOS ENSUES

In order for this strategy of controlled novelty to be effective, we need to have established a foundation of brand credibility and consistency. We can't surprise and delight a furious customer, nor can we create a moment of novelty when our audience is wading around in the unknown. Changing our branding, tweaking our logos, and launching new campaigns are all points at which we're tossing our audiences into the unknown and hoping that their right brains are able to bridge our old and new selves. When a brand makes a change—even a small one—it introduces a bit of chaos to its audience. And whether that change is the equivalent of a new haircut or facial reconstruction surgery, it's important that we tell an open and honest story to our audience about the changes. If your friend just got a nose job, and she tells you it was because her back hurt, you're probably going to piece together your own narrative because hers didn't make sense. Too often, we try to put a glossy sheen on the rationale behind a rebrand or new campaign without being truthful to our audience—and in the Internet age, they can tell.

The Gap made the mistake of "evolving" its iconic logo without explaining why, and most of you probably know exactly where this is headed.[12] When its customers reacted negatively to the new logo, The Gap changed its mind and told people it was all part of a crowdsourcing exercise to find a new logo, asking people for submissions. Then, after backlash from designers who saw the value of their discipline diminished by a major brand asking for free work, The Gap reverted to its original logo. That's a whole lot of chaos, and while I wasn't in the building for The Gap's branding conversations, it seems clear that there was as much chaos internally as there was externally. A clear vision was never communicated to its audience, and when the audience reacted negatively, no explanation was provided. Now *that's* chaos.

When British Petroleum (BP) decided to update its branding with a new logo and company name, people were initially skeptical. The broadly familiar BP logo was a simple green shield on which sat the serif yellow type "BP"—a logo the company had used for nearly 70 years (although its most consistent version wasn't finalized until 1989).[13] With all the tone deafness a single company can possibly muster, BP changed its logo in 2000 to a "Helios"—a symbol named after the Greek sun god—and declared the company's new name: Beyond Petroleum. It's the perfect rebrand for the company because the initials remained the same, meaning it wouldn't have to clean up anything it'd previously left behind. (Zing!)

BP declared that the rebrand represented its transformation into an eco-friendly company—it was going from being "part of the problem" to being "part of the solution."[14] Did you get the warm fuzzies? Me neither. Logos can do some powerful things, but turning a petroleum company into a champion for the environment is not one of them. The new BP logo has provided ammunition for skeptics and detractors at every turn. During the Deepwater Horizon oil spill and other environmental crises, naysayers created versions of BP's Helios dipped in oil or overlaid with dying animals. Sometimes they replaced the BP initials with BS, and so on.[15] The rationale simply didn't match up to the reality of the brand, and people didn't buy it.

Tropicana decided to change its packaging and logo in 2010 with absolutely disastrous results.[16] With a more modern font, a minimal aesthetic, and a greater emphasis on the "100% orange" message than on the Tropicana brand name, the agency behind the redesign explained that the rationale for the changes was to "take this brand and bring it or evolve it into a more current or modern state." Do you feel the lack of substance? I do. Customers had trouble recognizing the new packaging, and even when they did, they wondered whether or not they were buying the same product. The refocus on "100% orange," which was intended to put more emphasis on the "all natural" product attribute, actually caused loyal brand fans to question whether or not this represented a drop in product quality. Why else would the brand feel a need to stick that message in bold font on the front of its new package? Tropicana never explained the decision in depth to customers, so customers developed their own narratives. When we're thrown into chaos, we'll create our own order. And when it comes to brands and the intentions of capitalistic companies, we're not very generous about giving the benefit of the doubt. Between the cost of the agency and subsequent drop in sales, the rebrand is estimated to have cost Tropicana $50 million.

Most of our brands should strive to achieve an effect similar to a ride at Disney World. The people taking your brand's ride should feel safe and confident that they're going to have a positive experience. It shouldn't feel like riding an elevator, nor should it feel like riding a vintage roller coaster. Creating small, controlled pockets of novelty helps make experiences memorable and enjoyable. They allow us to break free of our represented world and experience the world directly and presently. Disney World rides tend to strike an elegant balance between a consistent narrative and elements of surprise.

Likewise, when we do create moments of novelty for our audiences, those moments ought to follow naturally from our brand platform. They should feel consistent with our brand and make contextual sense where we create them.

UNKNOWN, RIGHT BRAIN TERRITORY OFFERS A BROAD CREATIVE CANVAS FOR BRAND ENGAGEMENT

In right brain Id networks, brands tend to be less present. More often than not, brands are represented through organic conversations among users. People also tend to have more candid conversations about their beliefs in right brain space, and the lack of official brand presence in these networks allows user conversations to maintain near full control over brand perceptions. That's a massive opportunity for brands willing to embrace unexplored territory. And even for brands that aren't willing to engage directly, right brain networks offer a wealth of social listening insights. Because users in right brain space are in a mode of exploration, we have the opportunity to engage people with deeper and more immersive experiences. It also means that our success depends on our ability to stoke users' curiosity. Even simple tactics, like Charles Schwab's finance-related conversation prompts, lean naturally into the exploratory behavior of Id networks.

If you've used platforms like Twitter, Facebook, Instagram, and even LinkedIn for marketing, you've likely noticed that linking to outside content rarely drives as much engagement as on-platform content like images and videos. Even in organic space, Ego and Superego networks are filled with clickbaity headlines designed to draw people away from their feeds, but there is generally a strong resistance from users to disrupting their mode of light consumption. As users, we prefer to interact with things that keep us within our feeds, particularly in left brain space. However, this going-down-the-rabbit-hole phenomenon is built into many right brain networks. When a user sees a thread in the r/AskReddit community asking, "Now that the 2010s decade is ending, which trends are the most regrettable?", clicking into that thread is an exploratory behavior. It's the entryway to the rabbit hole. That's how even simple questions can amass millions of views and tens of thousands of comments in a few hours, which this one did. And in case you're curious, the top-voted answers were (1) YouTube prank channels masquerading as "social experiments," (2) the obnoxious challenge culture, and (3) the flat Earth theory. Bet you didn't expect that to still be a debate in 2019, did you, Copernicus?

As brands, when we ask a compelling question, we're creating territory for exploration. And best of all, the content is created in partnership with our audience. Coca-Cola put this strategy to use in a Super Bowl campaign on Reddit in 2016.[17] The brand had partnered with Marvel Studios to develop its Super Bowl TV spot, and prior to its airing, Coca-Cola asked comic book enthusiasts and bloggers to hype a "never before seen" matchup between two Marvel characters. To stoke the conversation further, Coca-Cola created an open-ended thread asking Redditors to get creative with their knowledge of the Marvel universe: "Which Marvel Super Hero matchup would make the best Big Game commercial?"

Seeding the thread first within Marvel communities, then eventually broadening its targeting to Reddit's front page, the brand generated a post filled with unique user-generated stories. Some users even wrote scripts about their favorite Marvel characters fighting over Cokes. Once the actual spot aired during the Super Bowl, the Coca-Cola team posted the video, sparking Redditors to share their ad organically across various Marvel communities and confirming that one Redditor had actually correctly guessed the matchup—Hulk versus Ant-Man. Coca-Cola gave Marvel fans license to get creative with this ad in a way that wouldn't be as comfortable in left brain networks. Because they were surrounded by fellow Marvel fans, engaged users knew their audience shared their interest. And even if they weren't professional writers, participants were able to express themselves creatively without social equity to lose. Coca-Cola harnessed this natural tendency toward creativity and conversation to drive a massive amount of organic sharing and deep engagement.

For campaigns to succeed in right brain territory, depth of experience is an important factor. Consider the previously mentioned examples of successful Id network campaigns—Cozmo Gets Lost in Reddit, Audi's Think Faster, Charles Schwab, Coca-Cola. Each campaign focused primarily on the experience of the people participating, and it delivered real depth for engaged users. This natural craving for explorable experiences is also reflected in the brands Id networks lift up organically. When it comes to gaming and entertainment brands, right brain networks are natural places for fan communities to form. And with fan communities come fan art, fiction, theories, discussions, and so on. The effect is so powerful that when Jonathan Nolan and Lisa Joy were writing the second season of HBO's *Westworld*, Nolan revealed on a panel, "Reddit has already figured out the third episode twist, so we're changing that right now."[18]

IN RIGHT BRAIN NETWORK TERRITORY, STRIVE TO CREATE EXPLORABLE TERRITORY

Depth of experience isn't something we take into account for most social media marketing. Most social platforms instruct us to create content as short and "snackable" as possible—and yes, that's a word platform reps have used to describe content best practices. While the "snackable" lens can effectively get us thinking about how to grab attention in a competitive feed, to truly capitalize on a successful grab for attention in Id networks, we should strive to aim our audience toward something actionable and meaningful. If we're sharing a life hack, we'd better make sure it works, and if we're providing a recipe, it'd better be thorough. If we're intent on engaging an audience in right brain space, we have a broad creative canvas with which to work, but we have to deliver.

In anticipation of Season 3 of the Netflix show *Stranger Things*, the Baskin-Robbins brand built an alternate-reality game (ARG) designed to re-engage fans of the first two seasons.[19] An ARG is a form of storytelling wherein a networked narrative is uncovered by solving subtle clues, often hidden in the real world either online or offline. The plot of *Stranger Things* Season 3 revolved around a fictional ice cream shop called Scoops Ahoy, and Baskin-Robbins found playful ways to build connections to the show—like themed ice cream specials and throwback-feeling ice cream parlor ads.

Given the show's 1980s setting, creative director Curt Mueller noted, "We realized there was a really good opportunity for either an

ARG or a very extravagant scavenger hunt that uses only 1985 technology. . . . [Players] had to use things like faxes and phones. They can't use the Internet as we know it today." The entry point for the ARG was hidden in a faux commercial for Scoops Ahoy. Two main characters introduce a new flavor of ice cream that will be "sailing into Baskin-Robbins," followed briefly by a 1-800 number. The spot accidentally aired weeks in advance of the actual ARG's launch, and by the time the game officially launched, a Reddit thread boasting over 1,000 comments had begun to coordinate on solving the puzzle.

I have a confession to make. Many of those 1,000 comments are from repeat commenters. Unlike most marketing tactics, ARGs aren't meant to cast the broadest net. That might seem counterintuitive to us as marketers, and creating an entirely separate ARG narrative to promote a TV show, which is itself a narrative, may seem like an awful lot of work. "A long walk for a ham sandwich," as one of my favorite creative directors used to say. But there's more to this strategy than creating a fun experience for a few thousand players.

From an efficiency perspective, our marketing efforts aim toward broadening our message to the widest possible audience, but broad, suited-for-the-masses campaigns don't ignite brand fanatics. That's where these campaigns centered on depth of experience, like ARGs, really shine. Successfully spiking conversation among brand fanatics can often generate earned reach through media coverage and organic sharing, and that's something Netflix's marketing department leans into regularly. While the Baskin-Robbins ARG may have been played by only a few thousand people (right brain engagement), the story of the ARG being undertaken and solved by Internet denizens generated articles in *The Drum*, *Mashable*, *Adweek*, gaming publications, and a range of other news sites. These articles transformed the actual experience of playing the ARG into an easy-to-digest narrative suited to left brain representation.

The puzzle itself received high praise from communities on Reddit and Discord for its design and narrative, and those are the elements that mattered to the people playing. In right brain territory, we're usually addressing communities with common interests rather than isolated individuals, so to drive meaningful engagement, we need to provide something that's compelling at the level of community. A well-designed

ARG that targets fans of a popular show is a perfect example. To be fair, *Stranger Things* is a bit of an outlier in that it has an army of fanatical fans, meaning Baskin-Robbins didn't have to do much prodding to set things in motion. It'd be much more difficult for them to execute an ARG without the relationship with the show—there aren't massive fan communities posting every day about Baskin-Robbins, which is the case with most brands. For traditional brands, campaigns like ARGs can still work. They'll just require juicier carrots at the end of their metaphorical sticks. And whenever possible, that carrot should appeal to the community more than to the individual.

Providing a depth of experience doesn't always mean massive productions and intricate ARG narratives. As with bringing novelty into left brain territory, we can create depth in subtle ways that point toward further explorable territory. The Honey Nut Cheerios brand received a major organic shoutout on Reddit for its campaign around honeybee-friendly wildflowers in 2017.[20]

A post in the r/pics community hit the front page of Reddit generating over 50,000 upvotes with the title, "Cheerios will send you 500 wildflower seeds for free to help save the honeybee (link in comments)." The language felt so on-message that I couldn't help but check the user history to see if this person was a brand representative. I remain convinced that this was actually just an ordinary user with whom the message resonated, so if you're the Cheerios marketing team giggling to yourselves about pulling one over on me, well done. The top comment within the thread pointed to the Cheerios website, which made the connection between the Honey Nut Cheerios "Buzzbee" mascot and the initiative to distribute wildflower seeds. Reddit has a broad representation of science-related communities, and the broader Reddit community loves to see smart solutions to environmental problems.

This kind of impactful, scrappy, strategic thinking is exactly the kind of initiative right brain communities love to rally around. It's the perfect example of a brand using its marketing dollars to drive awareness of a real problem, champion that problem, and create a straightforward action that allows people to help. That's not just my synopsis, either. The comment thread was filled with praise for marketers: "Kudos to the General Mills marketing team." "If this is how companies want to advertise, I can get behind it."

RIGHT BRAIN ENGAGEMENT SHOULD BE AS FUN TO OBSERVE AS IT IS TO PARTICIPATE IN

We've trained ourselves on left brain social networks to appeal to the lowest common denominator among our audiences. We ask questions like, "What's your favorite song?" because we know that a massive number of people can respond quickly to it. In right brain territory, we need to adjust that thinking. Rather than the lowest common denominator, we need to find the *greatest common factor*—something that challenges individuals and experts within a community to come forward with interesting, useful, unique perspectives. In right brain territory, our thread won't be judged by the number of responses. Rather, it'll be judged based on how interesting its responses are. Instead of asking, "What's your favorite song?", we might ask, "What's a fact about your favorite musician that not many people know?" We still want a large number of people to be able to answer the question, but we also want to build a conversation that's interesting to read.

Right brain networks also offer a unique opportunity to ignite fans of particular interests, hobbies, or even TV shows who are often too dispersed to effectively reach in left brain networks. When the Cartoon Network show *Rick and Morty* made reference to an obscure McDonald's dipping sauce that was available only during a promotion for the movie *Mulan* in 1998, fans of the show immediately started to knock on the McDonald's marketing team's metaphorical door with an opportunity. Following some noncommittal banter on Twitter, the brand enlisted its resident chefs to re-create the nearly 20-year-old sauce without publicly confirming its return. When it came time to seed the announcement, McDonald's took to Reddit and posted a cryptic message within the r/RickandMorty community.[21] The post read, "SOS 073017 2130 EST TWTR 3x.5GAL," and it was accompanied by a photo of three half-gallon containers of Szechuan Sauce. It wasn't exactly an ARG, but it contained a few references to the show that demonstrated McDonald's *Rick and Morty* fandom. Redditors upvoted the post to the top of the community, and McDonald's continued to engage fans within the comments of the post.

What started as a single post by McDonald's in the relatively small r/RickandMorty community set into motion a wave of conversations throughout various other Reddit communities. A post with nearly 40,000 upvotes in r/television noted that McDonald's had given one of the jugs of Szechuan Sauce to *Rick and Morty* creator Justin Roiland. A post in r/videos featured one of Reddit's favorite at-home chefs attempting to re-create the sauce in his home kitchen. A post in r/OutOfTheLoop, which allows Redditors to ask questions about trends they don't quite understand, explained why the entire site was losing its mind over a few bottles of McDonald's dipping sauce.

It's not often that a massive brand like McDonald's succeeds beyond even its own means, but that's exactly where McDonald's found itself after tantalizing *Rick and Morty* fans. While the brand had, in fact, re-created its cartoon-acclaimed sauce, it only supplied a few dozen packets to participating locations. So when *Rick and Morty* fans showed up en masse to McDonald's locations for their taste of the plunder, many of them were disappointed. And when I say "disappointed," I mean that they absolutely freaked out. Police were called to multiple McDonald's locations.[22]

The most infamous video features a young guy hopping up onto a McDonald's counter, screaming for Szechuan Sauce, stomping around like a petulant toddler, then falling to the floor screeching *Rick and Morty* references and rolling around before eventually performing the iconic Naruto run out of the restaurant.[23] For reference, Naruto is an anime character whose animators portray him running with his arms thrown back behind him. It's become synonymous with cringey Internet culture. Whether it was a self-aware "prank" or not, there was no shortage of unhappy *Rick and Morty* fans. Depth of experience matters. When we make a promise to right brain communities, we'd better deliver. Make enough Szechuan Sauce. The Internet never forgets.

Plenty of brands have tried the surprise-and-delight approach to social media, especially when platforms like Facebook and Twitter were first bursting onto the marketing scene. Giving away products and related value can grab attention and drive engagement when there's something in it for the people engaging, but the true brand hero moment often goes unnoticed in left brain networks. That's another meaningful differentiator of right brain networks' prioritization of the community above the individual user. Community members care about what happens to fellow community members, even at large scale.

In preparation for the release of the movie *Logan*, Fox Studios put the surprise-and-delight strategy to use on Reddit and demonstrated the power of advertising at the level of community. Following our theme of nontraditional advertising activations during traditional advertising moments, *Logan* took over the Reddit front page with a Super Bowl spot in 2017, noting, "Wolverine's getting his claws out for the last time," and asking Redditors, "What do you want to see?"[24] Not long after the comment thread opened, a superfan came out of the woodwork to answer with some specific requests. And a little snark:

> What we want to See is irrelevant as the movie is already shot and compiled together. However,
> - The Blue and Yellow Suit as seen at the end of The Wolverine 3 / Days of Future Past
> - A Hint of Mature Mystique, possibly portrayed buy Jennifer Coolidge
> - Fastball Special, with Logan throwing X-23 into the opponents position.
> - Deadpool dropping a piano on Logan as seen in Wolverine Origins #21

What you're not seeing in this reproduction of u/Spencerforhire83's comment is the thoroughly researched links embedded in each bullet to various comic book scenes, references, and actors to drive home his point.

When another user prodded, "This guy seems like he knows what he's talking about," u/Spencerforhire83 expanded on his passion for Marvel and love for Hugh Jackman:

> 3 Decades of Reading Comics, I have every MARVEL and DC Movie that has come out to video and some that have not (original Fantastic Four 1994). I know what I want in my superhero films.
>
> I actually met Hugh Jackman in the Seoul World Trade Center at the Quiznos, I heard murmuring coming from behind me from passers by while standing in line, I turned around, and there he was, better than 6 foot tall, and scruffy.

I said, MR JACKMAN! what are you doing here?

[He] responds, Im here for the movie. (Wolverine Origins opening that night). Whats good here? (that's right Hugh Jackman asked me for advice on a sandwich) I said the Italian with red onions, blue cheese toasted with olives) He Responds with, Alright then, that sounds good.

Did not ask him for autograph nor a picture, I thought it would be in bad form.

And I suppose I was also a bit Star Struck.

Also the Seoul World Trade center is the only place to get Blue Cheese with your sub in Seoul, The other Quiznoes in the city do not keep Blue Cheese in stock.

Other users piled onto the thread asking u/OfficialLoganMovie, the Fox Studios username behind the promotion, to take note. Fox eventually responded to the story with a simple comment: "Can you PM us your info?" The response alone received over 3,800 upvotes, and that was all Reddit needed to lose its collective mind.

Eventually, u/Spencerforhire83 updated his original comment, "EDIT: Apparently FOX Studios caught wind of this and they are flying me to New York to meet Hugh Jackman, and see Logan at a RED CARPET Screening! Thank you REDDIT!" He would go on to post updates of his journey throughout relevant Reddit communities. In fashion communities, he made posts asking for feedback on his "Red Carpet Casual" outfit.[25] In r/Movies and r/Xmen, he retold the story of the original thread and gushed about the movie itself.[26, 27] Another Redditor posted the ad's original thread into a community called r/BestOf, which curates iconic moments in the Reddit community's history, where it reached the front page.[28] Again. Dozens of posts later, the story had made its way throughout the Reddit platform for the cost of a round-trip plane ticket to New York and a seat at the red carpet screening. Not a bad deal for Fox.

Because Redditors feel kindred to other Redditors—because they feel like they're part of the same community—they care about what happens to each other. When something great happens to individuals in a community on Reddit, it's common for the whole community to rally around them to celebrate. Imagine Fox attempting a similar giveaway on Twitter. Maybe they tweet something like, "Tell us why you're the biggest Wolverine fan, and we might fly you out to the red carpet screening!", which gets to the point but feels transactional. Or maybe they just find someone organically on Twitter who's really excited about the movie and fly that person to the premier. Who cares? Maybe their 200 followers? Unless it's coordinated with additional promotion, the story just won't gain momentum. But because Redditors were invested in seeing u/Spencerforhire83 experience something unique and personally meaningful, the story spread far beyond Fox's ad buy.

As brands, it's important that we understand the nuances of these digital environments and the mindsets fostered by different structures of social networks. But we also operate with finite resources and often lofty expectations. It's important that we balance relevance for particular channels with efficiency in our creative output. As we elevate our view of the digital landscape, we can start to understand what types of tactics and campaigns suit themselves to left and right brain engagement.

In left brain networks, we're surrounded by a world of what we know—or what we've represented about our own knowledge. When chaos is introduced into that space, it's easy to overwhelm the precarious sense of known territory. The constructed world of what is known pales in scale to the world of the unknown, and it's all too easy for our facade of familiar comfort to be torn down. Simultaneously, too much order becomes boring for our audiences. Generally, our role in left brain space as brands is to create enough novelty to grab attention and move brand perception without tearing down what people already know about us.

In right brain space, our audience is in a mode of exploration, unfiltered expression, and communal connection. As brands, we ought to aim to provide interesting, novel territory for exploration by creating deep experiences and providing platforms on which our audience can dynamically cocreate meaning with us. Whether we construct exploratory space by delivering a high-budget production or simply prompt an interesting discussion, our role as a brand changes from creating badgeworthy content suited to individual expression to one of participation within a broader community. We can attract attention by leveraging the natural diversity present in most communities—by creating platforms for conversation that celebrate different perspectives or allow different kinds of knowledge to be expressed in interesting ways.

While left and right brain networks—and hemispheres—are worth analyzing separately, the two complement each other in important ways. As brands looking for as many efficiencies as can be afforded, it's important that we understand the relationship between the two. In the next chapter, we'll start to fit these strategies together into a coherent, holistic brand approach to digital engagement.

KEY TAKEAWAYS

- Our right and left brain hemispheres are suited to dealing with two major evolutionary problems: direct experience with a world of living things (right) and interpretation of that world in represented form to allow us to learn about that world (left).

- In Ego and Superego networks, we create representations of ourselves, which we use as tools to define ourselves in complex social environments. Ego and Superego networks can be considered left brain networks.

- In Id networks, we're in a mode of exploring new information and direct engagement with a world of unknown things. Id networks can be considered right brain networks.

- In left brain networks, we should strive to find a balance between maintaining brand consistency while introducing enough novelty to grab attention and improve brand perception.

- Right brain networks require a depth of experience that leans naturally into people's appetites for exploration, candid expression, and tendency to organize around like-minded communities.

THE MEME FLOW
Right Brain, Left Brain, and Right Brain Again

There are two basic ways we can talk about our deeply held beliefs. One way is to engage in a genuine, good-faith discussion in which we start with an open mind and pursue the truth. We put forth our perspectives about a subject, and we pay attention to the other perspectives presented in case we've missed something. In such a conversation, it's unlikely for any opinion to remain the same—more often than not, the mere act of engaging an outside perspective helps give dimension to a problem in a manner that our single perspective simply can't.

The other way to talk about our deeply held beliefs is to represent them. We're communicating something about ourselves and representing those selves to the world. We're putting parts of ourselves out into social space to define us, and we wear our beliefs to find like-minded people—or at least to have people acknowledge those parts of us. When we represent our beliefs, we're unlikely to change our minds not only because we aren't engaged at the level of challenging our beliefs but because changing our minds would mean altering parts of our identities.

In one scenario, we're engaged directly with the world and allowing our experience to affect our perspective. In the other, ideas become representations of self and identity. In the former case, we're manifesting qualities of the right hemisphere, and in the latter, the left. It's no wonder that dialogue about politics, religion, and most other polarizing topics tend to go nowhere productive in left brain networks like Twitter and Facebook.

Sometimes, we're looking for information and forming our opinions based on what we find. These are vulnerable moments for us because new information threatens the structures we've built atop what we already know. We don't want the whole structure to topple. But these vulnerable moments are deeply important for us as brands because that's when we affect how people really think about us. Reaching people effectively while they're representing their beliefs requires a different strategy than engaging people when they're actively forming those beliefs.

In Part I, "Memeology," we discussed the qualities share-driving social creative tends to exhibit. On one axis, we examined how content can be *badgeworthy* to help people represent themselves to their friends, like digital clothing, or it can be *bookmarkable*—simply useful and worth saving. On the other, content may be *commiserative*, relating to our everyday lives and inspiring us to do something here and now, or content can represent something we eventually *aspire* to do. These qualities also map to left and right brain perspectives about the world.

When content is badgeworthy or when it's something we aspire to do eventually, it's related to a representation of ourselves. The content we wear as badges to our friends helps us define who we are. Content geared to what we aspire toward relates to an internal simulation of ourselves at some future point—an optimistic version of whom we might become. When content is bookmarkable, commiserative, and inspires us to take real action in our everyday lives, it's appealing to right brain processes concerned with our immediate experience and engagement with the world in front of us.

In general, this can be a helpful consideration for creating content suited to right and left brain networks (Figure 9.1). When people are in modes of representation, we ought to arm them with content that's badgeworthy and aspirational. When people are in modes of exploration, we should strive to give them content that connects with their

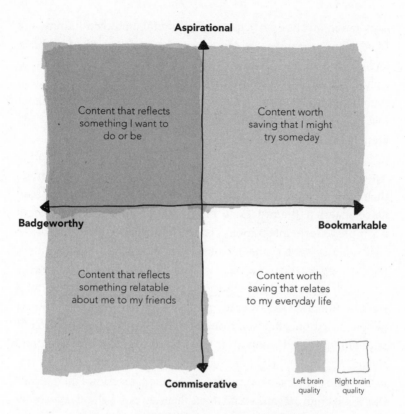

FIGURE 9.1 **Adding Value for Left and Right Brain**

interests and inspires action in the here and now. This isn't to say that left brain qualities should dictate every piece of content we develop for left brain networks, nor should we create only right brain content for right brain networks. In our everyday lives, we're constantly engaging both hemispheres, shifting perspectives fluidly between them. Just because we're participating in a right brain network doesn't mean a piece of content can't catch the attention of our left brain, and vice versa.

While content that demonstrates the left brain qualities of being badgeworthy and aspirational does tend to thrive in left brain networks, inspirational content may also grab our attention and shift us into a right brain perspective. Likewise, useful and inspirational content we've discovered through our right brain exploration may also serve us as badgeworthy left brain expression. If part of my right brain exploration involves participating in a photography community, and I find a funny meme in that community, I may well post it in left brain territory as a badge—"I'm a photographer, and from my perspective as a photographer, this is funny." In general, though, this is a good rule of thumb to consider during content development: content with qualities that appeal to the right brain will tend to thrive more naturally in right brain networks, and vice versa.

According to Iain McGilichrist, the natural flow of information between our hemispheres begins with experience in the right brain, then moves relevant information into the left brain to be processed.[1] Once analyzed, the processed information is returned to the right hemisphere for reintegration, hence McGilichrist's metaphor of the right brain as "master" and the left brain as "emissary." The same pattern is at work on broader scales with left and right brain social networks.

Much of the original content created on the Internet comes from right brain networks—after all, these are the networks that connect people based on interests, foster a sense of community, and consequently satisfy the conditions necessary for memes to form and spread. Members of right brain communities often take that content to left brain networks as ways of representing some part of their identities. Right brain networks tend to see themselves as behind-the-scenes observers of Internet culture, and left brain network activity is often discussed at a meta-level within right brain communities—a reintegration of sorts. Some popular right brain communities are organized to do exactly that—like r/BlackPeopleTwitter, which catalogs "Screenshots of Black people being hilarious or insightful on social media," or r/OldPeopleFacebook, which accumulates screenshots of old people misunderstanding how to use social media.

As brands, it's easy to reach people with the right message at the wrong time. Or the wrong message at the right time. When people approach us from the perspective of their right brains, they're genuinely looking for information or a helpful interaction from us. When people are starting to form an opinion about our brand or they are comparing our brand to others, they're engaged directly with their experience with us. What we say, how we act, and how they feel about their interaction with us will create a lasting impression. Customer service interactions, direct messages, and questions that seek genuine answers are moments of right brain engagement with our brands, and these are the proactive signals people give us to let us know they're receptive to connection with us. But when people tweet generally about us to their followers, use our product in a meme, or post a photo and tag us on Instagram, they're not *really* trying to engage us directly. They're using our brand to represent something about themselves or their lives. Both can be important moments but require different treatments from us.

Both the top and bottom of the purchase funnel tend to be moments of right brain engagement. Awareness, being the top of the funnel, is a right brain moment—it's our first impression. People can't represent something of which they're not aware, so when people truly notice us for the first time, our brand expressions inform how they represent us in their minds. Most brand thinkers understand the vital importance of a brand's first impression, and as our industry moves toward automation and efficiency, we risk underestimating how pivotal that first impression truly is. Where did they hear about us? From whom? In what context? Among what other brands? Favorably or unfavorably? These are the moments that we codify in our "consumer journey" slides but that we know deep down we can't reliably control or manufacture. In some cases, our first exposure may be through an ad or otherwise official brand communication, but for most medium to large brands, it's impossible to say exactly where a person's first real touchpoint is with us. This is where the intangible, immeasurable importance of our brand styling and reputation make their first impact: have we created a brand with enough magnetism to pull people toward us? And when they search for us, what do they find?

The middle of the purchase funnel, usually characterized by consideration and preference, is better understood through the lens of the left brain. Once we've become aware of a new product (right brain), we pass that information through to our left brain to fit it into our represented knowledge structure. What brands is this brand like? What do we know about its category? What do we know about its competition? What kinds of people buy these products, and am I that kind of person? The left brain is responsible for taking the unique experience of encountering this hypothetical new brand and fitting it into our working representation of the world.

Because we're dealing with representations in left brain space, the mode of interaction changes. If we're an aspiring streetwear fashion brand and someone posts an outfit trying to look edgy, we can easily undo any brand "coolness" we've built by commenting, "Cool look!" If we were *actually* cool, we'd be so used to this kind of thing happening that we'd hardly even notice. Or maybe we'd post some obscure emoji or hit the person's direct messages to see if he or she would like to have the photo featured on our account. This isn't meant to discourage brands from interacting with organic content. We just need to be mindful of what the person posting that content is hoping to achieve.

As bland as the term has become, customer service is another pivotal moment of right brain interaction with us. A person has a problem with an order, the product stopped working, or he or she needs to make an exchange. Except in cases like social media grandstanding in which a "customer service" inquiry is made loudly and publicly, customer service interactions tend to be personal and individual. They're not representations of experience—they're firsthand encounters with us that will eventually be categorized and stored. In a McKinsey study about the importance of customer service, 85 percent of customers who had positive experiences during emotionally charged brand interactions increased their investment, while 70 percent who had bad experiences showed demonstrable decreases.[2] Windows of right brain engagement, however brief, are critical moments for making lasting positive impressions.

When people mention our brand in a post, it's easy to misinterpret that as a cue for one-to-one interaction. But that's not what's happening, unless they've gone out of their way to make sure the message is sent solely and directly to us. Remember the Wendy's example of someone offering to buy everything on the menu, then posting a trash bag as proof? Wendy's responded, "Thanks for sharing your baby pictures," because the brand understood that the person tweeting at them wasn't its audience. The audience was the combination of its followers and the trash bag poster's followers who would see the interaction within their Twitter feeds. It's a battle between the brand's representation of itself and the poster's representation of the brand.

By addressing the audience and not our debate opponent, we bring to life our perspective and persona while reinforcing our boundaries. Because brands have become so gun-shy in social media, loud detractors are able to bully brands out of campaigns and into needless apologies. Lighthearted clapbacks show people that we're going to stand our ground. Netflix once retweeted a gif of a cast member from *Ru Paul's Drag Race* dancing on a pole wearing a lion costume, to which one follower responded, "Is this really what Netflix tweets. Is that really what they retweet. Really. For real." Netflix simply responded, "Yes." Its response generated over 100 *likes*—more than the tweet to which it had originally responded. As we all know, the outcome of an Internet debate is judged by *like* counts.

In left brain space, we know people are in the business of self-representation, and that's exactly what we ought to help them do. By creating content that represents our brands and the people who like our brand, we're able to lean into the kinds of content people hope to engage organically. When we create content suited to left brain engagement, we want to keep information as simple and accessible as possible and use verbiage that represents ourselves in relatable, easy-to-understand ways. That can be painful sometimes because we often have an intricate narrative about our brand that we want to share. We need to express that information too, just in the right (ha, get it?) place. When someone is compelled by our left brain content, we want to ensure that there is a corresponding right brain hub for research and information gathering about us.

EVERY BRAND MUST BALANCE ITS GENUINE EXPRESSION OF SELF WITH SCALABLE REPRESENTATION

One brand that's struck an admirable balance between easily consumable left brain content and right brain depth is Dannon's Activia brand. Activia probiotic yogurt bills itself as a specialty product particularly suited to gut health. Activia successfully differentiated itself from the crowded single-serve yogurt space by touting the health benefits of "probiotics," stating in a YouTube video featured on their website that "only Activia has billions of our live and active probiotics."[3] The key word there is "our." Activia contains a particular strain of probiotic called *bifidus regularis,* which is supposed to help maintain a healthy digestive system.[4] Actually, most kinds of yogurts contain similar amounts of probiotic cultures, and there are hundreds of products on the market that contain different strains of probiotics.[5] But Activia was the first to talk about it in a mainstream, easy-to-understand way. *Bifidus regularis* has undergone research funded by Dannon and has demonstrated some improvements in people with irritable bowel syndrome (IBS), but according to gastroenterologist Kirsten Tillisch, participants in these studies consumed Activia two to three times per day—significantly more often than an average person likely would.

The entire paragraph you just read is filled with information that's probably not particularly relevant to you. Unless you have IBS, in which case, I'm so sorry. *Bifidus regularis* probably didn't pique the curiosity of your left hemisphere. You probably didn't even *really* try to sound it out in your head. And that's the brilliance of the Activia brand. Dannon's strategy was to take this complex topic and condense it into consumable talking points that could resonate with the left hemisphere. Activia isn't a new product. It was launched in the 1980s in France under the name Danone Bio.[6, 7] It was introduced to the United States in 2006, reaching $130 million in sales, then grew another 50 percent the following year. By 2009, sales of Activia reached €2.6 billion globally, and Activia is credited with growing both health yogurt and probiotic product categories.

Activia's approach to messaging is as simple as it is brilliant. In one piece of Facebook creative, the brand leads with a closeup shot of a woman's abdomen, then superimposes the text, "Gut health that looks good on everyone."[8] The spot continues with a simple callout that says, "Probiotic + Prebiotic," without explaining what either of those words mean. The brand presumes that we've either heard of them and know them to be vaguely good for us, or that we've never heard of them before and hopefully draw the same conclusion. Another piece of creative from the same campaign uses similar visuals with captions that read, "Looking for probiotics? Found them!" as a woman drinks an Activia product. Another text card reads, "20 years of gut health research," then cycles through a series of different colored and shaped women's stomachs before finally resolving on a closeup of the product.

Not only are these the perfect sound bites for reaching the left brain but they also bypass the right brain's complexity filter by attaching themselves to established left brain structures. Activia presumes that health-conscious people have likely heard the word *probiotic* even if the full definition isn't obvious. By differentiating as *"the* probiotic yogurt," the brand attached itself to a preexisting, if slightly vague, left hemisphere category of "healthy food I should probably eat more often but that I don't really know where to find." Truthfully, any yogurt product can lay claim to probiotics, even if it doesn't specifically contain *bifidus regularis*. If our audience has a vague representation stored of the concept "probiotic" but has the problem of not knowing exactly where to get a probiotic, the hard work is already done. The right brain pitch has already been made, and Activia is able to circumvent the complexity of explaining the nuanced benefits of probiotics.

Most of us don't feel the need to do deep research into claims like, "Probiotics are good for you," because it's much easier to outsource our trust to trained professionals—or Karen from the office. She's always posting articles about this kind of stuff. But just in case we're curious for more information, Activia complements these light-and-quick left brain talking points with a robust website filled with research and information about probiotics, how they work, their health benefits, the "gut-brain connection," and so on.

As brands, it's vital that we balance our shorter-form selling points, which in all likelihood make up the bulk of our advertising and social media content, with a clear and deep articulation of why we do what we do or make what we make. Even if the majority of our audience doesn't access this depth of information, it wards off skeptics. Without a reliable information source about our brand, the claims of our left brain risk appearing to be facades—not that *any* marketer would *ever* make a claim that wasn't 100 percent true.

WITHOUT RIGHT BRAIN ANCHORS, LEFT BRAIN CLAIMS RISK FEELING DUPLICITOUS

Take Gwyneth Paltrow's brand Goop, for instance. Goop sells items like "Amethyst crystal-infused water bottles," which claim to "help tap into your own intuition," and "Psychic vampire repellents," which are so easy to use that one can simply "spray around the aura to protect from psychic attacks and emotional harm." Goop.com tries to balance these left brain claims with longer-form articles about how the crystals . . . use energy or like, vibrations? And, you know, how the different crystals work on different . . . frequencies. Or something. However, and this may come as a major surprise to you, the articles don't contain citations or links to any legitimate third-party sources.

The point is that crystals and probiotics are essentially the same. They're magic. I mean, not really, but as non-scientists, we've all heard positive claims about both. In general, we tend not to put on our lab coats and re-create the experiments ourselves. The difference is that probiotics have entire scientific disciplines actively engaged in figuring out how they work and why they're beneficial. Claims about crystals continue to build taller and taller scaffolding on already shaky left brain structures.

Every few months, Goop seems to inspire derisive new headlines like, "Gwyneth Paltrow's Goop Touted the 'Benefits' of Putting a Jade Egg in Your Vagina—Now It Must Pay" and, "Advertising Watchdog Files Complaint Against Gwyneth Paltrow's Goop for 'Deceptive' Health Claims." Amazingly, the Goop brand seems to maintain an insular community of believers, and it's hard to call Goop's transformation from a newsletter with 150,000 subscribers into a $250 million brand unsuccessful. How much of that success is driven by Paltrow's influence is hard to say, but Goop is in a difficult position in terms of growth in more mainstream markets. The brand relies on Paltrow's editorial voice and celebrity endorsement to maintain its relevance and engagement. Using a highly unscientific methodology of reviewing Goop's last 100 Instagram posts, as of this writing, 6 of the top 10 most popular posts are photos of Paltrow, despite her appearing in only 11 photos total.[9] So photos of Paltrow make up 60 percent of the most engaging content despite accounting for only 11 percent of the overall content.

It's unusual for brands to launch successfully with only left brain appeal, though it sometimes happens when celebrities and influencers throw around their endorsements. More often, startup founders and new brands trying to explain their value trip over themselves with more information than their audience can actually handle. They're immersed in the right brain experience of how they're thinking, what they're doing, and why it will matter to people. Their natural inclination is to convey the tactics and details that will (hopefully) make them successful and differentiate them from the market.

Fortunately, it's much easier to take a wide base of right brain qualities and process them into those left brain talking points that can hook people. Unfortunately, this process often relies on individual judgment and taste, especially for small companies, meaning it's easy to bury the lede because what appeals to a startup founder isn't always what appeals to a broad audience. However, if we use social media to gauge the effectiveness of that messaging and continue to optimize based on performance, we should eventually find our way to outputs that will catch left brain attention.

When we're dealing with people representing their political beliefs on Twitter, it's unlikely that any amount of nuanced discussion or research will sway the prevailing attitude. And we should expect the same of any entrenched belief that people are representing to the world as parts of their identities. Likewise, when we're engaged in a conversation with an open-minded community like r/ChangeMyView, simple representations of established beliefs are doomed to feel tone-deaf and disconnected. In order for us as brands to effectively reach people, we need to understand in which mode a person is engaged and adjust our approach accordingly. In left brain territory, providing people with content that represents them (and us) can help drive earned reach, solidify connection with our fans, and generate organic-feeling endorsements from them. In right brain territory, we need to stay more in tune with the nuances of the conversation in front of us, and we need to engage with it directly. In doing so, we'll be able to create genuinely positive experiences that dictate how and where we're categorized in left brain representation.

Our left brain hooks must be balanced with right brain anchors. In left brain territory, when messaging connects to our audience's pre-existing knowledge structures, it's better able to stick. That messaging should be as simple and accessible as possible, but it should be backed by a depth of information that supports our shorter-form claims. For some brands, that means creating attention-grabbing headlines about our revolutionary technology (left brain) alongside a thorough explanation of how and why that technology works (right brain). For others, it means using bite-sized messaging to point toward a deep and compelling story of who we are as a brand and why we do what we do.

Every brand starts with a tangible purpose—solving a problem, offering something of value, and so on. From that holistic, low-resolution picture, we begin the exercise that defines marketing as a discipline. We pull forward the features and elements that represent our brand well in the world. And if things are working properly, our audience's reaction to these messages return to inform how our brand operates. Succeeding in left and right brain territory isn't separate. It's part of a consistent cycle that follows naturally from how our brains experience the world.

KEY TAKEAWAYS

- The way we process information follows a predictable pattern. New information is experienced by the right hemisphere, the left brain extracts important details and fits them into its knowledge structures, and then the extracted information is passed back to the right hemisphere for reintegration.

- When engaged with our right brains, we're in a mode of forming and evolving our beliefs. This is a vulnerable and often brief window, characterized by unique, direct engagement with our brand—like reaching out to customer service.

- In a left brain context, we are representing our beliefs as expressions of our identities rather than engaging the beliefs themselves. General mentions of our brand without direct outreach to us is most often a left brain expression, and engagement on behalf of the brand should consider the user's goal of self representation.

FIVE LESSONS FOR BUILDING
AND HONING A SOCIAL STRATEGY

omcast. For most marketers, just reading the name is enough to send a shiver down the spine. Or mine, at least. Comcast is one of those brands that's not just fashionable to dislike—walk into a room of people who've dealt with the brand, and you can just about guarantee that someone has a personal horror story. To be fair, we really only notice Comcast—a telecommunications company that primarily supplies Internet, phone, and television access—when something goes wrong. Nonetheless, the Internet's hatred of Comcast runs deep.

In a 2015 roundup of the top Reddit posts of all time—not just in one particular community but across the hundred thousand plus active communities on the platform—a post about Comcast ranked number 6.[1] "Comcast." the post reads, "If you upvote this, it will show up on Google Images when people search Comcast, cable or internet service provider."[2] The attached image was of a Nazi flag—red background, central white circle, and large black swastika in the center. The post played on a familiar and very Reddit-y conception. Redditors recognize that highly upvoted posts tend to rank well on Google. By using particular keywords in a post title, there is a chance that the post will show up in Google's search results. It's a deeply meta form of participation—a boundary that Redditors push ad infinitum.

The post itself followed a long wave of backlash against Comcast both on and off Reddit. While stories of botched customer support were already enough to infuriate many Internet dwellers, Comcast supported the infamous Stop Online Piracy Act (SOPA) and PROTECT IP Act (PIPA), placing it square in the bull's-eye of Internet disdain.[3] While both SOPA and PIPA purportedly aimed to end online copyright infringements, both acts gave telecommunications companies new power to determine bandwidth distribution. Historically, Internet service providers have been considered "common carriers," much like airlines, taxicabs, and freight companies.[4] A common carrier is designated to serve the general public without discrimination, and SOPA and PIPA both aimed to remove that status. Internet denizens feared that companies like Comcast would have the authority to deprioritize sites they disliked, make deals with entrenched corporate superpowers, and disadvantage average Internet users. In short, you couldn't find a company Redditors hated more than Comcast.

In a shocking turn of events, Comcast created its own community on Reddit in 2016 called r/Comcast_Xfinity.[5] What I'm about to tell you may be alarming. You may not be ready for it. But it's the truth, and you need to hear it. Despite the customer service horror stories, throttling Internet speeds, even the support for SOPA and PIPA, Comcast has a deeply strategic, best-in-class presence on Reddit. There, I said it.

According to the community description, r/Comcast_Xfinity is "your official source on Reddit for help with Xfinity services," and, "If you have problems with your services, our experts are here to solve them." Rather than fleeing from the community that fostered such vitriol for its brand, Comcast dove straight into the belly of the beast and addressed the problem head-on. Well, not so much the PIPA and SOPA stuff, but it backed off on messaging its support for those. It's a brilliant example of acting on social listening and executing a strategy suited to a right brain, tangible experience with the brand. Customer service was one way for the brand to acknowledge the real concerns it had heard from the community. It was a genuine effort to add value.

The r/Comcast_Xfinity community is civil, it functions as intended, and most importantly, it provides a place to address problems. It fits naturally into the broader Reddit ecosystem. Prior to the formation of this community, it was natural for someone to mention a complaint about Comcast in a comment thread related to technology or Internet speeds. And inevitably, one bad customer service story bred more. It wasn't unusual for comment threads to spiral into a medley of Comcast customer service horror stories. But now, because the nature of Reddit is to be helpful for fellow community members, when someone mentions a problem with Comcast, it's natural for other users to direct that person to the r/Comcast_Xfinity community. And Comcast is usually very responsive and helpful.

Creativity and strategy are just as important in forming our channel strategies as they are in developing our content. No amount of research or referencing best practices could have generated this strategy for Comcast because it's generally uncharted territory. Branded subreddits are few and far between, and even fewer of them are active. Comcast arrived at this strategy through strategic social listening and genuine consideration for what they heard.

In this chapter, we'll explore some guidelines and suggestions for fitting this broader social exploration together into some actionable advice. It's important that these general guidelines are balanced by the particulars of your brand and the challenges it faces. What works for Comcast probably won't work for a boutique jewelry shop, and vice versa. As a strategist I worked with used to say, if you can take a strategy and swap in another brand without changing much, it's not good branding. As I recommend to all of my clients, great marketing starts with listening, and what we hear may vary massively among brands.

1. SOCIAL LISTENING IS CRITICAL TO BUILDING A SOCIAL MEDIA–SAVVY BRAND

One of the cornerstones on which great marketing—and social—strategy is built is listening. Throughout this book, I've described different social networks and communities as ecosystems, meme pools, and cultures. That's exactly how we ought to treat social networks and the cultures that reside within them. Listening is important for a few different reasons. In the most traditional sense, it's how we get feedback from our customers and noncustomers—we listen to what they want and how they react to our products and messaging.

But really listening also means understanding. Listening helps us figure out from which channel we'll get the most value and how we ought to interact within those channels. Listening enables us to act as natives within these cultures—or, at the very least, as conscientious tourists. That's better than being foreign invaders, which is how many brands are considered in social networks now. Unless our brand is freshly launched and in its own category, odds are that there are important messages for us to find and hear throughout the Internet.

There's a problem here, and it's related to the focused beam of attention manifested by our left hemispheres. When we focus on something, by definition, we're ignoring a bunch of other things. That's how experiments like the infamous "invisible gorilla" work.[6] If you're not familiar, psychologists Christopher Chabris and Daniel Simons developed an experiment in which participants watch a video of two teams passing basketballs back and forth. Participants are told to count the number of passes made. And while many people get the actual number of passes correct, only about 50 percent of viewers notice that during the video, a person dressed in a full gorilla costume walks between the players, beats its chest, and casually strolls off camera.

The invisible gorilla experiment has since become synonymous with "perceptual blindness"—when we focus our attention on one set of stimuli, we often become blind to others. Relatedly, we must also be careful not to fall into the echo chamber trap of "confirmation bias," in which we seek only evidence that supports our preexisting beliefs. As marketers, perceptual blindness and confirmation bias plague our industry. It's how we sit on the same stale "insights" year after year and wonder why our creative outputs aren't innovative. It's also how brands end up spending millions of dollars and months of planning producing tone-deaf spots like Pepsi's "Protests are silly, have a soda with Kendall Jenner" or Peloton's "My husband surprised me with an exercise bike to shame my body, so I made him a selfie documentary." If we start the creative process with a preconception of what the final outcome ought to be, our perspective loses integrity and the creative process breaks down.

True listening is more a right brain exercise than a left. Where our left brain focuses a beam of attention on something in particular, abstracting it from its context, the right brain interprets the world through a broader lens. The right brain, originally suited to predator detection, receives the world as it is presented to us and forms a fuller, contextualized picture of the world. When we jump straight into left brain "listening," we're essentially in a mode of pattern recognition. We have some preconceptions of what it is we'd like to find, and when we find a match, our preconception solidifies a little more. While we certainly need the left brain's skill set for focusing on particular points and analyzing what we find, we need the right brain's spatial awareness to establish the big picture first. All too often, when we go through the exercise of social listening, we report on what's going right rather than painting a true holistic picture. That's not so surprising given the tight leashes from which most social teams operate—many brands are quick to pull social budgets at the faintest hint of backlash. But the full picture—the good, the bad, and the ugly—is vital to our ability to stay relevant and self-aware as brands.

The listening process should start before we've even chosen which social networks we plan to prioritize. Ideally, we have access to powerful social listening tools such as Radian6, Sysomos, Brandwatch, or one of the many platforms that allow us to analyze social media trends, find patterns in how people talk about our brand and category, and spy on our competitors. More robust social listening platforms such as Radian6 and Sysomos often charge brands based on conversation volume for monitored terms, meaning they can get expensive, especially for broader-level listening. These tools tend to be more useful for brands with larger organic footprints and with high conversation volume. For smaller brands and startups, social listening can be an organic undertaking, using free offerings such as Google Analytics, Facebook Insights, Tweet Deck, and other platform-built exploration tools.

Because social media sites, especially Ego and Superego networks, tend to be predictive about recommending content and customizing user experiences, it's very difficult to find a truly agnostic view as a user. Social listening products can help us identify that bird's-eye view of the social landscape we'd be hard-pressed to find as users. But even simple exercises like searching for our brand name, keywords related to our category, and competitive brand names can provide powerful insights for us. Because branded accounts on most social networks also treat us as they would any other user, we can use native functionality to aid us in listening. If, for example, we establish a new branded Twitter account, we ought to follow influencers in our space as well as competitive brands, monitor hashtags related to our industry, and try to understand the relationships between them to provide insight into the types of conversations we might enter.

While social listening tools can be powerful ways to analyze this information, their automated reports and pretty charts can create too much distance between our analysis and reality. Helpful as they can be, it's important to remember that none of the users we hope to engage are looking at social media this way. For that reason, I encourage my teams and clients to post and interact directly within social platforms rather than using automated posting tools. It's easy to get lazy about scheduling a month's worth of content and letting the machine run. As much as we can, we should strive to participate in social networks the way other users do.

Listening should happen from the initial stages of channel selection all the way through evaluating which pieces of our branded content resonate best. In order to drive engagement, we need to pick channels on which our content has the potential to resonate. Goop isn't going to find many fans on Reddit, and *Call of Duty*'s latest version of Nazi Zombies probably isn't going to blow up on Pinterest. We ought to look for the kinds of content we hope to produce on behalf of our brand and identify the social networks on which that type of content thrives. In doing so, we not only can find meme pools in which our memes can compete but we can also learn from the nuances of format, voice, tone, and cultural norms how to create content that feels relevant and natural.

What communities, influencers, pages, and content aggregators tend to grow natural followings on the social networks of interest to us? If we're a fashion-related brand, Pinterest and Instagram are likely candidates for our priority social channels. If our brand's offering is complex or our content strategy is reliant on depth and discovery, we ought to look at networks like Reddit, Twitch, Imgur, Tumblr, Quora, and even smaller interest-based forums related to our brand territory. When we know our target audience fits a particular demographic—or that paid media and down-funnel objectives will dictate our success in social—more established advertising networks like Facebook and Google may be at the top of our channel priorities.

Listening should also be a priority at the level of the meme and meme machine. If we have some sense of the message we want to convey and the content we plan to distribute, we ought to pay close attention to the meme machines that propagate best. What characteristics do we find in common between viral pieces of content within that social network? Our goal here is to take the meme machine from its environment, infuse it with our own meme, and harness the evolutionary process to manifest our ideas to their greatest effect. As we release our meme machines into the wild, we'll likely start to see them fall into the familiar Pareto distribution—20 percent of our content will probably drive 80 percent of our results.

Performance evaluation is another critical form of listening. What can we hear from our audience about what we've made? And I don't just mean combing through the comments of our posts—having played the role of community manager for more than a few years for more than a few brands, I can tell you that nothing will make you lose hope in humanity faster than reading the comments on brands' social posts. Most networks with established advertising platforms provide us with robust, exportable analyses of our creative performance. Unfortunately, most brands don't put these reports to proper use.

Imagine that a month after launching our brand's social presence, we've achieved a modest engagement rate of 1.5 percent. If we create one batch of social creative per month, and we learn enough from our previous batch of content to improve by just 5 percent per month, we'll nearly double our overall engagement rate by the end of the year. Incremental learning is a vital part of the social creative process, and it's not enough to relegate the task to analysts. There are just too many ways to slice the data. Did shorter copy work better than longer copy? Did one piece of creative resonate particularly well with one demographic over another? Did hotter colors grab more attention than cooler colors? Did one content pillar outperform the others? A copywriter, an art director, a media planner, a community manager, and a strategist will all find different ways to slice performance data if they look hard enough. It was (probably) Isaac Asimov who said, "The most exciting phrase to hear in science, the one that heralds new discoveries, is not 'Eureka!' ('I found it!') but 'That's funny.'"[7]

Creative performance evaluations don't have to be overly complicated. The preferred format for these meetings among my teams was generally casual and almost brainstormlike. For each meeting, an analyst prepared a simple review of the last month's creative. Screenshots of each post were accompanied by one or two key metrics—true engagement rate, share rate, conversion rate, whatever had been deemed the priority performance indicators. Then, with everything up on the wall, the team just . . . talked. What did great? What didn't? Which was the most surprising? Who has a theory as to why?

Here are a few learnings from these meetings:

- When copy is superimposed on a post to contextualize an image—when the meme machine is completely encapsulated— posts generated 46 times more clicks of the share button.

- Recipes and crafts that include "process shots" drive significantly more engagement than static images of the final outcome.

- Nature photography tends to generate more engagement when accompanied by a quote or personal story.

- Complementary color schemes tend to grab more attention and generate more social actions.

- Static images and gifs tend to drive more earned reach than videos.

- Cute animals outperform everything else.

That last one is common sense, but hopefully it's clear how these kinds of learnings help a social creative team find a path to continual improvement.

A traditional creative performance report is a corpse. Its learnings are difficult to apply to the living world because they're rarely developed from the perspective of the people actually making the content. More often, performance metrics are used as leverage to prove value to a client or stakeholder. When performance evaluation becomes an active part of the creative process, the insights and learnings are tangible and alive. Plus, it makes social creative more fun. We all know that dopamine hit we get when we post something on a personal social media profile that gets some attention. If we can get our entire creative team aligned to the same evaluation of success, we all get to feel that dopamine rush when a brand post blows up.

When we arrive at a new learning, it's important that we codify that learning in a living document. And no, dropping data once a month into a shared Google doc isn't good enough. Past learnings should be part of every creative briefing for rounds of social creative. While veteran team members may feel this exercise to be redundant, maintaining a set of brand-specific best practices keeps us from making the same mistakes over and over again. It also helps to onboard new team members and provides an impartial third party for reference during disagreements about style and direction. Anchoring our teams in democratically sourced, data-backed learnings minimizes the clash of egos and helps to align different disciplines to the same goal. If you've ever worked in an ad agency, you know that minimizing clashes between egos is half the battle.

2. CHOOSE AS MANY CHANNELS AS YOU CAN DO WELL, AND DESIGNATE DISCRETE CHANNEL ROLES

When a new social network starts to become popular, parallel conversations arise in just about every brand organization. Should we be there? What would our presence look like? Can Intern Jonny take on another social media site? He's only handling seven right now, so . . . probably, right? I watched this happen with Facebook, Twitter, Instagram, Pinterest, Vine, Tumblr, and poor Google+ (you tried, guys). Then, I stoked those very same conversations when I joined Reddit in 2016, which is around the same time that brands also started to adopt

Snapchat. I gained another level of awareness of my own naïveté as I watched brand after brand dump money into Snapchat—an app that was originally designed for discretely sending nudes—while hearing that Reddit was a "brand safety concern." Years later, many large brands have broken through their hesitation with the Reddit platform to great effect, but what surprised me most about brands' willingness to jump into Snapchat was the lack of strategic rationale.

Joining a new social network as a brand is a big step, and it ought to be taken thoughtfully and strategically. Don't get me wrong, Snapchat is a strategic channel for some brands. Brands that find creative uses for lenses and augmented reality experiences and brands whose content fits particularly well into extremely short-form video are a perfect fit on the platform. But for brands that strive to earn reach, integrate into culture, and build a meaningful following, Snapchat is often an uphill battle.

Hype about a new emerging channel seems to short-circuit our strategic wiring. When AdAge publishes an article praising a brand's early adoption of an emerging channel, many brands have an inclination to chase the same success. Chasing "early-adopter" status is almost always a losing battle, unless it's executed with full consideration for the middle- to long-term implications for the brand. What will this new channel allow us to do that our current channels don't? How will we evaluate the success—or failure—of our participation in the new channel? How much resource and media budget can we reasonably allocate to it?

Even young brands have a tendency to spread themselves thin across a wide number of social channels. For smaller brands without big brand resources, this approach not only exhausts resources but it also almost guarantees low impact. When we create content that attempts to appeal to every channel, we'll likely achieve only lowest-common-denominator results from each of them. Conversely, investing ourselves fully into one or two channels humanizes us, allows us to engage in meaningful ways with our audience, and with consistency, builds the momentum we want from social media.

In brand building, we walk a fine line between strategic planning and real-world behavior. Brand builders in traditional agencies often lament the lengthy, exhaustive conversations behind every brand decision. What would it mean for us to change the hue of this brand color? What if we replaced this word on our packaging? Can we move the logo up four pixels? Social media has pushed us to think faster and forced us out of our lengthy conference room planning sessions because by the time our 10-person committee has agreed on the exact language to use in this tweet, the trending hashtag we hoped to engage has been all but forgotten. At a macro-level, that's a good thing for our industry. It has loosened the reins on driving a brand. But there is a risk in swinging too far into this "act first, ask questions later" approach.

In 2011, entrepreneur Eric Ries wrote a book called *The Lean Startup*, which was revolutionary, particularly in the world of tech.[8] The essential premise of the book is that companies, especially start-ups, ought to change their approach to building and launching products. Ries brilliantly identifies the often wasteful, needlessly long process most large companies have adopted in building and evolving their products. All too often, companies spend weeks, months, or years developing a product that is introduced to potential customers only after it's finished. What if customers wanted something slightly different? What if hearing feedback early on could inform the building of that product so that customers get what they really need?

Ries's proposed solution revolves around the *minimum viable product* (MVP). Rather than dropping a finished product in customers' laps, Ries recommends delivering the MVP to generate feedback throughout the development process. By delivering the MVP, organizations minimize the time and resources wasted during development and allow the customer to inform the product's ongoing evolution. With examples ranging from startups run out of garages to Fortune 500 companies, Ries makes a powerful case for the "lean startup method."

Lean startup thinking has made its way into social media thinking too. I suppose we have the common ground of Silicon Valley to thank for that. And in many ways, Ries's approach is an antidote to the stagnant, ultraconservative brand building process of the TV advertising era. While we can—and should—apply the tactics of Ries's "build-measure-learn" approach, we still have important lessons to glean from our more conservative branding forebears. As products, if we're valuable enough to our customers, there's a chance they'll wade through some missing features and broken code to bear with us. But as brands, we simply can't think that way. For brands, first impressions matter.

From determining which social networks in which we'll participate to what we optimize our content toward, we need to consider the full impression of someone encountering us. If we've spread ourselves too thin across too many channels, odds are that we're going to have shallow content for each platform and even shallower engagement to show for it. In many cases, a semi-active presence is worse than no presence at all. If a small fashion brand lazily posts the same product shots to 10 different social platforms, they're unlikely to make the impression they want to make, and they're certainly not going to sway any opinions. If their Instagram account only generates a few engagements per post, that doesn't bode well for users interested in attaching themselves to the brand as a form of self-expression.

I wish this next paragraph could tell you, "Here are the exact right social channels for your brand to use!" I'd even use an exclamation point so we could both get extra excited about it. But I can't do that. The right channel mix and strategy is different for every brand. As we try to answer this question for our brands, we should first ask ourselves what we're trying to accomplish. Are we trying to attach our brand to popular culture? Do we aspire to build a community, or are we satisfied with being a voice in a community we don't manage? Are we looking for down-funnel sales metrics as measures of success, or does our brand need to build upper-funnel awareness and affinity first? My advice is to choose as many channels as can be thoughtfully attended to and to designate specific goals for each. Sometimes those goals may overlap, but if they do, we should have a strong rationale as to why we shouldn't consolidate those channels.

The exception to this advice is *squatting*. Sometimes, squatting on a username or page that may be mistaken as an official brand presence is a worthwhile defensive tactic. It keeps users from trolling us with spoof accounts and demonstrates to users that we're at the very least aware of the platform. We don't necessarily have to execute a full content and engagement strategy for every channel on which we've secured a username, but whatever we do should feel intentional.

Squatted channels should be skinned to look and feel consistent with the brand. If we've secured a channel and we've themed it to look and feel like our brand, and we don't intend to use the channel to engage people, we simply need to make that clear to people. Even something as simple as a message to people who land on the page should suffice: "Hi, there, thanks for finding us! If you'd like to get in touch with us, you can find us on Twitter via @TheCatMassageInstitute or contact us directly through our website: www.TheCatMassageInstitute.com." (I wish that was a real website, but sadly, it isn't.)

When we choose to join a social network, our presence should embody what our brand aspires to be. That doesn't just mean creating content from our brand's perspective. It means that we're active, engaged, and invested. While there are certainly benefits to maintaining a wide social footprint, we're better off with one or two outstanding presences than we are with a handful of mediocre ones. We should look for a combination of factors in choosing our priority social networks. First, can the channel accomplish the goals we need to achieve? Second, will people there care about our message? And third, do we have the resources to ensure that our presence lives up to the brand we're trying to build?

3. MANIFEST BEHAVIORS WITH RIGHT BRAIN APPEAL, THEN TELL LEFT BRAIN STORIES ABOUT THEM

In the previous chapter, we examined how aspects of the right brain's perspective, characterized by presence with immediate experience, big picture thinking, and exploration of the unknown, correspond with behaviors in anonymous Id networks. Likewise, the left brain's represented version of the world, cleanly categorized and focused on the utility of the tools it's able to recognize, correspond with Ego and Superego networks, wherein we represent different aspects of ourselves. As we consider on which social networks our brand can make the biggest impact, we should be mindful of how we balance ourselves between these two modes of online expression.

As we might expect, left brain networks tend to have clearer lanes for interaction between users. These Ego and Superego networks also tend to have more developed tools for paid media distribution. Facebook/Instagram and Twitter are among the most developed advertising platforms the industry has ever seen. In general, left brain networks tend to be more discretely organized, they have more platform-enforced rules, and participation tends to be more formulaic. On Facebook, we can make posts, comment on other posts, and message the people with whom we have mutual connections. On Reddit, we're free to participate in over a hundred thousand interest-based communities, each of which has its own rules and cultures, and our mode of participation is more open-ended. Right brain networks tend to be less predictable in terms of how people—and brands—interact with one another. That can be a challenge or an opportunity for differentiation.

Left brain platforms like Facebook and Instagram have tight control over advertiser profiles and how many people those profiles are able to reach. Their algorithms are centralized and opaque—it isn't clear to us as users how a post worked its way into our feed. Because they're organized around individual user feeds, left brain platforms have the problem of balancing content to maintain user engagement. Too much advertiser content risks alienating users from the value they derive from the platform, while too little risks losing advertising clients. Earning reach on these platforms is extremely difficult without a baseline of paid media because the platforms themselves keep most organic advertiser content out of user feeds. An earned impression effectively takes dollars out of Facebook's pocket, so it's no surprise that brands' organic reach has been on a steady decline for years.

For challenger brands and brands striving to create organic impact in a social network, investing in Id network activity has greater potential payoff. Functionally, even more developed Id networks like Reddit maintain a clearer separation between paid and organic advertiser activity. That's largely dictated by the structure of the network itself—user pages aren't destinations. Communities are. Because communities play a greater role in content selection than the left brain networks' opaque algorithm equivalents, as brands, we have a clearer path to success. We have to win over the community rather than the platform itself.

When a community on Reddit collectively agrees that the content we've posted adds value, the Reddit platform treats our post just as it does any other user's. When an organic post reaches the front page of Reddit, the number of impressions generated can rival large media buys. In 2019, Reddit reported having 430 million monthly active users, and because the platform prioritizes community-level over user-level curation, savvy brands have real potential to drive massive amounts of organic reach and engagement.[9]

While right brain networks do have greater potential to create virality and word-of-mouth momentum for our brands, organic activity in general is much less predictable than paid media. For most brands, the optimal channel strategy requires a balance of both left and right brain networks. Left and right brain networks require different approaches, but that doesn't mean we can't build strategies that create synergy between them. Our right brains experience the world, and our left brains represent those experiences by telling stories, creating identities, and storing learnings for our future selves. Likewise, as brands, we should strive to create value adding experiences that appeal to the right brain, then tell left brain stories about those experiences.

Assuming we're still pretending to be the marketing team for The Cat Massage Institute, imagine that we decide to give away our patented cat massagers to owners whose cats have recently had . . . some kind of cat injury. A torn lickament. No wait, a purr-forated muscle. (I'm sorry.) Anyway, we give away our Cat Massager™ to a few people on Reddit—that's the behavior. Hopefully, those people now have a much more positive impression of us, and hopefully, they tell their stories to others within the Reddit community. One person posts in the r/AskVet community, and we're the top post in a community of over 66,000 people. Great! Even if we reached every single one of those people, that's probably a relatively small number compared to even a modest media buy. But now we have a story to tell.

Maybe our public relations team pitches a story about "Five Injured Cats Who Got Special Massages on Reddit." I'd click on that. Or maybe we create our own article or album titled, "Five Cats on Reddit who Needed Massages." I'm really going deep on the clickbait titles, but hopefully you get the point—behaviors are the foundation for expressing who our brand is to the world. To maximize the impact of those behaviors, we have to balance them with stories that represent us in ways that are suited to light engagements with a broad audience.

As a general rule, right brain networks tend to be more fruitful grounds for manifesting these behaviors, while the stories we tell should be suited to left brain networks. But this giveaway strategy could work on Twitter or Instagram too. The tactics and channels we choose to manifest behaviors and tell stories can fluctuate depending on where our behaviors and stories will resonate best. Old Spice did exactly that in a 2018 stunt that absolutely nobody saw coming—they created a new character class for *Dungeons and Dragons* players.[10]

The Old Spice brand recognized the power of igniting a fandom that may on the surface seem too niche to warrant engagement. *Dungeons and Dragons* is a tabletop role-playing fantasy game beloved by Internet dorks worldwide. When starting a new D&D campaign, players create characters based on different kinds of "classes," or archetypes. The barbarian class specializes in close combat, a cleric wields divine magic, and a bard . . . well, a bard plays magical music. Bards are the dorks among dorks. In a true first-of-its-kind brand move, Old Spice created a new class called The Gentleman. The Gentleman (or Gentle-woman) wasn't just a goofy, "Wouldn't it be funny if . . ." left brain representation of a character. It was a fully playable character, delivered with lore, special abilities, and a player sheet that looked and felt like something out of a traditional D&D book.

The Gentleman, like other D&D classes, gained special abilities over the course of leveling. Old Spice took liberties to create skills that were hilarious representations of its brand but had real application in a D&D game. The Gentleman started with an ability called "Punchline," characterized as "a humorous phrase to confound their enemies." At level 5, The Gentleman gained an ability called "I'm on a Horse," which allowed the character to "say, 'I'm on a horse' and a horse will appear beneath him." And yes, that's a reference to one of their own ads.

While Old Spice made the announcement of The Gentleman class on Twitter, one of the social channels in which they've invested heavily, the team engaged on Reddit when users in various D&D communities took note. Over 20 organic posts about The Gentleman were created throughout different subreddits. That may not seem like a lot, but sometimes one post in a relevant community is enough to ignite a fanbase. Old Spice reached the top of communities like r/DnD and r/Pathfinder_RPG, both of which are highly influential among fantasy role-players. Acclaim from these communities drove a wave of media coverage in *The Nerdist*, *The Gamer*, Comicbook.com, and a huge number of other gaming and D&D-related publications, citing the enthusiastic reception for The Gentleman among D&D players.[11, 12, 13]

Had Old Spice simply represented The Gentleman—had the company simply tweeted a mockup of what the player class might look like or asked Twitter, "If Old Spice made a D&D character, who would it be?", the reception and resulting media coverage would likely have been minimal. Old Spice dove headfirst into the behavior because it understood that the success of the stunt relied on the approval of real fans. If D&D communities rejected The Gentleman, the media coverage would never have snowballed.

One player wrote on r/DnD, "This is neat as shit that they would go out of their way to reach out to a community like that. . . . This is the best kind of commercial honestly."[14] Another responded, "What's crazy [is] it's not even half bad. I've seen more unbalanced options in Unearthed Arcana. Color me impressed." The depth, craft, and real applicability of The Gentleman won over users in right brain networks. The left brain practice of abstracting that behavior out into a consumable story broadened the campaign's appeal from "people who actively play *Dungeons and Dragons*" to "people who know vaguely what D&D is." That allowed the story to spread to Ego and Superego networks—if I come across this story, I can start a Facebook conversation about this with my friend who played D&D in high school, or I can make tongue-in-cheek jokes on Twitter about dorky D&D players finally wearing deodorant. Not that I would.

Whenever possible, we should strive to find these synergies between manifesting real behaviors in the world that have a tangible impact on people's lives (right brain) and telling those stories in ways that are generally interesting to a broad audience (left brain). Not only does that generate effective social content but it also maximizes the impact of everything we do. Old Spice generated thousands of shares across Twitter and Facebook by making something appreciated by nerds on Reddit. In order for our right brain behaviors to successfully engage people, they must connect with people in a real and tangible way. Without that genuine connection, the stories we tell feel shallow and contrived. The secret sauce isn't so secret—it's just difficult. We have to give people a reason to like us.

4. START YOUR CREATIVE PROCESS WITH THE MOST COMPETITIVE CONTENT ENVIRONMENTS IN MIND

Sugarcane farmers in Australia during the 1930s had a rough time. Their crops were being eaten by cane beetles, and in a desperate attempt to contain them, about a hundred South American cane toads were imported.[15] Indeed, the cane toads solved the beetle problem. And then some. Today, there are more than 1.5 billion cane toads in Australia, and they've conquered more than 386,000 square miles. Cane toads are a textbook example of what biologists call an "invasive species."

Most ecosystems are relatively insular, evolving without foreign species being rapidly introduced. That means predators and prey exist in an ongoing evolutionary arms race that keeps things relatively balanced. On a broad scale, this is an environmentally stable system. When a plant or animal evolves in one ecosystem and it is then introduced into another, it often fails to propagate because it hasn't evolved to survive in the new climate and among those other life-forms. But sometimes, invasive species like cane toads dominate an otherwise balanced ecosystem. Invasive species have a few particularly relevant traits to the meme metaphor you probably saw coming. Invasive species tend to reproduce easily and often. Invasive species also tend to move from more competitive environments into less competitive environments. That's not always the case—sometimes invasive species move laterally into approximately equally competitive environments. But, for example, it's unlikely that a species of climate-sensitive flower will invade the Arabian desert.

Memes follow a similar pattern. Invasive memes are ones formed in competitive meme pools and carry an evolutionary advantage over memes in less competitive meme pools. Be like the cane toad. Take the most successful memes from your most competitive meme pools, and allow them to invade less competitive meme pools.

For major brands, social media is often the absolute last consideration when planning content and establishing messaging hierarchy. But social networks are also the most competitive meme pools in which our brand messaging competes. More than ever, we see television programs borrow from social media for content. News programs and morning shows now rely on social media to indicate what's popular, as commentary on live events, to reference memes and trends—after Grumpy Cat blew up on Reddit, she had "interviews" with *Good Morning America*, the *TODAY Show* in Australia, and even *Forbes*.[16, 17, 18] Media flows downstream from the Internet, but for some reason, most large brands' advertising cycles revolve around TV and traditional media.

It's relatively easy for us to test ideas in social media. Social networks allow us to be less precious about polishing our assets, and sometimes content that's a little rough around the edges actually works better. When we're planning a major campaign, social networks ought to be our first stop rather than our last. When we want to test new campaign lines, concepts, funny skits, product demonstrations, and so on, social media provides us with a simple way to receive candid feedback at whatever scale we deem appropriate.

Even during our traditional creative processes, most of the memes we try don't survive. We cull our ideas by evaluating them against specific criteria. How effectively does the meme communicate the brand value? Will it solve the business problem the brand faces? As we weed out the ideas that fail these most basic criteria, we start to make stylistic and value judgments on behalf of our audiences. Will this concept grab people's attention? Does it feel true to what we know of their experience? Will they find it compelling? And while some advertisers have become very good at predicting the answers to these questions, we're still making educated guesses. Wouldn't we rather our audience give us some indication of which concepts are most interesting and relevant to them?

I'm not recommending that a brand's creative approach be crowdsourced. Most of the time, crowdsourcing is another path to the lowest common denominator of success. It's vital that we enter any creative exercise with a well-established strategy to frame our output. But the proverbial pendulum has been stuck far in the direction of finger-to-the-wind instincts of creative egos when we have abundant opportunities to hear feedback directly from our audiences.

In a traditional agency creative process, a broad brainstorming exercise generates an abundance of ideas. Then, a creative team, usually consisting of a copywriter and art director, begin down the frustrating road of concept submissions and rejections until they satisfy a creative team lead. And an account lead. And a strategy lead. And some random, unrelated VPs who inexplicably inserted themselves into the feedback process. Finally, the concepts are presented to a client, who feels a need to deliver a huge amount of feedback, proportionate to the huge amount of money they're paying the agency. Rinse and repeat three more times, and finally, things move to production.

Because the rest of the process has been so painful and wrought with approvals for every bit of minutia possible, the script becomes the bible. The process leaves no room for improvisation or opportunistic captures—you know, the things that keep videos from feeling overly scripted and contrived. The spot is unleashed on the world in 60-second, 30-second, and 15-second formats—then the pesky social team requests a 6-second version so that at the very least, when the video auto-plays in feed for 2 seconds, the team can put "30 percent view-through rate" on their recap slide.

Despite this robust process and massive investments of time, resources, and money, at no point have we consulted our audience. Throughout the process, we've generated hundreds, maybe thousands of ideas and culled all except a small handful. Why can't our audience help us choose which ideas to pursue and which to eliminate? If you're thinking, "creative egos," then touché. Here's an idea, though. Rather than going straight into full-on production, let's find the most simple, straightforward way to communicate our concept and promote it to a small audience on our social channels. If we decide we want to film real testimonials about how much people enjoyed our product, we might create some static images-with-quotes-superimposed and see how people react. If we want to feature an interesting life hack or way to use the product, we might use some simple phone photography to capture the concept. If we're choosing between a few jokes as openers in our TV spot, we might film low-production talking-head videos to see which resonate best.

Not only does light, low-production content humanize our brand and get our audience invested in our creative process but it also allows us to test the viability of various memes in a real, competitive environment. When we create a piece of content for a 30-second TV slot (a fishbowl), and we try to release our creation into the Internet (the ocean), our poor creative is likely to get swallowed immediately or wash quietly into the depths of YouTube alongside 11-year-olds' *Minecraft* gaming channels and daily chemtrail conspiracy vloggers.

There's nothing quite as painful as spending six months producing a piece of content that gets 12 views on YouTube and zero comments. At least backlash makes things exciting. But the truth is that the vast majority of branded content finds itself in the cold and lonely landfill of stuff that wasn't interesting enough to earn attention. Take the meme out of the lab. Let it run around. Take it through the obstacle course. See how it performs before putting it in the big race.

5. TIMING CAN BE AN EFFECTIVE TACTIC, BUT IT'S NOT A STRATEGY

Since Oreo's iconic "Dunk in the dark" moment during the 2013 Super Bowl, brands have been chasing real-time engagement as if it were the holy grail in social media. Some brands have gone so far as to create "newsroom" models for content creation equipped with TV monitors hosting charts that nobody actually looks at, community managers scouring for trends, and bored creative teams on deck to whip up timely but often insubstantial content. After all, that's how Oreo did it.

Oreo did more than buy a traditional Super Bowl spot during the game. It also assembled a "war room" social media team to create real-time content throughout the game. When the stadium's power went out, the social team took the opportunity to shine (no pun intended). They created a simple tweet that read, "Power out? No problem."[19] The tweet featured an image of an Oreo surrounded by darkness with a caption that read, "You can still dunk in the dark." The tweet generated over 14,000 retweets and nearly 7,000 *likes.* Coverage of Super Bowl ads were particularly enthusiastic about the tweet, with the first line of a *Huffington Post* article reading, "One of the most buzz-worthy ads of the Super Bowl on Sunday wasn't even a commercial—it was a mere tweet from Oreo during the blackout."[20]

While brilliantly executed and well received, the "Dunk in the dark" moment became a false idol for many major brands. Some attempted this 24/7 newsroom-style social strategy, which usually netted a high volume of extremely time relevant but ultimately low impact content. Some of my own teams scrapped perfectly valid social strategies following feedback that the output "wasn't time relevant enough." There are a few important elements of Oreo's success that aren't often factored into the evaluation. First, the Super Bowl is a rare moment in time with reach and awareness so broad that just about everyone in America knows what's happening. Second, the Super Bowl tends to be as much about the ads as it is about the sport. While 14,000 retweets and 7,000 *likes* is undoubtedly a high-performing tweet, it's unlikely that the tweet would have generated nearly as much media coverage as it did during a less advertiser-centric moment. Oreo was able to harness an audience of advertising beat writers looking for new angles on an annual story—"This year's best Super Bowl ad wasn't even a commercial!"

About a month prior to my writing this, a video, posted by an average user, reached the front page of Reddit titled, "Wendy's Training Video is what I wish we were still doing today."[21] The video isn't a spoof. It's actually a training video, likely from the 1980s. Or at least that's what the Internet suspects based on the whole "person gets sucked into the TV to learn how to cook hamburgers" plot. The post itself generated over 41,000 upvotes and 2,000 comments totally organically. We'd be hard pressed to find an ad for any brand that could intentionally reach the front page of Reddit with such velocity and positive sentiment.

A 1980s training video is as untimely as it gets, but there's something deeply compelling about it. It's a window into a previous era. It's also ultracheesy and reminiscent of the terrible info-tainment millennials were fed as children. The video wasn't meant for broad consumption, so it's like peeking behind the scenes as we watch. And this wasn't a case of "recently found footage" either. The video had been popularized by a radio host named Brian Fink on Twitter in 2018, where it had been reposted hundreds of times.[22] The same video reached the top of another Reddit community a few months prior and was shared in a smaller Reddit community three years before the front page blowup.[23, 24] The point is that timeliness is only one factor in the broader category of relevance. This Wendy's video could have been posted days, months, or years prior—or after—and it likely would still have generated the same level of engagement. The same can be said for much of the content we strive to create as brands: a timely post will eventually lose its relevance, but a relevant post doesn't always have to be timely.

Timeliness is important for a particular kind of content. It's important for content related to events that, in the words of *The Office* character Jim Halpert, "if you didn't see them live, you wouldn't really care that you didn't see them at all." Creating real-time content can indeed help a brand stand out from the noise, and it can signal to users that the brand is actually engaged in the conversation. But the short-ened planning process and robust network of approvals most brands require prior to posting make creating good timely content very diffi-cult, and unless the already complex content creative process happens in lockstep with a media promotion strategy, we're rolling the dice against network algorithms.

Before we fully commit to the tightrope walk of creating quality, timely content, most brands should get into a rhythm of creating high-performing evergreen content. If something is interesting, useful, or entertaining in its own right, the Internet doesn't care so much about when it was created. An album of life hacks from 1910 managed to generate nearly 5,000 upvotes on Reddit and over 500,000 views on Imgur, simply because they were interesting and useful.[25, 26] With the right framing, great content will remain viable long after it's created. Removing the pressure of faster-than-light turnaround and focusing on improving overall engagement will also hone our instincts when it comes time to make something that actually is time sensitive. If we haven't mastered engagement outside a time constraint, we're adding significantly more complexity and uncertainty to our process by trying to do so in tight time windows.

There are some cases where timeliness contributes meaningfully to social strategies, and this is in no way meant to diminish brands that successfully capture attention during events and around trends.

For brands with light and lean creative processes—usually smaller brands without lengthy approval processes—inserting the brand into real-time conversations can help us connect with new audiences and grow our organic reach. When an event is particularly relevant to our audience, participating in organic conversations can be a strong way to build connection between the brand and the event itself. Especially on platforms like Twitter, which prioritize timeliness and foster more real-time conversations, applying a lens of time relevance can lead to meaningful improvements to brand perception, relatability, and overall engagement.

While timing can be an effective tactic to utilize, it must be couched in a broader strategy and leveraged during moments of particularly high impact. Timeliness is not a strategy in and of itself. Tweeting trending hashtags can help us generate more organic reach, and particularly for new accounts and budding brands, it can be an effective way to get noticed. For the vast majority of social media creative development, maintaining a steady rhythm and focusing on incremental improvements by analyzing past performance will generate better return on investment. A great creative strategy is one that allows our brand to bring a unique and interesting perspective to a conversation. More often than not, great content today is still great content tomorrow.

KEY TAKEAWAYS

- Social listening is absolutely critical, and it should be considered an ongoing part of any brand's social media strategy. It should occur at the level of trend, of category, of brand, and of content itself.

- Choose as many social channels as can be well executed. Less is more when strapped for resources. One or two great brand presences will almost always trump a handful of mediocre ones.

- Create synergy between left and right brain strategies whenever possible. Manifest behaviors that reinforce brand positioning and connect meaningfully with people (right brain). Then tell stories about those behaviors in ways that appeal to a broad audience (left brain).

- Start the creative process with the most competitive channels in mind. It's easier for an engaging piece of content from social media to adapt to TV than the other way around.

- Utilize timing as a tactic when relevant to a broader strategy, but don't rely on real-time content to carry the social media strategy. Strive to create consistently high-engagement evergreen content before investing heavily in real-time content development.

CHAPTER 11

BUILDING BEST-IN-CLASS SOCIAL CAMPAIGNS EFFICIENTLY AND EFFECTIVELY

> When the people killed a buffalo, they did it with reverence. They gave thanks to the buffalo's spirit. They used every part of the buffalo they killed. The meat was their food. The skins were used for clothing and to cover their tipis. The hair stuffed their pillows and saddlebags. The sinews became their bowstrings. From the hooves, they made glue. They carried water in the bladders and stomachs. To give the buffalo honor, they painted the skull and placed it facing the rising sun.[1]
>
> —from "The Passing of the Buffalo," a Kiowa legend

Many of the Native American tribes who populated the American plains shared a common practice about hunting buffalo: use every part. It's a step beyond how we usually think about efficiency. These tribes weren't just interested in killing the maximum number of buffalo on a given hunting trip. They found ways to put every part of the animal to use.

Social media marketing is a lot like hunting buffalo. Just kidding, it isn't. But this sentiment is an extremely important part of putting the concepts from this book into practice. Much of the focus of this book is in finding meaningful differentiation between social networks, and while I believe understanding these nuances to be absolutely critical to good marketing strategy, nuance also presents challenges to the goals of scalability and efficiency. How can we create campaigns that are tailored to particular mindsets in different social networks while achieving scale and working within our available resources?

In previous chapters, we discussed the competitiveness of different meme pools—different environments in which content vies for attention. In purely pay-to-place media like TV and print, competition is more a question of media budget. There remain the questions of how strategically and creatively we might fill these spaces, but whether we make an incredible commercial or an absolutely abysmal one, we're likely going to reach the same number of people through our media buy.

Social media doesn't quite work that way. In social advertising, when we create a piece of content that performs extremely well, it has the potential to be shared, earn additional reach, make more efficient use of our media dollars, and generate organic traction. In part, that's why I recommend flipping the traditional creative funnel and beginning with social media—the qualitative and quantitative feedback we receive there can help us hone our creative for channels with more standard media. That's one example of using part of the buffalo we usually throw away. What comments do people make on our ads? Where does their viewership drop off? Which creative variation is the top performer? Most of that information is lost or, at best, included in recap reports, which is practically the same as getting lost.

In this chapter, we're going to apply the learnings from this book to a few theoretical advertising campaigns. For our first mock campaign, we'll truly start from scratch with a fresh brand—one with no background, history, or market share. Our hypothetical new brand makes a product with an established, long-standing competitor set—camping equipment. And since I'm writing this from the Bay Area, let's give our tent brand a fittingly hip tech name: Tent.ly.

EXAMPLE 1. LAUNCHING A BRAND WITH A COHESIVE BUT DIFFERENTIATED SOCIAL STRATEGY

Tent.ly makes premium quality tents that rival big-name competitors like The North Face and REI, but because Tent.ly isn't bound to brick-and-mortar sales and massive company infrastructure, it's able to sell tents for 20 percent less than most of its competitors. For Tent.ly, the category is already well established, and the use cases are obvious. Tent.ly's first hurdle as a brand is gaining credibility. Tent.ly hasn't developed its left brain territory for campers and hikers. It isn't a known quantity, and potential customers don't have a shared sense of the brand. Nobody outside the company knows how well Tent.ly's products will perform, and that's a big problem for a brand selling performance gear. How will its first wave of customers feel confident making a purchase?

To provide some initial stability and credibility, Tent.ly offers a five-year warranty on its tents. Any product defects or even wear and tear that impairs functionality will be repaired by the brand at no cost to the customer. A guarantee like that is an effective way to establish a goodwill relationship with new customers. It's a tactic used by many direct-to-consumer brands. Casper mattresses offers a 100-day, risk-free trial. Away suitcases also offers a 100-day, risk-free trial and an additional lifetime warranty for damaged parts. Especially for newcomer brands, it's not enough to simply outprice the competition in most cases. Not only does that become a race to the bottom when competitors start to play the same game, but consumers are also generally skeptical of the most cheaply priced items in a category.

To differentiate themselves from the competition, Tent.ly leans into its ability to make people feel at home in nature. Where brands like The North Face and REI often feature imagery from extreme conditions and aspirational settings, Tent.ly positions itself as bringing comfort and a feeling of home to the great outdoors. Its internal positioning statement is, "Tent.ly enables campers of all skill levels to feel at home in the midst of the world's natural beauty." Now the question is, how can Tent.ly live up to that promise?

After developing its brand personality and perspective, Tent.ly can start to think about how it might reach potential customers through different marketing channels. Tent.ly knows that its audience of camping and nature enthusiasts can be found in a wide range of channels—through out-of-home advertising near popular campgrounds, on nature- and camping-related TV programs, at trade shows, through email marketing, on shopping websites related to camping, through a variety of social media channels, and so on. Because Tent.ly needs to make extremely efficient use of its media dollars but also needs to grow its awareness, the brand decides to split its media budget. Half of the budget will be spent on hardworking, low-funnel tactics like paid search, programmatic advertising, and cost-per-click in-feed social ads. The other half of Tent.ly's budget will go toward ads tasked with increasing brand awareness and drumming up buzz among its target audience.

Because Tent.ly's stakeholders are hungry to get into the market, the brand first launches its lower-funnel marketing efforts using a range of photos of different products in different settings. Part of the Tent.ly team thinks that launching their lower-funnel marketing efforts will undermine a true brand launch, but the team also faces pressure from investors to start driving sales. While as marketers, we often want to plan our campaigns to feel as elegant and strategic as possible from start to finish, we have to remember that executions are never as clean as planning.

The sales data available prior to any brand-level marketing can actually serve as a strong benchmark for successful brand activity once it launches. If the team can show that 1 percent of the people who clicked on a paid search result converted to purchase prior to the branding campaign, and that number climbs to 2 percent after the branding campaign is in market, that's a strong indication that the brand marketing is changing broader perceptions. If it's sophisticated in terms of measurement and tagging, Tent.ly may even be able to connect brand awareness touchpoints with low-funnel ads targeting to measure the effect of its brand-level marketing.

Prior to launching its branding campaign, Tent.ly begins a social listening exercise to determine which channels it ought to prioritize. While the brand has enough financial backing for a strong launch campaign, it must be selective of where it reaches people and how. After studying volume of conversation, its competitive set, and its ultimate objectives, Tent.ly narrows down its channel mix. The marketing team decides to focus most of its activity on social channels where it can engage potential customers directly, and the team also has some interest in more traditional out-of-home advertising in particular markets.

Tent.ly knows that it needs robust targeting and a well-developed ads platform for at least one of its social channels. Because its lower-funnel ads are already using Facebook, the team decides to lean into Facebook as a priority channel. While the potential organic impact of Facebook is relatively low, the team recognizes that establishing a reputable presence on a platform that will carry much of its lower-funnel marketing will also help convert people to purchase. Should a potential customer come across one of Tent.ly's ads and decide to look more deeply into the brand, an active presence within the same channel will make a much more positive impression than an inactive page. On Facebook, Tent.ly plans to balance its low-funnel activity with content that drives engagement.

The team also recognizes the limitations of participating actively on Facebook. The potential to engage in organic conversations is limited. Organic reach is almost nonexistent. The vast majority of users are organized exclusively around their social networks, who may or may not also be interested in camping. Tent.ly decides to also prioritize participation in Reddit communities organized around camping and hiking. The tens of millions of subscribers to camping-related communities, connected through their common interests, allow Tent.ly to facilitate conversations directly with groups of people with strong potential to use its products. Tent.ly also knows that winning over Reddit's camping and hiking communities has a waterfall effect. Success on Reddit can affect opinions much more broadly, and because Reddit ranks particularly well in search, a positive thread on Reddit has the potential to be discovered by anyone researching the brand. While the team recognizes that the results from Reddit activity are less controllable, the potential payoff is massive.

Tent.ly also recognizes that one of the primary draws to camping and hiking is being surrounded by natural beauty. The visual nature of Instagram combined with the prominence of nature photography and related content provide a wide creativity territory for the brand to explore. As a new brand without a deep reservoir of content, the team also sees strong potential in partnering with influencers. Having a presence on Instagram, where many of its potential influencers have built their audiences, will also help maximize the impact of its influencer partnerships.

The Tent.ly team begins its creative briefing with the most competitive channels first, then works its way through less competitive channels. Social networks are more competitive than billboards, so that's where the team starts. Competitiveness between social channels can vary depending on vertical, but generally, it's worth starting at the bottom of the iceberg and working up—first Id networks, then Superego networks, then Ego networks. Tent.ly plans to start with an idea that's compelling to Reddit's camping and hiking communities, then find ways to expand its campaign to Instagram and Facebook.

During its marketing research and strategy explorations, Tent.ly found that one of the barriers to entry for campers and hikers of all experience levels is finding good locations. Many rely on brief conversations with park rangers or chance encounters with veteran campers to trade knowledge about great local hiking and camping spots. While apps like AllTrails provide comprehensive lists of available hikes in different areas, the reviews and recommendations feel manufactured and lack local flavor and expertise. Tent.ly decides to build its creative platform from this insight. Through a combination of organic community engagement and strategically placed paid media, Tent.ly will create an interactive, crowdsourced map designed to share local camping and hiking knowledge.

Tent.ly recognizes that in order to deeply engage communities like Reddit, the participation of the community must have a real stake in the development of the campaign. To drive meaningful participation, that participation must effect a meaningful outcome. Prior to fueling this experience with wider paid media, Tent.ly creates a series of simple posts designed to drive awareness and participation. The team identifies a few communities that have a high likelihood of finding value in Tent.ly's map. They look for communities that are large enough to be impactful, allow for open-ended engagement, and in which their participation as a brand won't break any rules.

The team creates a simple organic post in the r/Camping community, which boasts 1.4 million members:

> Post Title: Hey Reddit, we love camping, and we want better recommendations on where to explore next! What are your favorite local spots? (Also, we make tents.)
>
> Post Body: Hi there, Reddit! We're some folks from Tent.ly. We've been camping for a collective 35 years, and in the past, we could never afford top-quality tents. We quit our full-time jobs two years ago to start a tent company that could produce extremely high quality tents without the overhead of being a massive company so we can sell them for cheaper.
>
> Anyway, we have this marketing budget to spend, and rather than just sticking ads in your feed, we thought we'd use it to make something useful for campers and hikers.
>
> We created a map of the United States that's populated with all of the local and national parks we could find. If you've been to any of them, make a post on the map about how it was, what you liked and didn't like about it, whether you'd recommend it, etc. If enough people participate, we'll have an awesome map filled with local knowledge for the best camping and hiking spots around the country!
>
> What do you think? Anything you would add or change? If you can drop in some of your knowledge, we'd definitely appreciate it!

The voice and tone of an organic Reddit post should try to provide as much behind-the-curtain insight as possible. By introducing themselves as a passionate bunch who care about the same things their potential customers do, Tent.ly immediately establishes common ground with fellow outdoors enthusiasts in a way that feels authentic. The way Tent.ly describes the campaign is also casual—almost as if they're just other Redditors throwing around ideas. Not only does this provide some room for community members to evaluate the concept without advertiser ickiness attached to it, the team opens the door to new ideas, which allows people to feel invested in the campaign's success. By asking people what they think and if they have other ideas, Tent.ly underscores the fact that they care about the response. This isn't just another ad in a massive brand's marketing fleet—Tent.ly is demonstrating that they care to engage in real conversation about it.

There are a few ways this might go for Tent.ly. If everything is absolutely perfect about the post, its timing, competition in the algorithm, and so on, it could blow up and reach a massive audience of Redditors, beyond even the r/Camping community. It's an unlikely scenario, but it could happen—and the groundswell that follows these moments can be absolutely massive. When a new brand or website generates this kind of success and isn't ready for the spike in bandwidth, Reddit has been known to take websites down, lovingly referred to by the community as the "Reddit hug of death."

What's more likely is that the post resonates with some Redditors, also generates a few downvotes, and sits around the top or middle of the r/Camping community for a few hours. In this scenario, Tent.ly is likely to generate a good number of responses, some of which will be high quality in terms of participation or feedback. This level of success is replicable and relatively predictable with the right strategy in place. There is also a chance that Tent.ly's post receives a few downvotes off the bat, and it fades into oblivion. While that's far from the best-case scenario, it's still low risk, and Tent.ly can simply move on to another camping- or hiking-related community.

The payoff of organic posts is unpredictable. Even if Tent.ly does absolutely everything right, it's at the whim of the algorithm and whatever other content it's competing against that day. But posting organically accomplishes a few important things. First, it gives Tent.ly an initial burst of feedback from the target they hope to reach. If what they say to camping enthusiasts immediately generates negative feedback, it may be worthwhile for the team to reconsider their approach before broadcasting their message with paid media. Second, organic posting provides a footprint for Tent.ly, which signals to the community that they're savvy and invested in the outcome. Even if the organic post receives only mediocre engagement, when Tent.ly runs broader media on Reddit, users who view Tent.ly's profile will see its organic post. It's a way of demonstrating that the brand is engaged beyond the media buy, and especially for community engagement, that's important.

Let's assume Tent.ly's post receives a moderate to positive response. The brand can then create a promoted post on Reddit targeted to camping and hiking enthusiasts along the same lines as its organic one. Because promoted posts look and feel like organic posts, when they're relevant to the community, engagement within the comment threads of these posts can also feel very organic. Tent.ly takes 5 percent of its media budget to promote a post with much the same copy and sentiment as its organic post, except for a few tweaks they've made, based on the organic response.

Tent.ly responds to comments from Redditors across its organic and promoted posts, and the brand encourages people to participate by filling out their local area of the Tent.ly map. Over the course of two weeks, Tent.ly receives its first wave of about a hundred entries. While that may not sound like much, these first submissions are usually the most difficult to drive. They're also critical to creating the sense that this content is trending and active. Now the campaign can be targeted more broadly to specific geographies, interests adjacent to camping like outdoor photography, and other media strategies they use to reach the broadest relevant audience. Not only can media now broaden within the Reddit platform but Tent.ly can also begin to drive engagement with its other social channels. This is the true launch moment for the campaign—everything prior can be considered seeding and prelaunch. Across each of its social channels, Tent.ly allocates more of its media budget to driving participation in its crowdsourced map.

Prior to launching paid media on Instagram, the brand populates its handle with product photography in different natural environments, which they'd already commissioned. The team is very selective, choosing only photos with true aesthetic appeal—too much emphasis on the product will make the profile feel transactional and will discourage engagement. The team selects nine photos to fill a basic three-by-three grid, and it posts a few times per week organically to engage and grow its small following. Its first posts don't need to work too hard at engagement because there isn't much of an audience to engage yet. Rather, these initial photos are meant to represent the brand, the kinds of products it produces, and provide a feel for the content subscribers can expect in the future.

In addition to building out its own profile, the Tent.ly team part-ners with nature photography and camping influencers who have medium to large followings on Instagram. Tent.ly provides influenc-ers with tents, and it prompts its partners to take a recommendation from the brand's crowdsourced map. Influencers venture out to doc-ument their experiences at recommended campgrounds—providing live vlogging updates to their followers, posting photographs of their camp setups, sharing photographs of nature, and so on. Tent.ly shares and amplifies influencers' content, tags them in organic posts, com-ments on influencers' photos, and encourages influencers to do the same. In doing so, Tent.ly associates itself with these credible influ-encers and maximizes its potential for audience growth during the partnerships. The brand prompts influencers to share content with the hashtag #LoveMeTently, which connects influencer content and allows Tent.ly to draw a consistent thread between its partnerships and brand. It also provides a strong call to action for others in the com-munity to follow suit, participate in the crowdsourced map, and share their own content with the same hashtag.

On Facebook, Tent.ly uses similar but slightly varied photography to populate its profile, cover photo, and so on. The brand allows for about 50 percent overlap between Instagram and Facebook content. While duplicative content isn't always ideal, it's a useful way to max-imize the reach and impact of top content. It also helps to maintain some amount of organic reach by creating regular touchpoints with fol-lowers. The more often a user engages with its page's content, the more likely Tent.ly is to show up in their feed organically in subsequent posts.

The primary differentiator between Tent.ly's Facebook and Insta-gram strategies is in how it engages people. On Instagram the brand shares inspirational captions and quotes about nature, and it gener-ally allows the focus to remain on its photo and video content. On Facebook, Tent.ly encourages connection between friends and fosters engagement more directly. Tent.ly captions a photo of a beautiful hik-ing trail up a steep-looking mountain, "Tag someone who would climb this with you!" Its copy aims to evoke personal connections between friends to help grow organic reach.

As the crowdsourced map continues to populate with camping and hiking suggestions, the Tent.ly team curates different articles made up of lists of different hikes based on factors such as geography, experience level, and scenery. The team targets outdoor enthusiasts in Colorado with links to articles like "Campers' Top 10 Hikes in Colorado" or "8 Colorado Hikes off the Beaten Trail (with Incredible Views)." These article titles may feel a little clickbaity, but as long as we deliver what we promised on the other side of the link, this format of headline can be a strong draw. Not only that, people who wear camping and hiking as a badge may well share these posts with their networks as forms of self-expression—as if to say, "I'm such an outdoor enthusiast that I found these hikes that nobody else knew about." On Facebook and Instagram especially, Tent.ly aspires to aid people in expressing their love of the outdoors through the brand itself.

The Tent.ly team earmarked some of its media budget for out-of-home advertising in specific markets. This phase too can borrow campaign elements from content generated in social media. The team leverages top-performing photography from both its own shoots and its influencers' camping experiences on billboards surrounding airports and campgrounds in camping and hiking destinations. These billboards are designed first, to grab attention with striking photography; second, communicate the brand identity and its products; and third, to encourage connection with the brand through hashtags—"Share your best camping photos this trip with #LoveMeTently!"

Given the bandwidth, the team could also build incentives for engagement with its hashtag such as product giveaways, surprise and delights, or simply by amplifying great submissions through its own channels. Tent.ly's campaign ecosystem fits together in a way that's not only well suited to each of its channels but that creates efficiency between its activities in each. The dynamic nature of the campaign is interesting in and of itself. The brand meaning isn't created by the company in a lab. It's cocreated by participants in the campaign. Nobody wants to submit a photo to a contest if the submission is doomed to sit on some brand manager's hard drive for a decade. People submit photos they hope will get some kind of attention, engagement, and recognition. By designing the campaign both to use media dollars efficiently and to offer deeper points of connections, the brand builds sales, credibility, and word-of-mouth simultaneously.

EXAMPLE 2. REPOSITIONING A LEGACY TECH COMPANY TO MILLENNIALS AND GENERATION Z

More often than not, when planning a campaign, we have brand history with which to contend. It's rare that we have the challenge (and opportunity) to launch a brand from scratch. We're often in a position of fighting our own success too. Our brand has established itself as a market leader in one area and wants to evolve to capture another, or we're so well known for our work in one space that we build campaigns to share the spotlight with some other part of our business.

As brands grow and segment themselves across different lines of business, it's difficult to maintain cohesion. Especially when internal marketing teams compete for budget, it's easy for different segments to form antagonistic relationships with one another. One way this manifests for consumers is in arbitrary splits in brand social media presences. If we're an electronics company that makes computer processors, gaming accessories, office equipment, and virtual reality (VR) hardware, it may be tempting for our internal marketing organization to segment social presences across these different offerings. But to a potential customer, that can cause confusion and frustration, especially when we expect to interact with one consistent brand behind different products.

Imagine that we represent a large electronics company called Lumina. Lumina is a well-known, entrenched electronics manufacturer with dozens of products that suit a multitude of different markets. While some of Lumina's products are marketed to businesses, the majority of its brand-level budget is spent on consumer marketing. Lumina is generally considered a reliable electronics company among baby boomers, but it's lost market share among millennials and Gen Z. While Lumina is known for reliable, everyday products like computer parts, televisions, and smartphones, the company has invested heavily in innovation, particularly in the virtual reality space.

Rather than creating different social profiles for Lumina Computer, Lumina TV, and so on, the company maintains two kinds of social profiles on its chosen platforms—a primary, consumer-facing presence and separate Lumina for Business profiles where relevant. While this requires deeper levels of coordination among marketing teams across different Lumina products, it creates a smoother experience for customers interacting with the brand. To coordinate, Lumina's different marketing arms have established a brand-level strategy to maintain consistency across all of the company's consumer marketing efforts, and each team's work is evaluated according to this strategy for consistency.

Lumina briefs its creative agency to produce a campaign that will highlight the company's dedication to innovation by building awareness for its work in the virtual reality space. The budget is large, and the goal of the campaign is to position Lumina as both reliable and cutting-edge to millennials and Gen Z. Lumina has published regular press releases and drawn minimal press coverage about its virtual reality technology and research, but initial consumer research shows that very little of Lumina's Gen Z and millennial audiences associate the brand with innovation and new technology. The campaign must walk a fine line between positioning the brand to these audiences while remaining consistent and recognizable to Lumina's loyal customer base.

Because innovation is at the heart of the campaign, the team allocates almost no budget to transactional tactics like paid search and programmatic advertising. While these tactics can be cost-effective ways to convert people to purchase, they're not likely going to change people's perceptions about a well-known technology company. Instead, the team looks for channels in which its virtual reality technology and creative will shine the brightest.

Snapchat is a strong candidate for reaching millennials and Gen Z, and the team decides augmented-reality filters are a good creative canvas to communicate a message of innovation in an interesting way. Lumina also recognizes that as a budding technology, creators in virtual reality space are networked into tight communities where they have relatively insular (but deeply compelling) conversations. To reach virtual reality's early adopters, Lumina aspires to participate in conversations happening within virtual reality communities on Reddit where they can reach communities ranging from those specific to virtual reality to broader technology-related ones.

Lumina also recognizes that virtual reality is a deeply immersive technology. It's hard enough to capture the effect of virtual reality in a video, let alone in a competitive social feed. The brand decides that YouTube, Twitch, and other online streaming ads, which allow for more immersive content, should also play a role in the campaign ecosystem. Lastly, drawing insights from organic conversations within virtual reality communities and among first-time users, the team acknowledges that while seeing content about virtual reality can be engaging, it takes firsthand experience to truly understand the power of the technology. The team decides that an event activation should also fit into the campaign.

With Reddit, Snapchat, YouTube, Twitch, and event marketing in mind, Lumina's creative team comes up with the big idea: a massive game of *Minecraft* playable by people both online and in virtual reality headsets. *Minecraft* is a deeply loved sandbox video game that employs simple graphics and logic to allow players to form the world in which they're playing. The game is both relevant—boasting 480 million players in 2019—and nostalgic for the target audience.[2] *Minecraft* also has a special place in meme culture, which Lumina hopes will endear the brand to Internet tastemakers and nod to the brand's online savviness.

The team starts the campaign by interacting with various *Minecraft-* and virtual reality–related communities on Reddit. Again, starting at the bottom of the iceberg and working up through less competitive channels, the team spends a small amount of paid media to prompt *Minecraft* players and virtual reality communities on Reddit with the concept behind the campaign. After some initial research and dialogue with players, the team decides that rather than creating a *Minecraft* map themselves, it would be more interesting to have a shared map created dynamically by players.

The team creates its own Reddit community, and it uses Reddit's natural community algorithm to facilitate votes on different user-submitted maps. This new subreddit is relatively small, but the team evaluates its success in terms of the number of post submissions and depth of engagement rather than overall subscribership. Over the course of two weeks, the team maintains engagement with the broader *Minecraft* and virtual reality communities through regular updates. The Lumina team evaluates the top-voted entries and chooses one based on both popularity of voting and its developers' needs.

The Lumina team candidly explains to the Reddit community that there are some technical hurdles to jump before the map can be playable the way that they plan. Redditors appreciate the brand's candor, and a few offer to help playtest. Lumina now has a small focus group of dedicated players who can be brought into the experience during development. Lumina's agency partners with a development team to bring Reddit's map to life in a way that will allow players online and those using virtual reality hardware to play within the same world.

Lumina's creative team decides that Comic-Con is the perfect place to unveil its VR *Minecraft* experience. The creative open-endedness of the event, its strong attendance by Gen Z and millennials, and its attendees' affinity for new technology make the event a perfect setting to deliver the campaign in real life. In the lead-up to the event, Lumina teases some exciting VR experiences with a hint of tongue-in-cheek Internet humor, something the brand hasn't included in previous marketing but that is executed in a way that's consistent with its brand ethos. The goal leading up to Comic-Con is to maintain engagement with the Reddit community while building anticipation for the experience. In terms of left and right brain marketing, the event is Lumina's right brain–driven behavior. It's designed to drive as much participation as possible during the event, but the event is also intended to create compelling left brain stories for the brand to tell afterward.

As Comic-Con opens its doors, Lumina launches its first broadly reaching set of ads designed to maximize participation in the *Minecraft* map. Across its priority channels, Lumina reveals that within this *Minecraft* server is a hidden item, and the person who finds the item will win a free virtual reality home system. In reality, Lumina has hidden a number of different surprise and delights for participants to discover—product giveaways, special in-game items, and so on.

On Twitch and YouTube, Lumina shares teaser footage of its map, in which the team has created a series of impressive Comic-Con-inspired sculptures, buildings, and landscapes for players to explore. On Snapchat, Lumina creates an augmented-reality filter that takes a person's selfie video and turns it into a blocky *Minecraft*-style character—matching details such as clothing color, hair style, and accessories. When engaged users swipe up on the ad, they find that their *Minecraft* self is actually playable within Lumina's multiplayer map.

Meanwhile, Comic-Con attendees are experiencing the same world through Lumina's VR headset. The team captures video of the "Wow!" moment as event participants enter the world and interact with thousands of other players who've entered the map. Lumina's team also livestreams the players' perspectives organically on Twitch and YouTube, which allows other *Minecraft* players online to seek out those on the ground at Comic-Con. Online players form search parties for Comic-Con players. A game of hide-and-seek ensues. Players both online and at the event find creative ways to interact, spelling words with blocks, lining themselves up to shake virtual hands, building new sculptures, digging up hidden Easter eggs, and evolving the world in real time.

Over the course of the experience, millions of people were exposed to the content, hundreds of thousands of users viewed the livestreams, and tens of thousands of users actually entered the map. Not only has Lumina facilitated a fun and unexpected experience using its innovative technology, but the brand now also has a surplus of stories to tell. What did people build? How did they interact with one another? What were the funniest moments? What genuine connections were formed? How did different Reddit communities interact, and what memes did they create throughout the experience? The answers to each of these questions become fruitful territory for creating compelling postevent content. With the right approach to storytelling, the experience is relevant to audiences far beyond *Minecraft* players. The team recognizes that while the game was part of the initial draw, the stories the team plans to tell are more universal. The team treats the experience like a social experiment in the stories it tells.

Over the following months, Lumina serves a series of videos designed to highlight the funniest, most interesting, most surprising, and most earnest moments of interaction among people in its *Minecraft* map. The brand creates its hero spot, a 10-minute video that tells the full story of the campaign to those who are curious, but it promotes different 15- to 30-second vignettes across Reddit, Snapchat, Twitch, YouTube, and other streaming services.

Rather than using flashy graphics and filming actors pretending to have dramatic reactions to a virtual reality headset, Lumina created something genuinely unique. While *Minecraft* didn't show off its headset's maximum graphical power, it provided memorable experiences for thousands of players. The content derived from a real experience like this will almost always be more engaging and more positively received than overproduced ads created in a lab.

While Lumina expects a relatively small percentage of the people they reach with these stories to actually engage its *Minecraft* map first-hand, the depth of the campaign itself makes an impact on viewers. Lumina didn't just spend its marketing dollars talking about itself—it created something enjoyable, and as a result, the stories it tells don't feel entirely self-serving. The depth of the campaign and dedication to delivering an experience beyond a commercial shoot forms a strong impression with the millennial and Gen Z audience reached by its campaign.

EXAMPLE 3. PERFORMANCE MARKETING CAN BE ENGAGING TOO

Whether we're tasked with revitalizing a legacy brand or building a new one, we're often faced with a murky definition of success. Our marketing is tasked with carrying the brand forward, driving down-funnel goals, earning press coverage, and everything in between. Both new and old brands have challenges measuring marketing activity comprehensively. New brands rarely have solid baselines against which to compare a campaign's effect, and brands with history often have so much marketing activity happening that it can be difficult to pinpoint what drove which results.

Sometimes, though, we're afforded a unique opportunity and challenge to optimize our efforts toward a single success metric. The new generation of apps and online games is a good example; marketing these products revolves almost entirely around driving downloads. Even for free apps, the biggest marketing challenge tends to be driving download volume. Simple as driving downloads may seem, many of the same marketing challenges are present beneath the surface.

The term *performance marketing* is often used to describe marketing strategies that optimize toward one distinct down-funnel goal. In general, performance marketers are ruthless about optimizing toward that goal. Performance marketing goals usually include metrics such as driving downloads, installs, purchases, clicks, and follows. In more traditional advertising, creative and strategy sit at the top of the hierarchy. In performance marketing, customer data and analytics are the dominant forces, while creative and strategy tend to take a backseat.

A creative agency may approach a problem by first considering what impression the brand ought to make on a person it reaches. The performance marketer tends to start with as broad a pool of content as possible, then uses performance analytics to arrive at the winning strategy. Throughout this book, I've advocated for a balance of both approaches, but for even the most performance-driven marketers, it's worth considering user mindset, anchoring in a thoughtful brand purpose, and maximizing engagement.

Perhaps the first and easiest mistake to make is to consider performance marketing as separate from brand marketing. Internally, it can be useful to split budgets and talent between performance and brand marketing, but it's imperative that we remember that to a prospective customer, an ad is an ad. A person in our audience won't be privy to the distinction, so whatever reaches that person is actually achieving (or *not* achieving) both.

In the short term, aggressive performance marketing can seem like the most efficient and effective use of our media budgets. Performance marketing tends to achieve near-immediate results, and for new brands, the promise of quick results can be tempting. However, for the long-term health of our brands, we can't simply optimize our entire marketing strategy toward a single metric. Not only do we put ourselves at risk of building an entirely transactional relationship with our customers, but every dollar we spend marketing ourselves this way may be a step in the wrong direction. To use an extreme example, if we're a beauty app that's misguidedly spent $1 million driving downloads using a scandalous picture of a model in lingerie, and we find that 90 percent of our downloads have come from teenage men, we have a long, uphill battle against our own brand because we didn't consider the long-term implications of how we represented ourselves.

Fundamentally, performance marketing and brand marketing aren't at odds with one another. Performance marketing asks us, "What content will drive the absolute maximum number of conversions of this particular metric?" Brand marketing asks us, "What kind of content best expresses who we are as a company?" When a post from our brand reaches a person's feed, there isn't such a clear separation between the two, and perhaps as marketers, we shouldn't consider them so entirely separate either.

The answers to both the brand and performance marketing questions can be compatible. If we ask ourselves, "What kind of content that expresses who we are as a company also maximizes the number of meaningful actions our audience takes?", we find the middle ground between the two. The brand we aspire to be establishes a frame for us. By articulating our brand in a thoughtful way, we define who we do and don't want to be. The performance marketing mindset should be familiar to brand marketers who've spent a significant amount of time in social media; performance marketing simply challenges us to weigh our performance metrics more heavily. When paired with a strong measurement strategy, optimizing our ads toward conversions shouldn't be significantly harder than optimizing toward engagement—we're just taking the measurement a level deeper.

In this last example, imagine that we're marketing a new fashion app called Fitting Room. Fitting Room promises to let online shoppers try on clothing virtually from a wide selection of brands and retailers. Users simply take photos of themselves from various angles and enter their height and weight, and Fitting Room uses augmented-reality technology to dress the users in their desired garment. Fitting Room has agreements with major retailers and fashion brands to receive a percentage of the sale of each garment users' engage in the Fitting Room app, and the team is also exploring clothing sales from within the app itself. The app's target is generally women aged 18 to 34, but the team has found that men interested in fashion within the same age group are also using the app.

Fitting Room bootstrapped its way to development over the past two years. Through earned press and organic marketing efforts, Fitting Room accumulated its first 10,000 downloads. Fitting Room recently received its series A funding of $5 million to build additional features, polish the user experience, develop partnerships with more fashion labels, and grow the user base. Fitting Room must achieve 30,000 monthly active users in the next year to stay on track for its growth projections.

Currently, only 1,000 Fitting Room users of its initial 10,000 downloads are active monthly. The marketing team anticipates that some users who download the app simply won't use it regularly, and the team uses this 10 percent users-per-download rate to estimate its download requirement goal for the year. Fitting Room recognizes that its first 10,000 downloads, achieved primarily through organic word-of-mouth and press, are likely to be engaged at a higher rate than users who simply download the app through an ad. However, the team also anticipates that as the app adds features and improves its user experience, its engagement per download is likely to increase. The team maintains this optimistic estimate of 10 percent of downloads converting into regular users, planning to revisit the benchmark after ads launch and some initial data is available. To grow an additional 29,000 monthly active users, the team estimates that it will need about 300,000 downloads.

The Fitting Room team is small and integrated enough that its head of marketing talks regularly to its CEO and head of product. (Suspend your disbelief for a moment. It's a fictional example.) Until now, the product team has rolled out features and updates incrementally, allowing organic feedback from its engaged community to inform the product road map. With more feedback than resources in the lead-up to their recent funding round, the team accumulated plenty of feedback to inform six more months of development. Now, with its funding in place, the team knows what it needs to build in order to improve the app. The Fitting Room marketer wonders if this might be an opportunity to build anticipation for a release.

"But the app is already live?" Sure, it is. As proud of the product as the Fitting Room team is, the group knows that given all of the resources in the world, the current Fitting Room experience isn't everything they'd ideally deliver. With that in mind, the team explains to its user base that they are ecstatic to have such positive feedback from this community, and while they'd never anticipated this kind of response, they're taking the community's feedback into account for a major update. In three months, the team will upgrade its features, broaden its partnerships, and reveal a new Fitting Room experience. The team is looking for potential beta testers, aspiring fashion influencers, and up-and-coming designers to participate in their upcoming campaign. Anyone interested in joining their exclusive team of Fitting Room Friends should get in touch through a short application form. With more to come and the promise of regular development updates, the organic community's initial hesitations give way to excitement and appreciation.

Fitting Room recognizes that its brand represents more than its app's functionality. The brand enables people of all sizes and builds to buy fashion with confidence. That's the core of what Fitting Room hopes to represent to the world. The app opens fashion to a wide category of people interested in fashion but who've been previously excluded from the conversation—namely, anyone larger than a size double zero. With a $500,000 marketing budget for the next year, the team decides to create a campaign that celebrates diversity within the fashion scene—at-home makers, bedroom mirror stylists, up-and-coming designers, and nontraditional models.

The Fitting Room team decides to embody that message in a campaign that will culminate in its relaunch moment. Their launch plan has three main components. First, the team is working on major improvements to the app itself. Second, leaning into the organic interactions already taking place between users of the app, the team creates the Fitting Room Friends cohort, similar to a customer relationship management (CRM) system but a level deeper. The members of this group receive more personal communications from the Fitting Room team, have their own community hub in which to interact, test and offer feedback on new features, and are generally treated like insiders among Fitting Room users. While rare, some brands and products genuinely do facilitate community building around themselves, and in some cases, these brand-centric communities can serve a similar function to right brain, bottom-of-the-iceberg social networks.

The third component to the Fitting Room launch plan is a twist on a traditional influencer program. The Fitting Room team started an Instagram account when the app first launched, and while it's not a massive audience, the account has accumulated about a thousand followers organically. The team drafts a note designed to announce their search for fashion talent to be featured in their upcoming campaign. They share the call for entries with their budding Fitting Room Friends community first and then open the opportunity to the public through a post on Instagram.

Rather than writing a long caption to accompany a photo, the team designs a square-shaped image of text describing what they're looking for and how it connects to the Fitting Room brand. In doing so, Fitting Room optimizes its meme machine for sharing and virality. It's not sure it'll receive a massive response, but creating an image of its note both focuses the audience's attention on the primary goal and optimizes it for further sharing. The note can now be cross-posted, tagged, and screenshot, removing as many technical barriers as possible to sharing the message.

Initially receiving a few interested emails and comments in response to their call for talent, the team continues to encourage participation over the next few weeks. Thanks to its early earned press, the team is able to secure a few more stories in reputable fashion blogs to grow the reach of their campaign. "We believe fashion is for everyone! We're looking for up-and-coming designers and models to be featured in our upcoming campaign. Who don't we know about yet that we should?" At this early stage, the audience is twofold: first, aspiring designers and models, and second, friends of aspiring designers and models.

A few weeks later, Fitting Room has accumulated a few hundred applications to be part of its campaign. Everyone who submitted an application is welcomed into the Fitting Room Friends community (except a handful of troll entries), and the Fitting Room team selects 10 designers and 10 models to be featured in their campaign. The team introduces the Fitting Room Friends community to their selected talent, hosts a Q&A for the community and the selected models and designers, and encourages the community to continue to support one another throughout the campaign.

Partner models and designers are encouraged to share photos and videos that can be amplified across Fitting Room's social channels. The team provides prompts to their partners like, "What makes you passionate about fashion?" and "Where does the fashion industry need diversity the most?" The team creates regular organic updates featuring these different micro-influencers' responses, sharing their content, and encouraging people to follow them. As partners post content, Fitting Room also comments on and shares their posts. These organic engagements both boost the micro-influencers' reach (something they appreciate) and create a seamless way for these influencers' audiences to discover and follow Fitting Room. The Fitting Room team uses minimal media budget to promote their model and designer content to a small but relevant audience—targeting the followings of their micro-influencers, retargeting people who'd previously engaged the brand, and reaching followers of more recognizable fashion influencers and brands.

In preparation for launch day, the Fitting Room team hosts a photo shoot for their micro-influencers. The team hires a few photographers and videographers, rents a trendy-looking house for the shoot, and flies their partners in for a few days. Not only does this build the relationship between Fitting Room and its partners but it also provides ample opportunities to capture content ranging from professional photography to candid, behind-the-scenes moments.

Professional photographers capture models wearing designers' pieces, designers preparing their garments, and models being fitted. But the team also encourages partners to capture candid moments with their phones. Across their social profiles, partners share footage of behind-the-scenes moments of each other laughing, talking, browsing through sketchbooks, jumping into the pool, attending a fancy dinner, and so on. Fitting Room reposts and shares partners' organic content throughout the shoot, allowing the Fitting Room Friends and broader following to feel included.

As its videos and photos are polished into content for the launch, Fitting Room lines up press stories with various fashion blogs and publications. Information about the app updates are included but take a backseat to the real hook—exclusive fashion drops from up-and-coming designers, available only through the Fitting Room app, guaranteed to fit. The team features their micro-influencers front and center. After all, sharing the spotlight with up-and-coming partners is a clear way of living up to Fitting Room's brand promise of diversifying the fashion world's voices.

A few weeks from launch day, Fitting Room ramps up media to build anticipation for exclusive designer releases, encouraging people to download the app for access. Across Instagram, Snapchat, and TikTok, the brand promotes content ranging from silly selfie videos created by partners to polished videography from the shoot. While the creative varies widely between candid and polished, all of the content falls well within its brand strategy of representing diversity in fashion.

Because everything captured fits in the brand frame, it's simple for the team to optimize its media spend toward the content with the strongest download rate. That allows Fitting Room to walk the line between a branding campaign that also drives performance.

For Instagram, Fitting Room creates albums featuring different designers and models from its photo shoots. Each album starts with a serious, high-fashion-feeling photo but becomes more candid and casual as people swipe through. The last slide of each album is a selfie video from the designer and model introducing themselves and describing the inspiration behind their work, why they're in the industry, and so on. By balancing high-fashion aesthetics with the personalities behind the shoot, Fitting Room grabs the attention of its fashion-savvy audience while also communicating warmth and self-awareness. In the descriptions of these albums are different copy lines introducing the partners and explaining that on September 1, these pieces will go on sale through the Fitting Room app. Only 100 of each piece will be available, and every purchase is guaranteed to fit (or be retailored). Below the photo album is a button encouraging people to download the Fitting Room app.

On TikTok, the Fitting Room team promotes selfie videos of designers and models speaking to their audiences about their pieces, their inspiration, and how they'll be available for purchase. The team also posts clips from the photo shoot and reposts partners' content organically to maintain an active presence. Fitting Room encourages partners who are active on TikTok to create videos wearing their garments. The Fitting Room micro-influencers learn various TikTok dances and post them wearing their designs. A few of their posts earn a few hundred thousand views, growing Fitting Room's organic following and driving a recognizable bump in app downloads. The team doesn't anticipate a viral hit, but by posting organically and maximizing organic activity, Fitting Room positions itself for its maximum earned success. Its earned reach on TikTok is relatively low compared to the reach of its paid media, but its strong organic footprint helps maximize the impact of paid media by creating some grassroots awareness of the brand. As awareness grows about Fitting Room, people are more likely to interact with its content, which lowers the barriers to both paid and organic engagement.

On Snapchat, Fitting Room creates a series of short vertical videos using footage from its shoot combined with more candid phone video to tell quick narratives about the campaign. The videos themselves last only 10 seconds and use a few lines of on-video text to reinforce the narrative. These ads are less about driving engagement within the Snapchat environment and are aimed more at driving download volume and building awareness.

The team also purchases a few Snapchat geo-targeted filters in specific fashion-forward markets to encourage organic sharing and engagement. One filter reads, "*This* is high fashion," encouraging Snapchat users to post photos of themselves in whatever they're wearing—because fashion is for everyone. The team anticipates both serious and silly uses of the filter, which it embraces. By championing the "fashion for all" message, the brand taps into a preexisting mindset common among those interested in fashion. People engaging the Fitting Room filters are empowered to express themselves through the brand meaning, and because Snapchat connects people with their offline friends, it has a strong likelihood to spark conversations and inspire wider usage.

On launch day, Fitting Room ramps up media across all channels. The team unveils a full "runway show" video within their app and website, and clips of the video are used in cross-platform ads to build immediacy around the exclusive clothing launch. The team benefits from the strong press relationships they've built, and a few articles published the morning of the release help build word-of-mouth among online fashion communities. Having worked out the vast majority of the app's bugs during its development window, thanks in large part to Fitting Room Friends beta testers, the organic conversation remains focused on the models and influencers.

Almost immediately, 2 of the 10 garments sell out, and Fitting Room shares an update on its Instagram profile congratulating the two designers and models on their fast success. Not only does this feel like a selfless gesture but it also continues to build on the sense of activity, exclusivity, and the need for immediate action on the part of the audience. Over the course of the first day, one other garment sells out of its full 100 pieces, and the Fitting Room team maintains promotion of the remaining garments over the course of the following few days.

The team now has the option of restocking its most popular garments, partnering with more micro-influencers in the future, furthering their relationships with current micro-influencers, and so on. While the campaign was designed to build momentum for a particular moment, the team may continue to create similar partnerships in the future and release other exclusive designer clothing items. Having helped its first wave of partners grow significantly over the course of the campaign, Fitting Room also has the benefit of growing alongside its partners. These positive relationships between brands and personalities are often tangible to the audience; when an influencer actually enjoys working with a brand partner, it tends to show.

Not only did the Fitting Room brand use its media efficiently to drive downloads, it also created a brand moment designed to grab attention from the fashion community. Except for a few low-spend Snapchat filters, every paid placement the brand used to popularize its event and communicate its brand meaning also drove downloads of its app. Had Fitting Room focused on its features or the selection of clothing available for fitting, the creative would likely have been less engaging and would have failed to build word-of-mouth and advocacy.

If Fitting Room had applied a traditional performance marketing approach to driving downloads, the team may have been able to drive a comparable download count, but those users would have only a transactional relationship with the brand. Should a competitor come along and offer lower prices or better fits, Fitting Room is now in a position to defend itself because it stands for much more than an app to its engaged users and community.

REGARDLESS OF OBJECTIVE, MARKETING SHOULD BE ROOTED IN THE BRAND MEANING

The size, scale, and budget of a campaign will, in the vast majority of cases, affect the overall quantity of engagement we can drive as brands. But regardless of campaign size, we can find ways to build strong engagement. Even campaigns focused on down-funnel objectives benefit from creative and strategic thinking about how our messages— our memes—can grab attention, lean into organic conversation, and communicate our brand meaning. In doing so, we're able to earn reach beyond our media budget, make more efficient use of those media dollars by achieving stronger engagement rates, and build deeper connections with our audience.

Good strategists and creatives will evaluate their ideas at multiple levels of analysis. Is our idea big enough to grab attention? Is it connected to some broader cultural conversation? How will we bring that idea to life on the various channels in which our brand participates? How does our idea relate to the kinds of content and connections to which people already gravitate in those channels? How will each piece of content appear within those environments? What organic sources of inspiration can we find to inspire our content approach? How can we ensure that our content is as accessible, shareable, and attention grabbing as possible? From idea to execution, from capturing broad attention to manifesting our memes in the most efficient ways possible, building optimal social media campaigns requires that we think far beyond ourselves as brands and understand the environments in which we plan to reach people.

KEY TAKEAWAYS

- Great social campaigns maximize their efficiency by ensuring that each component of a campaign has not only a specific goal but also has some bearing on the overall outcome of the campaign.

- To drive meaningful participation, that participation must effect a meaningful outcome. When asking for user-generated content (UGC), ensure that the creative output will be interesting, and put UGC to work in the campaign itself.

- Brand behavior and storytelling are two essential halves of brand marketing. In order to tell great stories, our brand must have done something great.

- For even the most performance-oriented marketing teams, a social media campaign should be rooted in the brand meaning and ensure that it is building toward long-term brand growth.

THE NEGLECTED
RIGHT HEMISPHERE
Balancing Storytelling with Experience Building

I t was an otherwise normal Saturday, save for a few run-of-the-mill branded April Fools' Day gags. Burger King announced fake Whopper-flavored toothpaste.[1] Bush's baked beans mocked up a fake jelly beans product. Jim Beam pretended to come out with "Jim Beans," a canned baked beans product. Coffee mate posted about a coffee-flavored coffee creamer. Lots of bean stuff was happening. Are you bored yet?

On that day, something else happened. Something magical that will go down in Internet history. On April Fools' Day 2017, Reddit unveiled an "experiment" via a community called r/Place.[2, 3] When its metaphorical doors opened, r/Place was a simple 1,000-by-1,000-pixel blank canvas. Beneath the canvas was a short set of instructions that read almost like a poem:

> There is an empty canvas.
> You may place a tile upon it, but you must wait to place another.
> Individually you can create something.
> Together you can create something more.[4]

The concept was as simple as it was elegant. Anyone with a Reddit account could visit this community and interact with the shared canvas. Participants could choose 1 of 16 different colored tiles to place in any space on the canvas—regardless of whether or not that particular tile was occupied. After placing a tile, a timer started, which kept that user from placing another tile for about 10 minutes. As the instructions allude, an individual user could create something simple, given some dedication and a few hours. But if participants could rally their communities together, they could create much more. That's exactly what they did.

Admittedly, the beginning of the r/Place experiment was a little rocky. As you might expect, the first large-scale creation on the canvas was a big red penis.[5] But the novelty of the dick joke wore off quickly, and soon, different factions began to form. In the bottom right corner of the canvas, a group that called themselves The Blue Corner started to paint the entire canvas blue. In response, a group called Green Lattice started to create a more sophisticated pattern of green and black tiles starting in the upper right corner of the canvas. Another faction soon formed called Rainbow Road, in reference to a racing map in the video game *Mario Kart*, which involved an even more sophisticated diagonal rainbow pattern and worked its way across the canvas.

The complexity of Redditors' creations only increased throughout the experiment. Communities throughout Reddit found creative ways to represent themselves. Using shared spreadsheets and designated latitudinal and longitudinal coordinates, communities pushed the boundaries of online coordination on an ever-evolving, chaotic, shared canvas. Location-based communities created flags.[6] Video game communities represented pixelated characters from nearly every game imaginable. Some participants even created versions of Van Gogh's *Starry Night* and da Vinci's *Mona Lisa*. He-Man, Dat Boi, Pepe, Club Penguin, that picture of Peyton Manning looking over his shoulder in his black ski mask, and "no step on snek" all made appearances on the final canvas. A Windows 95–inspired taskbar and a Runescape-derived "Connection lost" message attempted to break the canvas's fourth wall. People, ideologies, countries, memes, and ideas from all corners of Reddit found homes on the r/Place canvas.

Many of the designs were complex beyond belief. *Ars Technica* writer Sam Machkovech pointed out that creating even something as simple as a single letter required significant coordination among users: "A reasonably perceptible Roman character requires no less than 24 pixels, so more than 24 Reddit users were needed to not only fill in that single letter's pixels, but also to stand guard for immediate follow-up vandalism." Somehow, Redditors managed to write not just letters or words but an entire section of dialogue from the *Star Wars* prequels between Chancellor Palpatine and Anakin Skywalker. Beginning with, "Did you ever hear the tragedy of Darth Plagueis The Wise?" the story had become what we Internet dorks refer to as "copypasta," text that is frequently copied and pasted seemingly at random into usually unrelated conversations. All 732 characters are legible in the final image of r/Place. By Machkovech's math, that required the ongoing coordination of about 17,500 Redditors.

April 2017 was a particularly contentious time on the Internet. Following the 2016 election and President Trump's inauguration, tensions were high on both sides of the political divide. But somehow, none of that showed up in r/Place. Politics simply didn't gain traction. There is no Republican or Democratic flaming to be found on the final r/Place canvas. A handful of attempts to broadcast political messages can be found briefly in timelapses of the evolution of the r/Place canvas, but they were quickly covered by representations of interests, passions, memes, flags, logos, and so on. The beauty of the r/Place experiment was that it made hateful messages much more difficult to broadcast than constructive ones.

Maintaining a spot on the canvas required people to be passionate and coordinated in order to keep their place. As the canvas evolved, some communities' spaces impeded on others', and borders had to be negotiated. Where country flags butted up against others, some communities created heart-shaped bridges between the two—reflecting their neighbors' flags' colors where the heart shape overlapped with their own. When the German flag "invaded" the French flag, which most Redditors interpreted as a pixelated World War II joke, Redditors extended the French flag and represented the United Nations' Dove of Peace symbol at the intersection. Even The Blue Corner, Green Lattice, and Rainbow Road groups were allowed to maintain parts of their original real estate, though scaled back to make room for others.

Machkovech analyzed what made r/Place so different from most online discourse, and his conclusion is a lesson for every brand and company participating in social media. The constructive power of coordination exhibited in r/Place is completely antithetical to what we usually read about in headlines regarding people interacting in social media. He explained, "An individual social-network user can devote time to creating multiple accounts and carpet-bombing specific targets with emotional and psychological attacks. An r/place user had to unite an army of persistent voices over long stretches of time to preserve a minuscule bit of pixel real estate." While in everyday social network interactions it's very easy to share a hateful message that has outweighed impact on the recipient, the r/Place experiment and Reddit's community-driven nature empowered constructive messages to drown out the hateful ones.

The r/Place experiment accomplished something at which so many social networks fail: it provided space for people to interact in ways that embraced their commonalities, celebrated their differences, magnified what was constructive, and minimized what wasn't. Not only did this silly April Fools' Day experiment achieve all of that, but it did so without the need for censorship. Because the entire experience was made up of individual pixels, "content" couldn't be easily removed. But it didn't have to be. The r/Place community did display rules, but those rules were extremely simple: be creative, be civil, follow sitewide rules, and don't post personal information. The output of the experiment wasn't manufactured by platform enforcement or policing. It was the organic result of people participating in the structure of the experience, perhaps also influenced by Reddit's cultural backdrop.

Too often, criticisms leveled against social media fail to recognize its power to unite people. Different social network structures breed vastly different kinds of behaviors and mindsets. How people are connected to one another and how they're identified yield drastic changes in the ways in which people relate to one another. When we start to understand how these often-overlooked factors of social network structure affect user mindsets, the driving forces behind problematic online behaviors become much more clear. When people are anonymous, organized around their common interests, identify as part of a broader community, and are given license to express creativity at a community-wide scale, it's natural for them to coordinate in ways that are positive and constructive.

The r/Place experiment, like much of the Reddit community itself, manifested the right brain characteristics of being expressive and explorative. It allowed people to coordinate and create without concern for their public persona. Had r/Place run on a platform like Facebook, Twitter, or Instagram, it's unlikely that the result would have been as coherent and constructive. That's not because the people are different. It's because the structure of their interactions is different. When people are in a mode of representing themselves, we can't expect them to engage as their most candid, vulnerable selves. Likewise, when people are engaged in a mode of exploration and candor, we shouldn't expect their behaviors and expressions to represent themselves the same ways they might when tied to their offline identities.

The fault line between these two very different modes of engagement is responsible for many of the problematic behaviors we see in social networks. When an anonymous user on Twitter sends a mean message to a person who is representing themselves and their beliefs, we have a conflict between right and left brain modes of experience. The mean message sender is engaged directly with their experience of the recipient's representation. But because the recipient is in a mode of representing a version of themselves, the message feels particularly harsh. While the sender may be attacking an idea, the recipient feels attacked personally. Superego networks like Twitter and Instagram are particularly fertile ground for these clashes of perspective because they allow for both identity-based and anonymous users to interact in the same space. It's easier to be candid and honest anonymously, and it's also easier to be nasty and hateful anonymously. Hate directed toward us is easier to shrug off as anonymous users than when we're representing public parts of our selves.

Even when things are going smoothly, left brain Ego and Superego networks are often criticized for creating echo chambers. But that's exactly what we ought to expect from interactions among people's representations of themselves. It's natural for us to attract representations that align with our own. Beyond that, most left brain networks are actually designed to create "echo chambers." Their algorithms are built to find the content with which we as individual users are most likely to engage. And except for content that deeply infuriates us, the content we're most likely to engage is the content with which we agree.

An echo chamber is only a problem when we believe that it represents a true, holistic picture of the outside world. The social networks themselves aren't as much a problem as how we relate to them. A feed filled with what we enjoy can be a wonderful thing. But in the same way that we don't grow and develop by exclusively eating candy, we also need to expose ourselves to content that isn't aligned with our individual beliefs. Right brain networks like Reddit and other interest-based online communities are in many ways antidotes to the echo chamber problem because they prioritize a community-level perspective over an individual one. Inarguably, social networks have the power to create echo chambers by curating content specifically for us as individuals. But social networks also have the power to expose us to new and different perspectives we wouldn't likely encounter in our everyday lives.

As brands, we've skewed our social media participation and ad spends heavily toward left brain networks. That's logical given that Facebook/Instagram and Twitter have the most developed social advertising platforms. The importance of presence in these left brain networks is undeniable. They help us build legitimacy, establish "known territory" for our brands, target very specific demographics, and when done right, grow our reach through the endorsement of our fans. However, as we seek to integrate into culture, convert new brand fans, and change broader brand perceptions, we must also find ways to engage people in right brain territory.

Admittedly, brands that have engaged right brain communities have done so with mixed success. Sometimes, outlier brands like UNIQLO become so integral to the community that they're received like members of the tribe. More often, brands receive negative feedback, are banned for self-promotion, or simply fail to gain traction. The ways in which we've learned to approach left brain social networks don't often translate to success in right brain networks. Rather than representing ourselves as individual brands to groups of other individuals, when we seek to engage right brain networks, we need to understand that we're participating in and addressing a community.

In previous examples of success in right brain Id networks, we've examined experiences like Anki's Cozmo Lost in Reddit, Audi's Think Faster, and Charles Schwab's open-ended prompts. One of the common threads through these experiences is that they're reliant on the community to be fun and meaningful. It wouldn't be any fun to navigate Cozmo through the escape rooms alone. The Audi Think Faster Ask Me Anything (AMA) series format works only when lots of people are asking interesting questions. An open-ended prompt is only interesting to engage when others have offered interesting or insightful perspectives.

TO ENGAGE PEOPLE'S RIGHT BRAINS, CREATE SOMETHING EXPLORABLE

Another approach to engaging a community as a brand is to provide tools that the community will find interesting and valuable. In doing so, we can add value for a community in a way that is not only unobtrusive but also enables the community to do more together. The r/Place experiment inspired an Adobe integration with Reddit called r/Layer, which launched in September 2019.[7] The r/Layer experience, a play on Adobe's Photoshop product and its use of "layers" to create images, started similarly as a blank canvas. But rather than users placing individual pixels, Redditors were given a set of simple drawing tools with which they contributed layers to a massive group drawing— kind of like a giant digital graffiti wall.

Over the course of five days, more than 150,000 unique drawings were contributed to r/Layer, and they ranged from professional art to memes to references to r/Place—even The Blue Corner showed up![8, 9] While creations weren't quite as community reliant on the r/Layer canvas—each layer could be considered its own finished piece—different layers played on one another throughout the course of the experience. When one Redditor started to draw a blacktop road near the top of the canvas, others helped build its infrastructure, briefly creating a highway across the entirety of the canvas.[10] Redditors similarly represented interests, memes, and the like—sneakers, video game characters, Wilson from *Castaway*, Bobby from *King of the Hill*, Mike Wazowski from *Monsters Inc.*, the AOL Running Man logo, and so on.

Not only did the r/Layer experience spark conversations within its designated community, echoes of r/Layer spread far throughout Reddit and beyond. It appeared on KnowYourMeme.com, and it generated organic time-lapse videos on YouTube. Some creators even made tutorials to help new participants learn how to use the tools.[11, 12, 13] The experience didn't just create one story to tell—it created many. Communities throughout Reddit not only participated in the experience but also brought their drawings back to the communities that inspired them. Organic posts reached the top of a wide range of subreddits— video game communities like r/Stellaris, location-based communities like r/Portugal, meme communities like r/EmojiPasta (which is like copypasta but with emojis), music communities like r/Greenday, and even a community for open discussion about sexuality for young people called r/BisexualTeens.[14, 15, 16, 17, 18]

Adobe's role in the experience was very different from how it participates in other social networks, and it executed the campaign brilliantly. In the lead-up to the campaign, Adobe promoted gifs it had cocreated with acclaimed gif maker u/hero0fwar, a lead moderator in influential Reddit communities like r/HighQualityGifs and r/reactiongifs.[19, 20] Not only did this collaboration net Adobe effective content perfectly suited to the Reddit ecosystem, it also allowed the brand to borrow credibility from his rare influencer-like status among Reddit communities. Adobe used traditional advertising space to surround the experience with relevant ads, but they weren't intrusive. In doing so, the brand lived up to its positioning as a champion of creativity by enabling a massive community to create something together.

These experiences that succeed in engaging right brain communities are often the antithesis of what we've come to accept as "social media best practices." They aren't short. They don't fit into six-second video slots. Often, they aren't even particularly time sensitive. They're deep, expressive, and communal. They allow people to infuse the experiences with their own meaning and, as a result, create interesting stories. As brands, we can't help but be protective of ourselves. These open-ended engagements can make us feel particularly vulnerable. But we must also recognize that regardless of whether or not we acknowledge it, our brand and its meaning are the cocreations of ourselves and the cultures that surround us. When we participate in social media, regardless of whether we're in right or left brain space, we need to embrace that dynamic rather than fight it. Otherwise, we risk becoming stale, stagnant, and out of touch.

SOCIAL MEDIA PUSHES BRANDS TO BE MORE THAN TRANSPARENT—IT REQUIRES US TO ACT IN ACCORDANCE WITH WHAT WE SAY

Social media is changing our industry at a rapid rate. In many ways, it already has, but we're only beginning to feel the transformation in store for how brands communicate with their audiences. Social media pushes us to be more self-aware of our brands and their roles in people's lives. It forces us to confront the reactions and expressions of our audiences in ways that are more tangible and immediate than any marketing channel since knocking on doors. Social media manifests different versions of our audiences, and it requires that we understand the nuances of these different selves to reach our audiences effectively.

From the earliest social media strategies, we understood that the "matching luggage" approach to campaign building felt wrong. We knew that our TV spot wasn't the optimal asset for engaging people on Facebook or Twitter. But rarely did we articulate the underlying, "Why?" As we continue to evolve our understanding of how best to reach people in different online spaces, it's more important than ever for us to understand that social media platforms aren't just websites. They're not just apps on people's smartphones. Social networks are real, tangible places where people go. They're environments in which people express and represent themselves, that inform how people perceive themselves and the world around them, and that evolve their social norms and cultures. We don't "go on" social media. We enter into it.

As new as social media feels and as fast as its different cultures evolve, many of our core marketing strategies remain relevant. In some ways, social media pushes us back to basics: create something of value, show it to people who will find it valuable, be consistent, and act in accordance with what you say. The era of TV branding, which put us at arm's length from our audiences, has given way to the return of close proximity to the people with whom our brands seek to connect. As a result, our industry is being forced to trim the proverbial fat—to forgo the preciousness of our brands in vacuums, to be authentic and self-aware, and to find genuine points of connection with people. Social media represents a much-needed reality check for our industry. It won't necessarily oust legacy brands, but it will continue to reward those with strategies rooted in self (and cultural) awareness.

Advertising and *marketing* are dirty words on the Internet. While we've come to simply accept this antagonistic relationship with our audiences, the reason isn't simply "because people hate ads." In a 2016 survey, 83 percent of Internet users agreed that not all ads are bad and that they'd preferably only block obnoxious ones.[21] An additional 77 percent agreed that given the option, they'd prefer to filter ads rather than block them completely. Brands—and advertising—have genuine value to add to people's experiences online.

Unfortunately, we advertisers have engaged in an evolutionary arms race with our audience's attention. We continue to load more ads per page, and we find ways to make those ads louder, brighter, flashier, and more obtrusive. In the aforementioned survey, 91 percent of respondents agreed that ads were more intrusive compared to those served in 2013 and 2014, and 87 percent reported seeing more ads in general. This relationship between marketers and our audiences is untenable. We can't build brands by attacking our customers' attention or by hijacking trends. We build brands by demonstrating our value to the people who will find us valuable.

As I close this book, I'd like to challenge our industry to consider the right brain behaviors that enable our left brain storytelling. Are we behaving in the world in ways that are consistent with our positioning and the value we bring to people? What behaviors can we manifest in the world that add real value for our audiences? Once we've answered those questions, the stories we tell become more genuine. When we stop attacking their attention, our audiences can let down their guards. We can rebuild our relationships based on mutually added value.

As marketers, we're equipped with pools of money intended to express the value of the brands we represent. If our goal is to change people's minds about us, it's not enough for us to simply tell a story. We can spend all of the production budget in the world and still create an ad that's ineffective if the story feels disconnected from our audiences and the cultures in which they participate. If we truly want to maximize our marketing budgets and get people to think differently about us, we need to embody living articulations of what we want our brands to represent. In doing so, we move a step beyond transparency into what really endears us to our audiences in the age of social media— we act in accordance with what we say. That's what people expect from other people, and it's the only sustainable way to build trust.

Fortunately for us, the Internet provides a broad canvas for creating experiences and representing ourselves in ways that attract people. We may find our audiences engaged in pure self-expression and in modes of curiosity, in which we can deliver explorable experiences, interact with naturally forming communities, and lean into people's creative drives. And we may find our audiences in spaces in which they're representing themselves socially, in which we can aid them in expressing those representations, represent ourselves in ways that are aspirational or genuinely relatable, and facilitate connections between people. The possibilities are limited only by our creativity.

Look for what people value. Try to understand why they value it. Create something they'll genuinely enjoy. Then, tell stories about it.

Notes

CHAPTER 1

1. Shifman, Limor. *Memes*. Cambridge, MA: The MIT Press, 2014.
2. Dawkins, Richard. *The Selfish Gene: 40th Anniversary Edition*. Oxford: Oxford University Press, 2016.
3. Blackmore, Susan, and Richard Dawkins. *The Meme Machine*. Oxford: Oxford University Press, 2000.
4. Shifman, *Memes*.
5. r/shittyfoodporn. "When Payday Is Still Two Days Away." reddit. Accessed January 10, 2020. https://www.reddit.com/r/shittyfoodporn /comments/9yb873/when_payday_is_still_two_days_away/.
6. Aurelius, Marcus. *Meditations*. Translated by Albert Wittstock and Martin Hammond. Introduction by Christopher Gill. Oxford: Oxford University Press, 2013.
7. "Shifts for 2020: Multisensory Multipliers." Facebook IQ. Accessed January 10, 2020. https://www.facebook.com/business/news/insights /shifts-for-2020-multisensory-multipliers.

CHAPTER 2

1. "The Ice Water Challenge." Cancer Society Auckland. Accessed January 10, 2020. https://web.archive.org/web/20140819082259/https://www.cancer societyauckland.org.nz/newsandmedia.
2. Federer, Joe. "4 Reasons You're Seeing More Videos on Facebook Than Ever." THAT'S FICTION, May 2, 2015. http://www.thatsfiction .com/latest-work/2015/5/2/4-reasons-youre-seeing-more-videos-on -facebook-than-ever.

3. Shaban, Hamza. "Digital Advertising to Surpass Print and TV for the First Time, Report Says." *The Washington Post*. WP Company, March 7, 2019. https://www.washingtonpost.com/technology/2019/02/20/digital-advertising-surpass-print-tv-first-time-report-says/?noredirect=on&utm_term=.2afae4360624.

CHAPTER 3

1. "The History of Word of Mouth Marketing." The Free Library. Accessed January 11, 2020. https://www.thefreelibrary.com/Thehistoryofwordofmouthmarketing.-a0134908667.
2. Louis Vuitton. "Virgil Abloh Staples Edition." Facebook. Accessed January 11, 2020. https://www.facebook.com/watch/?v=2334680580142899.
3. Wendy's. "Buy Our Cheeseburgers." Twitter. Accessed January 11, 2020. https://twitter.com/Wendys/status/1012398470903291904.
4. "Slaps Roof of Car." Know Your Meme, June 28, 2018. https://knowyourmeme.com/memes/slaps-roof-of-car.
5. Small, Deborah. "Hearts, Minds and Money: Maximizing Charitable Giving." Interview by Knoledge@Wharton. Wharton Education. Accessed January 11, 2020. https://knowledge.wharton.upenn.edu/article/maximizing-charitable-giving/.
6. Naumann, Robert K., Janie M. Ondracek, Samuel Reiter, Mark Shein-Idelson, Maria Antonietta Tosches, Tracy M Yamawaki, and Gilles Laurent. "The Reptilian Brain." National Center for Biotechnology Information, April 20, 2015. https://www.ncbi.nlm.nih.gov/pmc/articles/PMC4406946/.
7. r/Starterpacks. "The 'Every Cheap Italian Restaurant' Starter Pack." reddit. Accessed January 11, 2020. https://www.reddit.com/r/starterpacks/comments/akcryr/the_every_cheap_italian_restaurant_starter_pack/.
8. Brita. "'I'm Trying to Save Money Now' Starter Pack from Your Friends at Brita (r/FellowKids, Here We Come!)." reddit. Accessed January 11, 2020. https://www.reddit.com/user/Brita_Official/comments/8xsra0/im_trying_to_save_money_now_starter_pack_from/.
9. Brita. "Wow, Reddit! 100 Posts in r/Fellowkids and Counting, We're Flattered. Remember to Fill up Your Brita, All That Salt Must Be Making You Thirsty!" reddit. Accessed January 11, 2020. https://www.reddit.com/user/Brita_Official/comments/984hyt/wow_reddit_100_posts_in_rfellowkids_and_counting/.

CHAPTER 4

1. Victor, Anucyia. "Zilla Van Den Born Boasts of Trekking in Asia Using Photos Taken in Home Town." *Daily Mail Online*, September 9, 2014. https://www.dailymail.co.uk/travel/travel_news/article-2749306/What -scam-Student-boasts-friends-trekking-Asia-visiting-stunning-beaches -tasting-local-cuisine-meeting-Buddhist-monks-using-FAKE-photos -taken-home-town.html.

2. Hunt, Melissa G., Rachel Marx, Courtney Lipson, and Jordyn Young. "No More FOMO: Limiting Social Media Decreases Loneliness and Depression." *Journal of Social and Clinical Psychology* 37, no. 10 (2018): 751–768. https://doi.org/10.1521/jscp.2018.37.10.751.

3. Williams, Shawna. "Human Species May Be Much Older Than Previously Thought." *The Scientist Magazine*, September 29, 2017. https://www.the -scientist.com/news-opinion/human-species-may-be-much-older-than -previously-thought-30819.

4. "Don't Believe Facebook; You Only Have 150 Friends." NPR, June 5, 2011. https://www.npr.org/2011/06/04/136723316/dont-believe- facebook-you-only-have-150-friends.

5. Knapton, Sarah. "Facebook Users Have 155 Friends—but Would Trust Just Four in a Crisis." *The Telegraph*. Telegraph Media Group, January 20, 2016. https://www.telegraph.co.uk/news/science/science-news /12108412/Facebook-users-have-155-friends-but-would-trust-just-four -in-a-crisis.html.

6. Clement, J. "Global Social Media Account Ownership 2018." Statista, July 22, 2019. https://www.statista.com/statistics/788084/number-of -social-media-accounts/.

7. McKie, Robin. "How Hunting with Wolves Helped Humans Outsmart the Neanderthals." *The Guardian*. Guardian News and Media, March 1, 2015. https://www.theguardian.com/science/2015/mar/01/hunting-with -wolves-humans-conquered-the-world-neanderthal-evolution.

8. Bedell, Geraldine. "Rates of Depression Have Soared in Teenagers. What Are We Doing Wrong?" *The Independent*. Independent Digital News and Media, February 27, 2016. https://www.independent.co.uk/life- style/health-and-families/features/teenage-mental-health-crisis-rates-of -depression-have-soared-in-the-past-25-years-a6894676.html.

9. Cramer, Shirley, and Dr. Becky Inkster. "#StatusOfMind Social Media and Young People's Mental Health and Wellbeing." *Royal Society for Public Health*, May 2017. https://www.rsph.org.uk/our-work/campaigns /status-of-mind.html.

10. Scribner, Herb. "63 Percent of Instagram Users Report Being 'Miserable.' Here's Why." *Deseret News*. June 25, 2018. https://www.deseret.com/2018 /6/25/20647615/63-percent-of-instagram-users-report-being-miserable -here-s-why.

11. Houser, Kristin. "Surprise! Reddit Is Actually Helping People Battle Mental Illness." *Futurism*. Neoscope, April 20, 2018. https://futurism .com/neoscope/reddit-depression-mental-illness.

12. Marx, Christopher, Cord Benecke, and Antje Gumz. "Talking Cure Models: A Framework of Analysis." *Frontiers in Psychology* 8 (2017). https://doi.org/10.3389/fpsyg.2017.01589.

13. Peterson, Jordan B. "Biblical Series VIII: The Phenomenology of the Divine." YouTube, July 27, 2017. https://www.youtube.com/watch?v= UoQdp2prfmM.

14. Litman, Jordan A. "Epistemic Curiosity." *Encyclopedia of the Sciences of Learning*, 2012, 1162–1165. https://doi.org/10.1007/978-1-4419-1428 -6_1645.

15. r/Showerthoughts. "'I Add 'Reddit' after Every Question I Search on Google Because I Trust You All More Than Other Strangers.'" reddit, September 24, 2016. https://www.reddit.com/r/Showerthoughts /comments/54btqq/i_add_reddit_after_every_question_i_search_on/.

16. McCoy, Terrence. "4chan: The 'Shock Post' Site That Hosted the Private Jennifer Lawrence Photos." *The Washington Post*. WP Company, September 2, 2014. https://www.washingtonpost.com/news/morning -mix/wp/2014/09/02/the-shadowy-world-of-4chan-the-shock-post-site -that-hosted-the-private-jennifer-lawrence-photos/.

17. Clement, J. "Global Social Media Account Ownership 2018."

CHAPTER 5

1. Dove US. "Dove Real Beauty Sketches | You're More Beautiful Than You Think." YouTube, April 14, 2013. https://www.youtube.com/watch?v= XpaOjMXyJGk.

2. Bahadur, Nina. "How Dove Tried to Change the Conversation About Female Beauty." *HuffPost*, December 7, 2017. https://www.huffpost.com /entry/dove-real-beauty-campaign-turns-10_n_4575940.

3. Dinesh, Disha. "11 Awesome Facebook Campaigns to Inspire You." *DreamGrow*, July 10, 2019. https://www.dreamgrow.com/11-awesome -inspiring-facebook-campaings/.

4. Brett, Brian. "The Psychology of Sharing: Why Do People Share Online?" *New York Times*, July 13, 2011. https://web.archive.org/web /20160922145048/http://nytmarketing.whsites.net/mediakit/pos/POS _PUBLIC0819.php. Additional information available here: https://www .businesswire.com/news/home/20110713005971/en/New-York-Times -Completes-Research-%E2%80%98Psychology-Sharing%E2%80%99.

5. Ziploc Brand. "Cheesecake Stuffed Strawberries." Facebook, March 9, 2015. https://www.facebook.com/Ziploc/photos/a.329236260422251 /947546951924509/?type=3&theater.

6. Ziploc Brand. "DIY Tie-Dye Crayons." Facebook, September 18, 2015. https://www.facebook.com/Ziploc/photos/a.329236260422251 /1049744868371383/?type=3&theater.

7. Ziploc Brand. "Pecan Pie Bark." Facebook, November 17, 2015. https://www.facebook.com/Ziploc/photos/a.329236260422251 /1068198406526029/?type=3&theater.

8. Ziploc Brand. "Easy Pomegranate Juice." Facebook, July 26, 2014. https://www.facebook.com/Ziploc/photos/a.329236260422251 /820978114581394/?type=3&theater.

9. "Snapchat Advertising Formats." Snapchat for Business. Accessed January 14, 2020. https://forbusiness.snapchat.com/advertising.

10. Johnson, Lauren. "Taco Bell's Cinco De Mayo Snapchat Lens Was Viewed 224 Million Times." *Adweek*, May 11, 2016. https://www.adweek .com/digital/taco-bells-cinco-de-mayo-snapchat-lens-was-viewed-224 -million-times-171390/.

11. "I'm Getting Ready for Small Business Saturday, Nov 30. Are You?" American Express. Accessed January 14, 2020. https://www .americanexpress.com/us/small-business/shop-small/.

12. Vasquez, Natalia. "11 Examples of Branded Snapchat Filters & Lenses That Worked." *Medium*. Comms Planning, February 28, 2017. https:// medium.com/comms-planning/11-branded-snapchat-filters-that -worked-94a808afa682.

13. "Sony Pictures' Venom Snapchat Campaign Drove 1 Million Incremental Movie Ticket Sales." Snapchat for Business. Accessed January 14, 2020. https://forbusiness.snapchat.com/inspiration/sony-pictures-venom -snapchat-campaign-drove-1-million-incremental-movie.

14. "Snapchat Ad Examples & Success Stories: Snapchat for Business." Snapchat for Business. Accessed January 14, 2020. https://forbusiness .snapchat.com/inspiration.

15. "Squatty Potty." Facebook. Accessed January 14, 2020. https://www .facebook.com/squattypotty/.

16. Squatty Potty. "This Unicorn Changed the Way I Poop." Facebook, October 2015. https://www.facebook.com/squattypotty/videos /925884884149638/.

CHAPTER 6

1. Freud, Sigmund. *Civilization and Its Discontents*. New York, NY: Norton, 2010.

2. Shaw, Beau. "Historical Context for the Writings of Sigmund Freud." Columbia College. https://www.college.columbia.edu/core/content /writings-sigmund-freud/context.

3. Cramer, Shirley, and Dr. Becky Inkster. "#StatusOfMind Social Media and Young People's Mental Health and Wellbeing."

4. "30 Minutes of Daily Meditation Can Stave Off Anxiety And Depression." *HuffPost*, January 7, 2014. https://www.huffingtonpost.co.uk/entry /anxiety-and-depression-meditation_n_4549618.

5. Turner, Laura. "Is Twitter Making You More Anxious?" *The Atlantic*. Atlantic Media Company, July 19, 2017. https://www.theatlantic.com /technology/archive/2017/07/how-twitter-fuels-anxiety/534021/.

6. R/GA. "Beats by Dre Straight Outta Compton—The Shorty Awards." The Shorty Awards. Accessed January 14, 2020. https://shortyawards.com /8th/straight-outta-3.

7. "How Heinz Harnessed the Power of Twitter and Got 1 Billion Impressions in 48 Hours." Twitter Marketing. Accessed January 14, 2020. https://marketing.twitter.com/na/en/success-stories/how-heinz -harnessed-the-power-of-twitter-and-got-one-billion-impressions.

8. Heinz Ketchup. "Looks Like Chicago Is Among the First to Get Dipped in #Mayochup!" Twitter, September 19, 2018. https://twitter.com /HeinzKetchup_US/status/1042390349468053504.

9. *Buzzfeed*. "@Buzzfeedtasty." Instagram. Accessed January 14, 2020. https://www.instagram.com/buzzfeedtasty/?hl=en.

10. "Lowe's Fix in Six: Using 'The New' to Create 'Know-How.'" The 4A's. Accessed January 14, 2020. https://www.aaaa.org/wp-content/uploads /legacy-pdfs/BBDO-LowesFixinSix-HM.pdf.

11. Lowe's Home Improvement. "Stripped Screw? No Problem, Just Use a Rubber Band." Vine, April 19, 2013. https://vine.co/42084afe-ccfe-4682 -ba31-671e3dcbe768.

12. Lowe's Home Improvement. "Use a Cookie Cutter and a Hammer for Perfect Pumpkin Carving." Vine, October 24, 2014. https://vine.co /63b4200c-0fc4-4636-8e2d-f5e5ede518a2.

13. Lowe's Home Improvement. "Use Tape to Measure the Distance Between Holes, Then Put the Tape on the Wall." Vine, May 17, 2013. https://vine .co/a422ca28-3b0d-486c-9919-4ecb3d009d8b.

14. Lowe's Home Improvement. "Lighten up! DEWALT 2-PC 20V Combo Kit Was $199, Will Be $149 on Black Friday." Vine, November 12, 2014. https://vine.co/v/OiFHAJ7OqEF.

15. Lowe's Home Improvement. "Use a Cookie Cutter and a Hammer for Perfect Pumpkin Carving!" Facebook, October 25, 2014. https://www.facebook.com/lowes/videos/10152384851961231/?v= 10152384851961231&redirect=false.

16. GoPro. "@GoPro." Twitter. Accessed January 14, 2020. https://twitter .com/GoPro.

17. GoPro. "@GoPro." Instagram. Accessed January 14, 2020. https://www .instagram.com/ggopro/.

18. Lewin, Michelle. "@michelle_lewin." Instagram. Accessed January 14, 2020. https://www.instagram.com/michelle_lewin/?hl=en.

19. Greene, Kai. "@kaigreene." Instagram. Accessed January 14, 2020. https://www.instagram.com/kaigreene/?hl=en.

20. Panda, Simeon. "@simeonpanda." Instagram. Accessed January 14, 2020. https://www.instagram.com/simeonpanda/?hl=en.

21. Thomas, Giles. "[23] Best Instagram Marketing Campaigns for Growth in 2019." RisePro, May 30, 2019. https://risepro.co/instagram-marketing -campaign/.

22. @citysage. "'In Honor of Valentine's Day @madewell1937 Asked Me to Share Some Things I Love . . . like the First Cup of Morning Coffee, the Comfiest Goes- . . . ." Instagram, February 14, 2014. https://www .instagram.com/p/kZ3ZLUIJ_t/.

23. Madewell. "Inspo: Your Pics." Accessed January 14, 2020. https://www .madewell.com/inspo-community-denimmadewell-landing.html.

24. Wendy's. "Thanks for Sharing Your Baby Pictures." Twitter, December 18, 2017. https://twitter.com/Wendys/status/942854646070235137.

CHAPTER 7

1. Isaacson, Walter. "How to Fix the Internet." *The Atlantic*, December 15, 2016. https://www.theatlantic.com/technology/archive/2016/12/how-to -fix-the-internet/510797/.

2. Whittaker, Zack. "New York's Anonymity Ban: Why Should the Web Be Any Different?" *ZDNet*, May 26, 2012. https://www.zdnet.com/article /new-yorks-anonymity-ban-why-should-the-web-be-any-different/.

3. Barton, Eric. "The Danger of Online Anonymity." *BBC*, March 9, 2015. https://www.bbc.com/worklife/article/20150309-the-danger-of-online -anonymity.

4. "Top Sites in the United States." Alexa. Accessed January 15, 2020. https://www.alexa.com/topsites/countries/US.

5. North, Anna. "The Double-Edged Sword of Online Anonymity." *The New York Times*, May 15, 2015. https://takingnote.blogs.nytimes.com /2015/05/15/the-double-edged-sword-of-online-anonymity/.

6. "The Power of Community: A Research Project by Reddit & YPulse." YPulse, September 18, 2019. https://www.ypulse.com/2019/09/18 /ypulse-x-reddit-whitepaper-the-power-of-community/.

7. Kendall, Todd D., and John E. Walker. "Pornography, Rape, and the Internet." July 2007. https://www.semanticscholar.org/paper /Pornography%2C-Rape%2C-and-the-Internet-Kendall-Walker /602ddbdd604afe9cbd31c97f01d941fa637f271a.

8. Hill, Catey. "Study Finds Online Porn May Reduce the Incidence of Rape." nydailynews.com. *New York Daily News*, January 11, 2019. https:// www.nydailynews.com/news/money/study-finds-online-porn-reduce -incidence-rape-article-1.390028.

9. Landsburg, Steven E. "Proof That Internet Porn Prevents Rape." *Slate Magazine*, October 30, 2006. https://slate.com/culture/2006/10/proof -that-internet-porn-prevents-rape.html.

10. Jung, C. G. *Psychology and Religion: West and East*. Hove: Routledge, 2014.

11. Beck, Martin. "How a Fashion Brand Drives 20% of Daily Online Revenue from a Single Reddit Post." Marketing Land, October 20, 2015. https://marketingland.com/how-a-fashion-brand-drives-20-of-daily -online-revenue-from-a-single-reddit-post-147309.

12. "I'm on My Phone, so I Can't Access the One from Last Year (Doesn't Load on Mobile)..." reddit, February 24, 2017. Accessed January 20, 2020. https://www.reddit.com/r/malefashionadvice/comments/5w1a56 /mfa_psa_the_uniqlo_linen_shirts_from_this_season/de7h9be/.

13. Dyda, Arielle. "u/midnight1214." reddit, April 27, 2012. https://www .reddit.com/user/midnight1214.

14. "PSA: Uniqlo on 5th Ave Claim the Free Heattech Vouchers Are No Longer Accepted." reddit, December 16, 2016. https://www.reddit.com /r/frugalmalefashion/comments/5ir0e6/psa_uniqlo_on_5th_ave_claim _the_free_heattech/.

15. "Teachers of Reddit, What's the Saddest Thing You've Ever Found out about a Student?" reddit, March 7, 2017. https://www.reddit .com/r/AskReddit/comments/5y3ax2/teachers_of_reddit_whats_the _saddest_thing_youve/dene3x8/?context=8&depth=9.

16. "Shoutout to u/midnight1214 (Our Friendly Uniqlo Reddit Rep) for This Kind Gesture on AskReddit." reddit, March 8, 2017. https://www .reddit.com/r/malefashionadvice/comments/5y8oz6/shoutout_to _umidnight1214_our_friendly_uniqlo/.

17. "Molly's Trip to France." reddit, March 8, 2017. https://www.reddit.com /r/donate/comments/5y8tfx/mollys_trip_to_france/.

18. "The Basic Bastard Wardrobe: British Budget Edition." reddit, September 18, 2019. https://www.reddit.com/r/malefashionadvice/comments /d5zhqw/the_basic_bastard_wardrobe_british_budget_edition/.

19. "Best of Uniqlo?" reddit, October 22, 2019. https://www.reddit.com /r/femalefashionadvice/comments/dllr6x/best_of_uniqlo/.

20. "My Friend Is About to Ask His Girlfriend to Marry Her and I'm the Only One Who Knows How Unfaithful She Is. Do I Say Anything?" reddit, April 28, 2019. https://www.reddit.com/r/relationship_advice /comments/bicdpm/my_friend_is_about_to_ask_his_girlfriend_to _marry/.

21. "What Are Some Things That Guys Misinterpret from Women as 'She's Interested in Me'?" reddit, November 28, 2018. https://www.reddit.com /r/AskWomen/comments/a15seh/what_are_some_things_that_guys _misinterpret_from/.

22. "Serious—Won Lottery, Paid off All Debts, Terrified of Financial Advisors and Investing. Advice?" reddit, May 17, 2015. https://www.reddit.com/r/personalfinance/comments/36bp59/serious_won_lottery_paid_of_all_debts_terrified/.

23. "Hey Reddit, Your Friends at Charles Schwab Here. What's Something You're Doing Today to Set Yourself up for Success Tomorrow?" reddit. Charles Schwab, February 23, 2018. https://www.reddit.com/comments/7zrq4l/hey_reddit_your_friends_at_charles_schwab_here/.

24. "What Does 'Wealthy' Mean to You? Here's Where Some of the Top US Cities Draw the Line between 'Financial Comfort' and 'Wealth' (from Your Friends at Charles Schwab)." reddit. Charles Schwab, June 14, 2018. https://www.reddit.com/user/Schwab_Official/comments/8r4yxg/what_does_wealthy_mean_to_you_heres_where_some_of/.

25. "Hey Reddit, Charles Schwab Team Here with a Question. What's Your Approach to Tracking Gains and Losses in Your Trading History and Learning from Your Past?" reddit. Charles Schwab, November 20, 2018. https://www.reddit.com/user/Schwab_Official/comments/9ywffe/hey_reddit_charles_schwab_team_here_with_a/.

26. "Kodiak, Alaska Welcomes Pitbull." YouTube. Walmart, August 10, 2012. https://www.youtube.com/watch?v=2NrllHwHq7w.

27. Berman, Taylor. "In Victory for the Internet, Pitbull Visits Alaska, Receives Gift of Bear Spray." Gawker, July 30, 2012. https://gawker.com/5930334/in-victory-for-the-internet-pitbull-visits-alaska-receives-gift-of-bear-spray.

28. "U.S. Census Bureau QuickFacts: Kodiak City, Alaska." Census Bureau QuickFacts, July 1, 2018. https://www.census.gov/quickfacts/fact/table/kodiakcityalaska/PST045218.

29. "Mountain Dew Naming Campaign Melts Down After Online Hijacking." *HuffPost*, August 13, 2012. https://www.huffpost.com/entry/4chan-mountain-dew-n_1773076.

30. "Taylor Swift Foils Prank with Donation to School for the Deaf." *Rolling Stone*, June 25, 2018. https://www.rollingstone.com/music/music-country/taylor-swift-counters-4chan-prank-with-donation-to-school-for-the-deaf-102935/.

31. "William Lashua's Birthday." Know Your Meme, November 20, 2019. https://knowyourmeme.com/memes/events/william-lashuas-birthday.

32. Ingram, Mathew. "4chan Decides to Do Something Nice for a Change." Gigaom, September 2, 2010. https://gigaom.com/2010/09/02/4chan-decides-to-do-something-nice-for-a-change/.

33. AnonymousHasASoul. "William J Lashua's Birthday Party!" YouTube, September 5, 2010. https://www.youtube.com/watch?v=UzqNkIkj3rE.

34. "Think Faster, The World's Fastest AMA." M/H VCCP. Audi. Accessed January 15, 2020. https://mtzhf.com/work/audi-think-faster-the-worlds-fastest-ama.

35. "I am Barack Obama, President of the United States—AMA." reddit, August 29, 2012. https://www.reddit.com/r/IAmA/comments/z1c9z/i_am_barack_obama_president_of_the_united_states/.

36. "I'm Bill Gates, co-chair of the Bill & Melinda Gates Foundation. Ask Me Anything." reddit, February 27, 2018. https://www.reddit.com/r/IAmA/comments/80ow6w/im_bill_gates_cochair_of_the_bill_melinda_gates/.

37. "We Are Edward Snowden, Laura Poitras and Glenn Greenwald from the Oscar-Winning Documentary CITIZENFOUR. AUAA." reddit, February 23, 2015. https://www.reddit.com/r/IAmA/comments/2wwdep/we_are_edward_snowden_laura_poitras_and_glenn/.

38. "I am Dr. Jane Goodall, a Scientist, Conservationist, Peacemaker, and Mentor. AMA." reddit, September 13, 2017. https://www.reddit.com/r/IAmA/comments/6zvwqe/i_am_dr_jane_goodall_a_scientist_conservationist/.

39. "IamA Vacuum Repair Technician, and I Can't Believe People Really Wanted It, but, AMA!" reddit, October 28, 2013. https://www.reddit.com/r/IAmA/comments/1pe2bd/iama_vacuum_repair_technician_and_i_cant_believe/.

40. "IamA Vacuum Repair Technician, and I Can't Believe People Really Wanted It, but, AMA!"

41. Ifeanyi, KC. "Reddit's First-Ever Interactive Livestream Stars a Very Lost Robot." *Fast Company*, November 14, 2017. https://www.fastcompany.com/40495819/reddits-first-ever-interactive-livestream-stars-a-very-lost-robot.

42. "I Only Believe This Is Live, When a Dog Makes a Shit." reddit, November 14, 2017. https://www.reddit.com/r/promos/comments/7ct3se/we_did_it_reddit_cozmo_has_finally_escaped_from/dptf4m1/.

43. u/SpookyBlackCat. "This Is the Best Use of Obvious Advertising on the Internet!!!" reddit, November 14, 2017. https://www.reddit.com/r/promos/comments/7ct3se/we_did_it_reddit_cozmo_has_finally_escaped_from/dptguk9/.

44. u/mumbalakumbala. "Commenters—You Are Doing an Awesome Job, This Is All in All a Pretty Impressive . . . " reddit, November 14, 2017. https://www.reddit.com/r/promos/comments/7ct3se/we_did_it_reddit_cozmo_has_finally_escaped_from/dptgvx2/.

CHAPTER 8

1. Jefferson, Brandie. "Splitting the Difference: One Person, Two Minds: The Source: Washington University in St. Louis." *The Source*. Washington University, June 1, 2018. https://source.wustl.edu/2018/05/splitting-the -difference-one-person-two-minds/.

2. Bloom, Juliana S., and George W. Hynd. "The Role of the Corpus Callosum in Interhemispheric Transfer of Information: Excitation or Inhibition?" *Neuropsychology Review* 15, no. 2 (2005): 59–71. https://doi .org/10.1007/s11065-005-6252-y.

3. Halpern, M. E., Onur Güntürkün, William D. Hopkins, and Lesley J. Rogers. "Lateralization of the Vertebrate Brain: Taking the Side of Model Systems." *Journal of Neuroscience* 25, no. 45 (September 2005): 10351– 10357. https://doi.org/10.1523/jneurosci.3439-05.2005.

4. McGilchrist, Iain. *The Master and His Emissary: the Divided Brain and the Making of the Western World*. New Haven, CT: Yale University Press, 2019.

5. Karenina, Karina, Andrey Giljov, Janeane Ingram, Victoria J. Rowntree, and Yegor Malashichev. "Lateralization of Mother–Infant Interactions in a Diverse Range of Mammal Species." *Nature Ecology & Evolution* 1, no. 2 (September 2017). https://doi.org/10.1038/s41559-016-0030.

6. Gotter, Ana, and Timothy J. Legg. "What Is Capgras Syndrome?" *Healthline*, May 1, 2017. https://www.healthline.com/health/capgras -syndrome.

7. Renzi, E. De, D. Perani, G.a. Carlesimo, M.c. Silveri, and F. Fazio. "Prosopagnosia Can Be Associated with Damage Confined to the Right Hemisphere—An MRI and PET Study and a Review of the Literature." *Neuropsychologia* 32, no. 8 (1994): 893–902. https://doi.org/10.1016 /0028-3932(94)90041-8.

8. Migliore, Lauren. "The Aha! Moment: The Science Behind Creative Insight." *Brain World*, May 28, 2019. https://brainworldmagazine.com /aha-moment-science-behind-creative-insight/.

9. Sherman, Lauren. "High-Low Collaborations Democratised Fashion. But What Did They Do for the Designers?" *The Business of Fashion*, September 19, 2019. https:// www.businessoffashion.com/articles/news-analysis/high-low-collaborations -democratised-fashion-but-what-did-they-do-for-the-designers.

10. "Target Celebrates 20 Years of Designer Partnership with an Anniversary Collection." Target Corporate, August 1, 2019. https://corporate.target .com/article/2019/08/20-years-anniversary-collection.

11. Heath, Dan, and Chip Heath. *The Power of Moments*. Random House UK, 2017.

12. Ellis, Blake. "New Gap Logo Ignites Firestorm." *CNNMoney*. Cable News Network, October 8, 2010. https://money.cnn.com/2010/10/08/news /companies/gap_logo/index.htm.

13. Yarwood, Andrew. "A Brief History of 5 Iconic Oil Business Brands." Fircroft, March 27, 2019. https://www.fircroft.com/blogs/a-brief-history -of-5-iconic-oil-business-brands-98627135823.

14. "BP: Case Study." *Landor*. Accessed January 16, 2020. https://landor.com /work/bp.

15. Hardy, Tony. "10 Rebranding Failures and How Much They Cost." Canny, December 17, 2019. https://www.canny-creative.com/10-rebranding -failures-how-much-they-cost/.

16. Andrivet, Marion. "What to Learn from Tropicana's Packaging Redesign Failure?" *The Branding Journal*, June 2, 2019. https://www .thebrandingjournal.com/2015/05/what-to-learn-from-tropicanas -packaging-redesign-failure/.

17. "Which Marvel Super Hero Matchup Would Make the Best Big Game Commercial? (Most Persuasive Answers Win a Year of Gold)." reddit. Coca-Cola, December 22, 2015. https://www.reddit.com/comments /3xvstd/which_marvel_super_hero_matchup_would_make_the/.

18. Hooton, Christopher. "Westworld Season 2 Will 'Fuck with the Metaphysical.'" *The Independent*, March 27, 2017. https://www .independent.co.uk/arts-entertainment/tv/news/westworld-season -2-plot-reddit-storyline-jonathan-nolan-details-news-a7651506.html.

19. Nelson, Samantha. "How Baskin Robbins Built a Stranger Things Alternate Reality Game Using 1985 Tech." Gaming Street, August 15, 2019. https://www.gamingstreet.com/baskin-robbins-stranger-things -arg/.

20. u/Northern_Nomad. "Cheerios Will Send You 500 Wildflower Seeds for Free to Help Save the Honeybee (Link in Comments)." reddit, March 15, 2017. https://www.reddit.com/r/pics/comments/5zmio2 /cheerios_will_send_you_500_wildflower_seeds_for/.

21. "SOS 073017 2130 EST TWTR 3x.5GAL." reddit. McDonald's, July 30, 2017. https://www.reddit.com/r/rickandmorty/comments/6qis8y/sos _073017_2130_est_twtr_3x5gal/.

22. Alexander, Julia, and Ben Kuchera. "How a Rick and Morty Joke Led to a McDonald's Szechuan Sauce Controversy." *Polygon*, October 12, 2017. https://www.polygon.com/2017/10/12/16464374/rick-and-morty -mcdonalds-szechuan-sauce.

23. "RICK AND MORTY MCDONALD'S SZECHUAN SAUCE FREAKOUT!!!! (ORIGINAL VIDEO)." YouTube. Chairman Mar, October 8, 2017. https://www.youtube.com/watch?v=-GC5rAX0xHg.

24. "Watch the New *Logan* Big Game Spot Below! Wolverine's Getting His Claws out for the Last Time. What Do You Want to See?" reddit. FOX Studios, February 1, 2017. https://www.reddit.com/r/promos/comments/5ri3jc/watch_the_new_logan_big_game_spot_below/.

25. u/Spencerforhire83. "I Have Been Invited to Red Carpet Screening for the Movie Logan . . ." reddit, February 15, 2017. https://www.reddit.com/r/malefashionadvice/comments/5u7h86/i_have_been_invited_to_red_carpet_screening_for/.

26. u/Spencerforhire83. "Last Week I Commented About Meeting Hugh Jackman in Seoul Years Ago . . ." reddit, February 15, 2017. https://www.reddit.com/r/movies/comments/5u7fwr/last_week_i_commented_about_meeting_hugh_jackman/.

27. u/Spencerforhire83. "I Met Hugh Jackman in 2009, Fox Studios Heard About My Story and Decided to Fly Me to the New York Premier of Logan. Needless to Say, It Was AWESOME." reddit, February 26, 2017. https://www.reddit.com/r/xmen/comments/5waowm/i_met_hugh_jackman_in_2009_fox_studios_heard/.

28. "Huge X-Men Fan Talks About a Quiznos Encounter with Hugh Jackman . . ." reddit, February 6, 2017. https://www.reddit.com/r/bestof/comments/5sg0op/huge_xmen_fan_talks_about_a_quiznos_encounter/.

CHAPTER 9

1. McGilchrist, Iain. *The Master and His Emissary: The Divided Brain and the Making of the Western World*. New Haven, CT: Yale University Press, 2019.

2. Beaujean, Marc, Jonathon Davidson, and Stacey Madge. "The 'Moment of Truth' in Customer Service." McKinsey & Company, February 2006. https://www.mckinsey.com/business-functions/organization/our-insights/the-moment-of-truth-in-customer-service.

3. "How Do Probiotics Work?: Activia® Probiotic Yogurt." Activia, June 21, 2019. https://www.activia.us.com/what-are-probiotics/how-do-probiotics-work.

4. Corleone, Jill. "What Is the Difference Between Activia and Regular Yogurt?" LIVESTRONG.COM. Leaf Group. Accessed January 17, 2020. https://www.livestrong.com/article/449851-what-is-the-difference-between-activia-regular-yogurt/.

5. Aubrey, Allison. "Confusion at the Yogurt Aisle? Time for Probiotics 101." NPR, July 9, 2012. https://www.npr.org/sections/thesalt/2012/07/09/156381323/confusion-at-the-yogurt-aisle-time-for-probiotics-101.

6. "Activia." *Wikipedia*. Wikimedia Foundation, June 8, 2007. https://en.wikipedia.org/wiki/Activia.

7. Zak, Lena. "Healthy Year Ahead for Yoghurts." *Food Mag*, March 25, 2009. https://www.foodmag.com.au/healthy-year-ahead-for-yoghurts/.

8. Activia. Facebook. Dannon. Accessed January 5, 2020. https://www.facebook.com/watch/?v=424575311693782. (Note: Video has since been deleted.)

9. @Goop. Instagram, Accessed December 21, 2019. https://www.instagram.com/goop/?hl=en. Reviewed 100 most recent posts, dating back to November 17, 2019.

CHAPTER 10

1. Lee, Joel. "The 10 Highest Rated Reddit Posts of All Time." MakeUseOf, July 20, 2015. https://www.makeuseof.com/tag/10-top-rated-reddit-posts-time/.

2. "Comcast. If You Vote This up, It Will Show up on Google Images When People Google Search Comcast, Cable or Internet Service Provider." reddit, February 21, 2015. https://www.reddit.com/r/circlejerk/comments/2wou7z/comcast_if_you_vote_this_up_it_will_show_up_on/.

3. Goldman, David. "SOPA and PIPA Attract Huge Lobbying on Both Sides." *CNNMoney*. Cable News Network, January 25, 2012. https://money.cnn.com/2012/01/25/technology/sopa_pipa_lobby/index.htm.

4. "What Is a Common Carrier?" Findlaw. Accessed January 17, 2020. https://injury.findlaw.com/torts-and-personal-injuries/what-is-a-common-carrier.html.

5. "r/Comcast_Xfinity." reddit. Comcast Xfinity, March 20, 2016. https://www.reddit.com/r/Comcast_Xfinity/.

6. Bloom, Paul. "What We Miss." *The New York Times*, June 4, 2010. https://www.nytimes.com/2010/06/06/books/review/Bloom-t.html.

7. "The Most Exciting Phrase in Science Is Not 'Eureka!' But 'That's Funny...'" Quote Investigator, November 26, 2018. https://quoteinvestigator.com/2015/03/02/eureka-funny/.

8. Ries, Eric. *Lean Startup*. New York, NY: Portfolio Penguin, 2017.

9. "Where Stories Are Born." reddit. Accessed January 12, 2020. https://www.redditinc.com/press.

10. @OldSpice. "Download This New Old Spice Gentleman Class for the Greatest Role Playing Game of All Time . . ." Twitter. Old Spice, February 7, 2018. https://twitter.com/OldSpice/status/961362988019064832.

11. Marnell, Blair. "Old Spice Created a 'Gentleman Class' for Dungeons & Dragons." *Nerdist*, February 8, 2018. https://nerdist.com/article/dungeons-and-dragons-gentleman-class-old-spice/.

12. Solorzano, Sergio. "Old Spice Creates New 'Gentleman' Class for Dungeons & Dragons (and Pathfinder!)." *TheGamer*, February 22, 2018. https://www.thegamer.com/old-spice-dungeons-dragons-pathfinder-gentleman-class/.

13. Hoffer, Christian. "Old Spice Creates New Playable Class for 'Dungeons and Dragons.'" ComicBook.com, February 8, 2018. https://comicbook .com/gaming/2018/02/08/dungeons-and-dragons-old-spice-/.

14. "Old Spice Created a DnD Class! The Gentleman!" reddit, February 7, 2018. https://www.reddit.com/r/DnD/comments/7w1r8p/old_spice _created_a_dnd_class_the_gentleman/dtx1yrv/.

15. Israel, Brett. "Cane Toads Invade, Conquer Australia." LiveScience, June 24, 2010. https://www.livescience.com/29560-cane-toad-conquest -invades-australia.html.

16. The TODAY Show Australia. "Reporter Can't Stop Laughing at Grumpy Cat." YouTube, August 18, 2013. https://www.youtube.com/watch?v= BW8Aleq2Hn0.

17. Good Morning America. "Grumpy Cat Interview 2013 on 'GMA.'" YouTube. ABC News, March 22, 2013. https://www.youtube.com/watch ?v=skwUUiDtKpA.

18. Forbes. "Grumpy Cat: The Forbes Interview." YouTube. Forbes Life, March 25, 2013. https://www.youtube.com/watch?v=S0x6CjnWRZ8.

19. @Oreo. "Power out? No Problem. Pic.twitter.com/dnQ7pOgC." Twitter, February 4, 2013. https://twitter.com/Oreo/status/298246571718483968.

20. "Oreo Sends 'Brilliant' Tweet During Super Bowl Blackout." HuffPost, April 6, 2013. https://www.huffpost.com/entry/oreos-super-bowl-tweet -dunk-dark_n_2615333.

21. "Wendy's Training Video Is What I Wish We Were Still Doing Today." reddit, November 10, 2019. https://www.reddit.com/r/videos/comments /ducbu2/wendys_training_video_is_what_i_wish_we_were/.

22. Matthews, Toni. "A Guy Found Wendy's Training Videos from 80's & They're Just as Hilarious as You Think." InspireMore, January 10, 2018. https://www.inspiremore.com/wendys-training-videos/.

23. "80's Wendy's Training Video for New Hires." reddit, September 5, 2019. https://www.reddit.com/r/Cringetopia/comments/d03cm9/80s_wendys _training_video_for_new_hires/.

24. "Wendy's Training Video Regarding Hot Drinks." reddit, May 20, 2016. https://www.reddit.com/r/NotTimAndEric/comments/4k9dia/wendys _training_video_regarding_hot_drinks/.

25. "Old School—Cigarette Card Life Hacks from 1900–1910." reddit, August 2, 2014. https://www.reddit.com/r/lifehacks/comments/2cfy1q /old_school_cigarette_card_life_hacks_from_1900_to/.

26. "Old School—Cigarette Card Life Hacks from 1900–1910." Imgur, August 2, 2014. https://imgur.com/a/ShP0d.

CHAPTER 11

1. "The Passing of the Buffalo." First People. Accessed March 31, 2020. https://www.firstpeople.us/FP-Html-Legends/ThePassingoftheBuffalo -Kiowa.html.
2. Bailey, Dustin. "Minecraft Player Count Reaches 480 Million." PCGamesN, November 11, 2019. https://www.pcgamesn.com/minecraft /minecraft-player-count.

CHAPTER 12

1. Sollosi, Mary. "April Fools' Day 2017: The Best Brand Pranks." EW.com, April 1, 2017. https://ew.com/news/2017/04/01/april-fools-day-2017 -brand-pranks/.
2. Machkovech, Sam. "Did Reddit's April Fools' Gag Solve the Issue of Online Hate Speech?" Ars Technica, April 4, 2017. https://arstechnica .com/gaming/2017/04/in-memoriam-reddits-72-hour-live-graffiti-wall -as-a-social-experiment/.
3. http://www.reddit.com/r/Place.
4. Machkovech, Sam. "Did Reddit's April Fools' Gag Solve the Issue of Online Hate Speech?"
5. Gurkengewuerz. "Reddit Place (/r/Place)—FULL 72h (90fps) TIMELAPSE." YouTube, April 3, 2017. https://www.youtube.com/watch ?v=XnRCZK3KjUY.
6. "r/Place—Place Final Canvas (Well Done, Everyone!)." reddit, April 3, 2017. https://www.reddit.com/r/place/comments/6385gl/place_final _canvas_well_done_everyone/.
7. Asarch, Steven. "How to Make Works of Art with Reddit Layer." Newsweek, September 11, 2019. https://www.newsweek.com/reddit -layer-what-how-use-new-adobe-1458798.
8. "r/Layer." reddit, June 24, 2014. https://www.reddit.com/r/layer.
9. "Collaborations on Layer." reddit, October 8, 2019. https://www.reddit .com/r/Layer/comments/df6k5m/collaborations_on_layer/.
10. chrispie. "1 Day of r/Layer Timelapse." YouTube, September 13, 2019. https://www.youtube.com/watch?v=MtW1U5d6zHI.
11. "/r/Layer." Know Your Meme, September 12, 2019. https://knowyour meme.com/memes/sites/rlayer.
12. chrispie. "1 Day of r/Layer Timelapse."
13. Gauging Gadgets. "Reddit r/Layer Subreddit Artwork Overview and Tutorial: How to Add a Layer." YouTube, September 10, 2019. https:// www.youtube.com/watch?v=xdYpVq567Vg.
14. "Made My Fave Empire Leader in r/Layer!" reddit, September 12, 2019. https://www.reddit.com/r/Stellaris/comments/d39na3/made_my_fave _empire_leader_in_rlayer/.

15. "On 🄱eddit's 🄲ommunity Layer 🄿roject r/Layer." reddit, September 12, 2019. https://www.reddit.com/r/emojipasta/comments/d36o7a/on _eddits_ommunity_layer_roject_rlayer/.

16. "Agora Que Temos o r/Layer Nada Como Relembrar Glórias Passadas!" reddit, September 12, 2019. https://www.reddit.com /r/portugal/comments/d34pge/agora_que_temos_o_rlayer_nada_como _relembrar/.

17. "SOMEONE PLEASE DRAW THIS ON R/LAYER! IT WON'T WORK FOR ME." reddit, September 10, 2019. https://www.reddit.com /r/greenday/comments/d2fz9e/someone_please_draw_this_on_rlayer _it_wont_work/.

18. "Almost Instantly Someone Wrote 'Yeet' on Top of the Bi Flag I Put on r/Layer Lol." reddit, September 10, 2019. https://www.reddit.com /r/BisexualTeens/comments/d2btrp/almost_instantly_someone_wrote _yeet_on_top_of_the/.

19. "r/OutOfTheLoop—What's Going on with u/hero0fwar and Why Are Adobe Ads so Obsessed with Him?" reddit, October 3, 2019. https:// www.reddit.com/r/OutOfTheLoop/comments/dctth8/whats_going_on _with_uhero0fwar_and_why_are_adobe/.

20. "u/hero0fwar." reddit, February 4, 2010. https://www.reddit.com/user /hero0fwar.

21. An, Mimi. "Why People Block Ads (and What It Means for Marketers and Advertisers)." *HubSpot* Blog, July 13, 2016. https://blog.hubspot.com /marketing/why-people-block-ads-and-what-it-means-for-marketers -and-advertisers.

Bibliography

"30 Minutes of Daily Meditation Can Stave Off Anxiety And Depression." *Huff-Post*, January 7, 2014. https://www.huffingtonpost.co.uk/entry/anxiety-and-depression-meditation_n_4549618.

@citysage. " 'In Honor of Valentine's Day @madewell1937 Asked Me to Share Some Things I Love . . . like the First Cup of Morning Coffee, the Comfiest Goes-. . . ." Instagram, February 14, 2014. https://www.instagram.com/p/kZ3ZLUIJ_t/.

@Goop. Instagram, Accessed December 21, 2019. https://www.instagram.com/goop/?hl=en. Reviewed 100 most recent posts, dating back to November 17, 2019.

@OldSpice. "Download This New Old Spice Gentleman Class for the Greatest Role Playing Game of All Time . . . ." Twitter. Old Spice, February 7, 2018. https://twitter.com/OldSpice/status/961362988019064832.

@Oreo. "Power out? No Problem. Pic.twitter.com/dnQ7pOgC." Twitter, February 4, 2013. https://twitter.com/Oreo/status/298246571718483968.

Activia. Facebook. Dannon. Accessed January 5, 2020. https://www.facebook.com/watch/?v=424575311693782. (Note: Video has since been deleted.)

"Activia." *Wikipedia*. Wikimedia Foundation, June 8, 2007. https://en.wikipedia.org/wiki/Activia.

"Agora Que Temos o r/Layer Nada Como Relembrar Glórias Passadas!" reddit, September 12, 2019. https://www.reddit.com/r/portugal/comments/d34pge/agora_que_temos_o_rlayer_nada_como_relembrar/.

Alexander, Julia, and Ben Kuchera. "How a *Rick and Morty* Joke Led to a McDonald's Szechuan Sauce Controversy." *Polygon*, October 12, 2017. https://www.polygon.com/2017/10/12/16464374/rick-and-morty-mcdonalds-szechuan-sauce.

"Almost Instantly Someone Wrote 'Yeet' on Top of the Bi Flag I Put on r/Layer Lol." reddit, September 10, 2019. https://www.reddit.com /r/BisexualTeens/comments/d2btrp/almost_instantly_someone_wrote _yeet_on_top_of_the/.

An, Mimi. "Why People Block Ads (and What It Means for Marketers and Advertisers)." *HubSpot* Blog, July 13, 2016. https://blog.hubspot.com /marketing/why-people-block-ads-and-what-it-means-for-marketers -and-advertisers.

Andrivet, Marion. "What to Learn from Tropicana's Packaging Redesign Failure?" *The Branding Journal*, June 2, 2019. https://www .thebrandingjournal.com/2015/05/what-to-learn-from-tropicanas -packaging-redesign-failure/.

AnonymousHasASoul. "William J Lashua's Birthday Party!" YouTube, September 5, 2010. https://www.youtube.com/watch?v=UzqNkIkj3rE.

Asarch, Steven. "How to Make Works of Art with Reddit Layer." *Newsweek*, September 11, 2019. https://www.newsweek.com/reddit-layer-what-how -use-new-adobe-1458798.

Aubrey, Allison. "Confusion at the Yogurt Aisle? Time for Probiotics 101." NPR, July 9, 2012. https://www.npr.org/sections/thesalt/2012/07/09 /156381323/confusion-at-the-yogurt-aisle-time-for-probiotics-101.

Aurelius, Marcus. *Meditations*. Translated by Albert Wittstock and Martin Hammond. Introduction by Christopher Gill. Oxford: Oxford University Press, 2013.

Bahadur, Nina. "How Dove Tried to Change the Conversation About Female Beauty." HuffPost, December 7, 2017. https://www.huffpost.com/entry /dove-real-beauty-campaign-turns-10_n_4575940.

Bailey, Dustin. "Minecraft Player Count Reaches 480 Million." *PCGamesN*, November 11, 2019. https://www.pcgamesn.com/minecraft/minecraft -player-count.

Barton, Eric. "The Danger of Online Anonymity." *BBC*, March 9, 2015. https://www.bbc.com/worklife/article/20150309-the-danger-of-online -anonymity.

Beaujean, Marc, Jonathon Davidson, and Stacey Madge. "The 'Moment of Truth' in Customer Service." McKinsey & Company, February 2006. https://www.mckinsey.com/business-functions/organization/our -insights/the-moment-of-truth-in-customer-service.

Beck, Martin. "How a Fashion Brand Drives 20% of Daily Online Revenue from a Single Reddit Post." *Marketing Land*, October 20, 2015. https:// marketingland.com/how-a-fashion-brand-drives-20-of-daily-online -revenue-from-a-single-reddit-post-147309.

Bedell, Geraldine. "Rates of Depression Have Soared in Teenagers. What Are We Doing Wrong?" *The Independent*. Independent Digital News and Media, February 27, 2016. https://www.independent.co.uk/life-style

/health-and-families/features/teenage-mental-health-crisis-rates-of
-depression-have-soared-in-the-past-25-years-a6894676.html.

Berman, Taylor. "In Victory for the Internet, Pitbull Visits Alaska, Receives Gift of Bear Spray." *Gawker*, July 30, 2012. https://gawker.com/5930334 /in-victory-for-the-internet-pitbull-visits-alaska-receives-gift-of-bear -spray.

"Best of Uniqlo?" reddit, October 22, 2019. https://www.reddit.com /r/femalefashionadvice/comments/dllr6x/best_of_uniqlo/.

Blackmore, Susan, and Richard Dawkins. *The Meme Machine*. Oxford: Oxford University Press, 2000.

Bloom, Juliana S., and George W. Hynd. "The Role of the Corpus Callosum in Interhemispheric Transfer of Information: Excitation or Inhibition?" *Neuropsychology Review* 15, no. 2 (2005): 59–71. https://doi.org/10.1007 /s11065-005-6252-y.

Bloom, Paul. "What We Miss." *The New York Times*, June 4, 2010. https://www .nytimes.com/2010/06/06/books/review/Bloom-t.html.

"BP: Case Study." *Landor*. Accessed January 16, 2020. https://landor.com /work/bp.

Brett, Brian. "The Psychology of Sharing: Why Do People Share Online?" *The New York Times*, July 13, 2011. https://web.archive.org/web /20160922145048/http://nytmarketing.whsites.net/mediakit/pos/POS _PUBLIC0819.php. Additional information available here: https://www .businesswire.com/news/home/20110713005971/en/New-York-Times -Completes-Research-%E2%80%98Psychology-Sharing%E2%80%99.

Brita. "Wow, Reddit! 100 Posts in r/Fellowkids and Counting, We're Flattered. Remember to Fill up Your Brita, All That Salt Must Be Making You Thirsty!" reddit. Accessed January 11, 2020. https://www.reddit .com/user/Brita_Official/comments/984hyt/wow_reddit_100_posts_in _rfellowkids_and_counting/.

Brita. " 'I'm Trying to Save Money Now' Starter Pack from Your Friends at Brita (r/FellowKids, Here We Come!)." reddit. Accessed January 11, 2020. https://www.reddit.com/user/Brita_Official/comments/8xsra0/im _trying_to_save_money_now_starter_pack_from/.

Buzzfeed. "@Buzzfeedtasty." Instagram. Accessed January 14, 2020. https:// www.instagram.com/buzzfeedtasty/?hl=en.

chrispie. "1 Day of r/Layer Timelapse." YouTube, September 13, 2019. https:// www.youtube.com/watch?v=MtW1U5d6zHI.

Clement, J. "Facebook Users Worldwide 2019." Statista, November 19, 2019. https://www.statista.com/statistics/264810/number-of-monthly-active -facebook-users-worldwide/.

Clement, J. "Global Social Media Account Ownership 2018." Statista, April 22, 2020. https://www.statista.com/statistics/788084/number-of-social -media-accounts/.

"CMV: Ted Cruz Would Be Worse for the US Than Trump." reddit, April 16, 2016. https://www.reddit.com/r/changemyview/comments/4f2sb3/cmv_ted_cruz_would_be_worse_for_the_us_than_trump/.

"Collaborations on Layer." reddit, October 8, 2019. https://www.reddit.com/r/Layer/comments/df6k5m/collaborations_on_layer/.

"Comcast. If You Vote This up, It Will Show up on Google Images When People Google Search Comcast, Cable or Internet Service Provider." reddit, February 21, 2015. https://www.reddit.com/r/circlejerk/comments/2wou7z/comcast_if_you_vote_this_up_it_will_show_up_on/.

Corleone, Jill. "What Is the Difference Between Activia and Regular Yogurt?" LIVESTRONG.COM. Leaf Group. Accessed January 17, 2020. https://www.livestrong.com/article/449851-what-is-the-difference-between-activia-regular-yogurt/.

Cramer, Shirley, and Dr. Becky Inkster. "#StatusOfMind Social Media and Young People's Mental Health and Wellbeing."

Dawkins, Richard. *The Selfish Gene: 40th Anniversary Edition*. Oxford: Oxford University Press, 2016.

Dinesh, Disha. "11 Awesome Facebook Campaigns to Inspire You." *DreamGrow*, July 10, 2019. https://www.dreamgrow.com/11-awesome-inspiring-facebook-campaings/.

"Don't Believe Facebook; You Only Have 150 Friends." NPR, June 5, 2011. https://www.npr.org/2011/06/04/136723316/dont-believe-facebook-you-only-have-150-friends.

Dove US. "Dove Real Beauty Sketches | You'Re More Beautiful Than You Think." YouTube, April 14, 2013. https://www.youtube.com/watch?v=XpaOjMXyJGk.

Dyda, Arielle. "u/midnight1214." reddit, April 27, 2012. https://www.reddit.com/user/midnight1214.

Ellis, Blake. "New Gap Logo Ignites Firestorm." *CNNMoney*. Cable News Network, October 8, 2010. https://money.cnn.com/2010/10/08/news/companies/gap_logo/index.htm.

Federer, Joe. "4 Reasons You're Seeing More Videos on Facebook than Ever." THAT'S FICTION, May 2, 2015. http://www.thatsfiction.com/latest-work/2015/5/2/4-reasons-youre-seeing-more-videos-on-facebook-than-ever.

Forbes. "Grumpy Cat: The Forbes Interview." YouTube. Forbes Life, March 25, 2013. https://www.youtube.com/watch?v=S0x6CjnWRZ8.

Freud, Sigmund. *Civilization and Its Discontents*. New York, NY: Norton, 2010.

Gauging Gadgets. "Reddit r/Layer Subreddit Artwork Overview and Tutorial—How to Add a Layer." YouTube, September 10, 2019. https://www.youtube.com/watch?v=xdYpVq567Vg.

GoPro. "@GoPro." Instagram. Accessed January 14, 2020. https://www
.instagram.com/ggopro/.

GoPro. "@GoPro." Twitter. Accessed January 14, 2020. https://twitter.com
/GoPro.

Goldman, David. "SOPA and PIPA Attract Huge Lobbying on Both Sides."
CNNMoney. Cable News Network, January 25, 2012. https://money.cnn
.com/2012/01/25/technology/sopa_pipa_lobby/index.htm.

Good Morning America. "Grumpy Cat Interview 2013 on 'GMA.'" You-
Tube. *ABC News*, March 22, 2013. https://www.youtube.com/watch?v=
skwUUiDtKpA.

Gotter, Ana, and Timothy J. Legg. "What Is Capgras Syndrome?" *Healthline*,
May 1, 2017. https://www.healthline.com/health/capgras-syndrome.

Greene, Kai. "@kaigreene." Instagram. Accessed January 14, 2020. https://
www.instagram.com/kaigreene/?hl=en.

Gurkengewuerz. "Reddit Place (/r/Place)—FULL 72h (90fps) TIMELAPSE."
YouTube, April 3, 2017. https://www.youtube.com/watch?v=
XnRCZK3KjUY.

Halpern, M. E., Onur Güntürkün, William D. Hopkins, and Lesley J. Rogers. "Lateralization of the Vertebrate Brain: Taking the Side of Model
Systems." *Journal of Neuroscience* 25, no. 45 (September 2005): 10351–
10357. https://doi.org/10.1523/jneurosci.3439-05.2005.

Hardy, Tony. "10 Rebranding Failures and How Much They Cost." Canny,
December 17, 2019. https://www.canny-creative.com/10-rebranding
-failures-how-much-they-cost/.

Heath, Dan, and Chip Heath. *The Power of Moments*. Random House
UK, 2017.

Heinz Ketchup. "Looks like Chicago Is Among the First to Get Dipped
in #Mayochup!" Twitter, September 19, 2018. https://twitter.com
/HeinzKetchup_US/status/1042390349468053504.

"Hey Reddit, Charles Schwab Team Here with a Question. What's Your
Approach to Tracking Gains and Losses in Your Trading History and
Learning from Your Past?" reddit. Charles Schwab, November 20, 2018.
https://www.reddit.com/user/Schwab_Official/comments/9ywffe/hey
_reddit_charles_schwab_team_here_with_a/.

"Hey Reddit, Your Friends at Charles Schwab Here. What's Something You're
Doing Today to Set Yourself up for Success Tomorrow?" reddit. Charles
Schwab, February 23, 2018. https://www.reddit.com/comments/7zrq4l
/hey_reddit_your_friends_at_charles_schwab_here/.

"Hillary Clinton Favorable Rating: *HuffPost* Pollster." *The Huffington Post*.
Accessed January 17, 2020. https://elections.huffingtonpost.com/pollster
/hillary-clinton-favorable-rating.

Hill, Catey. "Study Finds Online Porn May Reduce the Incidence of Rape." nydailynews.com. *New York Daily News*, January 11, 2019. https://www.nydailynews.com/news/money/study-finds-online-porn-reduce-incidence-rape-article-1.390028.

Hoffer, Christian. "Old Spice Creates New Playable Class for 'Dungeons and Dragons.'" ComicBook.com, February 8, 2018. https://comicbook.com/gaming/2018/02/08/dungeons-and-dragons-old-spice-/.

Hooton, Christopher. "Westworld Season 2 Will 'Fuck with the Metaphysical.'" *The Independent*, March 27, 2017. https://www.independent.co.uk/arts-entertainment/tv/news/westworld-season-2-plot-reddit-storyline-jonathan-nolan-details-news-a7651506.html.

Houser, Kristin. "Surprise! Reddit Is Actually Helping People Battle Mental Illness." Futurism. Neoscope, April 20, 2018. https://futurism.com/neoscope/reddit-depression-mental-illness.

"How Do Probiotics Work?: Activia® Probiotic Yogurt." Activia, June 21, 2019. https://www.activia.us.com/what-are-probiotics/how-do-probiotics-work.

"How Heinz Harnessed the Power of Twitter and Got 1 Billion Impressions in 48 Hours." Twitter Marketing. Accessed January 14, 2020. https://marketing.twitter.com/na/en/success-stories/how-heinz-harnessed-the-power-of-twitter-and-got-one-billion-impressions.

"Huge X-Men Fan Talks About a Quiznos Encounter with Hugh Jackman . . . ." reddit, February 6, 2017. https://www.reddit.com/r/bestof/comments/5sg0op/huge_xmen_fan_talks_about_a_quiznos_encounter/.

Hunt, Melissa G., Rachel Marx, Courtney Lipson, and Jordyn Young. "No More FOMO: Limiting Social Media Decreases Loneliness and Depression." *Journal of Social and Clinical Psychology* 37, no. 10 (2018): 751–768. https://doi.org/10.1521/jscp.2018.37.10.751.

"I Add 'Reddit' After Every Question I Search on Google Because I Trust You All More than Other Strangers." reddit, September 24, 2016. https://www.reddit.com/r/Showerthoughts/comments/54btqq/i_add_reddit_after_every_question_i_search_on/.

"I am Barack Obama, President of the United States—AMA." reddit, August 29, 2012. https://www.reddit.com/r/IAmA/comments/z1c9z/i_am_barack_obama_president_of_the_united_states/.

"I am Dr. Jane Goodall, a Scientist, Conservationist, Peacemaker, and Mentor. AMA." reddit, September 13, 2017. https://www.reddit.com/r/IAmA/comments/6zvwqe/i_am_dr_jane_goodall_a_scientist_conservationist/.

"IamA Vacuum Repair Technician, and I Can't Believe People Really Wanted It, but, AMA!" reddit, October 28, 2013. https://www.reddit.com/r/IAmA/comments/1pe2bd/iama_vacuum_repair_technician_and_i_cant_believe/.

Ifeanyi, KC. "Reddit's First-Ever Interactive Livestream Stars a Very Lost Robot." *Fast Company*, November 14, 2017. https://www.fastcompany .com/40495819/reddits-first-ever-interactive-livestream-stars-a-very -lost-robot.

"I'm Bill Gates, Co-chair of the Bill & Melinda Gates Foundation. Ask Me Anything." reddit, February 27, 2018. https://www.reddit.com /r/IAmA/comments/80ow6w/im_bill_gates_cochair_of_the_bill_melinda_gates/.

"I'm Getting Ready for Small Business Saturday, Nov 30. Are You?" American Express. Accessed January 14, 2020. https://www.americanexpress.com /us/small-business/shop-small/.

"I'm on My Phone, so I Can't Access the One from Last Year (Doesn't Load on Mobile) . . . ." reddit, February 24, 2017. Accessed January 20, 2020. https://www.reddit.com/r/malefashionadvice/comments/5w1a56/mfa _psa_the_uniqlo_linen_shirts_from_this_season/de7h9be/.

Ingram, Mathew. "4chan Decides to Do Something Nice for a Change." Gigaom, September 2, 2010. https://gigaom.com/2010/09/02/4chan -decides-to-do-something-nice-for-a-change/.

"I Only Believe This Is Live, When a Dog Makes a Shit." reddit, November 14, 2017. https://www.reddit.com/r/promos/comments/7ct3se/we_did_it _reddit_cozmo_has_finally_escaped_from/dptf4m1/.

Isaacson, Walter. "How to Fix the Internet." *The Atlantic*, December 15, 2016. https://www.theatlantic.com/technology/archive/2016/12/how-to-fix -the-internet/510797/.

Israel, Brett. "Cane Toads Invade, Conquer Australia." *LiveScience*, June 24, 2010. https://www.livescience.com/29560-cane-toad-conquest-invades -australia.html.

Jefferson, Brandie. "Splitting the Difference: One Person, Two Minds: The Source: Washington University in St. Louis." *The Source*. Washington University, June 1, 2018. https://source.wustl.edu/2018/05/splitting-the -difference-one-person-two-minds/.

Johnson, Lauren. "Taco Bell's Cinco De Mayo Snapchat Lens Was Viewed 224 Million Times." *Adweek*, May 11, 2016. https://www.adweek.com/digital /taco-bells-cinco-de-mayo-snapchat-lens-was-viewed-224-million -times-171390/.

Jung, C. G. *Psychology and Religion: West and East.* Hove: Routledge, 2014.

Karenina, Karina, Andrey Giljov, Janeane Ingram, Victoria J. Rowntree, and Yegor Malashichev. "Lateralization of Mother–Infant Interactions in a Diverse Range of Mammal Species." *Nature Ecology & Evolution* 1, no. 2 (September 2017). https://doi.org/10.1038/s41559-016-0030.

Kendall, Todd D., and John E. Walker. "Pornography, Rape, and the Internet." July 2007. https://www.semanticscholar.org/paper/Pornography%2C -Rape%2C-and-the-Internet-Kendall-Walker/602ddbdd604afe9cbd31c 97f01d941fa637f271a.

"Kodiak, Alaska, Welcomes Pitbull." YouTube. Walmart, August 10, 2012. https://www.youtube.com/watch?v=2NrllHwHq7w.

Landsburg, Steven E. "Proof That Internet Porn Prevents Rape." *Slate Magazine*, October 30, 2006. https://slate.com/culture/2006/10/proof-that -internet-porn-prevents-rape.html.

Lee, Joel. "The 10 Highest Rated Reddit Posts of All Time." MakeUseOf, July 20, 2015. https://www.makeuseof.com/tag/10-top-rated-reddit-posts -time/.

Lewin, Michelle. "@michelle_lewin." Instagram. Accessed January 14, 2020. https://www.instagram.com/michelle_lewin/?hl=en.

Litman, Jordan A. "Epistemic Curiosity." *Encyclopedia of the Sciences of Learning*, 2012, 1162–1165. https://doi.org/10.1007/978-1-4419-1428-6_1645.

Louis Vuitton. "Virgil Abloh Staples Edition." Facebook. Accessed January 11, 2020. https://www.facebook.com/watch/?v=2334680580142899.

"Lowe's Fix in Six: Using 'The New' to Create 'Know-How.'" The 4A's. Accessed January 14, 2020. https://www.aaaa.org/wp-content/uploads/legacy-pdfs /BBDO-LowesFixinSix-HM.pdf.

Lowe's Home Improvement. "Stripped Screw? No Problem, Just Use a Rubber Band." Vine, April 19, 2013. https://vine.co/v/bU61aqq2YOp.

Lowe's Home Improvement. "Use Tape to Measure the Distance between Holes, Then Put the Tape on the Wall." Vine, May 17, 2013. https://vine .co/v/bEFQXmnWrOP.

Lowe's Home Improvement. "Use a Cookie Cutter and a Hammer for Perfect Pumpkin Carving!" Facebook, October 25, 2014. https://www.facebook .com/lowes/videos/10152384851961231/?v=10152384851961231& redirect=false.

Lowe's Home Improvement. "Use a Cookie Cutter and a Hammer for Perfect Pumpkin Carving." Vine, October 24, 2014. https://vine.co /v/Oh5EM3auMAr.

Lowe's Home Improvement. "Lighten up! DEWALT 2-PC 20V Combo Kit was $199, will be $149 on Black Friday." Vine, November 12, 2014. https:// vine.co/v/OiFHAJ7OqEF.

Machkovech, Sam. "Did Reddit's April Fools' Gag Solve the Issue of Online Hate Speech?" *Ars Technica*, April 4, 2017. https://arstechnica.com /gaming/2017/04/in-memoriam-reddits-72-hour-live-graffiti-wall-as -a-social-experiment/.

"Made My Fave Empire Leader in r/Layer!" reddit, September 12, 2019. https://www.reddit.com/r/Stellaris/comments/d39na3/made_my_fave _empire_leader_in_rlayer/.

Madewell. "Inspo: Your Pics." Accessed January 14, 2020. https://www .madewell.com/inspo-community-denimmadewell-landing.html.

Mander, Jason. "Internet Users Have Average of 7 Social Accounts." Global-WebIndex Blog, June 9, 2016. https://blog.globalwebindex.com/chart-of-the-day/internet-users-have-average-of-7-social-accounts/.

Marnell, Blair. "Old Spice Created a 'Gentleman Class' for Dungeons & Dragons." *Nerdist*, February 8, 2018. https://nerdist.com/article/dungeons-and-dragons-gentleman-class-old-spice/.

Marx, Christopher, Cord Benecke, and Antje Gumz. "Talking Cure Models: A Framework of Analysis." *Frontiers in Psychology* 8 (2017). https://doi.org/10.3389/fpsyg.2017.01589.

Matthews, Toni. "A Guy Found Wendy's Training Videos from 80's & They're Just as Hilarious as You Think." *InspireMore*, January 10, 2018. https://www.inspiremore.com/wendys-training-videos/.

McCoy, Terrence. "4chan: The 'Shock Post' Site That Hosted the Private Jennifer Lawrence Photos." *The Washington Post*. WP Company, September 2, 2014. https://www.washingtonpost.com/news/morning-mix/wp/2014/09/02/the-shadowy-world-of-4chan-the-shock-post-site-that-hosted-the-private-jennifer-lawrence-photos/.

McGilchrist, Iain. *The Master and His Emissary: The Divided Brain and the Making of the Western World*. New Haven, CT: Yale University Press, 2019.

McKie, Robin. "How Hunting with Wolves Helped Humans Outsmart the Neanderthals." *The Guardian*. Guardian News and Media, March 1, 2015. https://www.theguardian.com/science/2015/mar/01/hunting-with-wolves-humans-conquered-the-world-neanderthal-evolution.

Migliore, Lauren. "The Aha! Moment: The Science Behind Creative Insight." *Brain World*, May 28, 2019. https://brainworldmagazine.com/aha-moment-science-behind-creative-insight/.

"Molly's Trip to France." reddit, March 8, 2017. https://www.reddit.com/r/donate/comments/5y8tfx/mollys_trip_to_france/.

"Mountain Dew Naming Campaign Melts Down After Online Hijacking." *HuffPost*, August 13, 2012. https://www.huffpost.com/entry/4chan-mountain-dew_n_1773076.

"My Friend Is About to Ask His Girlfriend to Marry [Him] and I'm the Only One Who Knows How Unfaithful She Is. Do I Say Anything?" reddit, April 28, 2019. https://www.reddit.com/r/relationship_advice/comments/bicdpm/my_friend_is_about_to_ask_his_girlfriend_to_marry/.

Naumann, Robert K., Janie M. Ondracek, Samuel Reiter, Mark Shein-Idelson, Maria Antonietta Tosches, Tracy M. Yamawaki, and Gilles Laurent. "The Reptilian Brain." *National Center for Biotechnology Information*, April 20, 2015. https://www.ncbi.nlm.nih.gov/pmc/articles/PMC4406946/.

Nelson, Samantha. "How Baskin Robbins Built a *Stranger Things* Alternate Reality Game Using 1985 Tech." *Gaming Street*, August 15, 2019. https://www.gamingstreet.com/baskin-robbins-stranger-things-arg/.

North, Anna. "The Double-Edged Sword of Online Anonymity." *The New York Times*, May 15, 2015. https://takingnote.blogs.nytimes.com/2015/05/15/the-double-edged-sword-of-online-anonymity/.

"Old School—Cigarette Card Life Hacks from 1900 to 1910." reddit, August 2, 2014. https://www.reddit.com/r/lifehacks/comments/2cfy1q/old_school_cigarette_card_life_hacks_from_1900_to/.

"Old School—Cigarette Card Life Hacks from 1900-1910." Imgur, August 2, 2014. https://imgur.com/a/ShP0d.

"Old Spice Created a DnD Class! The Gentleman!" reddit, February 7, 2018. https://www.reddit.com/r/DnD/comments/7w1r8p/old_spice_created_a_dnd_class_the_gentleman/dtx1yrv/.

"On Beddit's Bommunity Layer Broject r/Layer." reddit, September 12, 2019. https://www.reddit.com/r/emojipasta/comments/d3607a/on_eddits_ommunity_layer_roject_rlayer/.

"Oreo Sends 'Brilliant' Tweet During Super Bowl Blackout." *HuffPost*, April 6, 2013. https://www.huffpost.com/entry/oreos-super-bowl-tweet-dunk-dark_n_2615333.

"Owning Libs Is so Easy, and Liberals Are so Dumb, That They Own Themselves!" reddit, December 14, 2018. https://www.reddit.com/r/The_Donald/comments/a65268/owning_libs_is_so_easy_and_liberals_are_so_dumb/.

Panda, Simeon. "@simeonpanda." Instagram. Accessed January 14, 2020. https://www.instagram.com/simeonpanda/?hl=en.

Peterson, Jordan B. "Biblical Series VIII: The Phenomenology of the Divine." YouTube, July 27, 2017. https://www.youtube.com/watch?v=UoQdp2prfmM.

"PSA: Uniqlo on 5th Ave Claim the Free Heattech Vouchers Are No Longer Accepted." reddit, December 16, 2016. https://www.reddit.com/r/frugalmalefashion/comments/5ir0e6/psa_uniqlo_on_5th_ave_claim_the_free_heattech/.

"r/Comcast_Xfinity." reddit. Comcast Xfinity, March 20, 2016. https://www.reddit.com/r/Comcast_Xfinity/.

Renzi, E. De, D. Perani, G.a. Carlesimo, M.c. Silveri, and F. Fazio. "Prosopagnosia Can Be Associated with Damage Confined to the Right Hemisphere—An MRI and PET Study and a Review of the Literature." *Neuropsychologia* 32, no. 8 (1994): 893–902. https://doi.org/10.1016/0028-3932(94)90041-8.

R/GA. "Beats By Dre Straight Outta Compton: The Shorty Awards." The Shorty Awards. Accessed January 14, 2020. https://shortyawards.com/8th/straight-outta-3.

"*RICK AND MORTY* MCDONALD'S SZECHUAN SAUCE FREAKOUT!!!! (ORIGINAL VIDEO)." YouTube. Chairman Mar, October 8, 2017. https://www.youtube.com/watch?v=-GC5rAX0xHg.

Ries, Eric. *Lean Startup*. Place of publication not identified: Portfolio Penguin, 2017.

"/r/Layer." Know Your Meme, September 12, 2019. https://knowyourmeme.com/memes/sites/rlayer.

"r/Layer." reddit, June 24, 2014. https://www.reddit.com/r/layer.

"r/OutOfTheLoop—What's Going on with u/hero0fwar and Why Are Adobe Ads so Obsessed with Him?" reddit, October 3, 2019. https://www.reddit.com/r/OutOfTheLoop/comments/dctth8/whats_going_on_with_uhero0fwar_and_why_are_adobe/.

"r/Place—Place Final Canvas (Well Done, Everyone!)." reddit, April 3, 2017. https://www.reddit.com/r/place/comments/6385gl/place_final_canvas_well_done_everyone/.

r/shittyfoodporn. "When Payday Is Still Two Days Away." reddit. Accessed January 10, 2020. https://www.reddit.com/r/shittyfoodporn/comments/9yb873/when_payday_is_still_two_days_away/.

r/Starterpacks. "The 'Every Cheap Italian Restaurant' Starter Pack." Accessed January 11, 2020. https://www.reddit.com/r/starterpacks/comments/akcryr/the_every_cheap_italian_restaurant_starter_pack/.

"Serious—Won Lottery, Paid off All Debts, Terrified of Financial Advisors and Investing. Advice?" reddit, May 17, 2015. https://www.reddit.com/r/personalfinance/comments/36bp59/serious_won_lottery_paid_of_all_debts_terrified/.

Shaban, Hamza. "Digital Advertising to Surpass Print and TV for the First Time, Report Says." *The Washington Post*. WP Company, March 7, 2019. https://www.washingtonpost.com/technology/2019/02/20/digital-advertising-surpass-print-tv-first-time-report-says/?noredirect=on&utm_term=.2afae4360624.

Shaw, Beau. "Historical Context for the Writings of Sigmund Freud." Columbia College. Accessed January 14, 2020. https://www.college.columbia.edu/core/content/writings-sigmund-freud/context.

Sherman, Lauren. "High-Low Collaborations Democratised Fashion. But What Did They Do for the Designers?" *The Business of Fashion*, September 19, 2019. https://www.businessoffashion.com/articles/news-analysis/high-low-collaborations-democratised-fashion-but-what-did-they-do-for-the-designers.

Shifman, Limor. *Memes*. Cambridge, MA: The MIT Press, 2014.

"Shifts for 2020: Multisensory Multipliers." Facebook IQ. Accessed January 10, 2020. https://www.facebook.com/business/news/insights/shifts-for-2020-multisensory-multipliers.

"Shoutout to u/midnight1214 (Our Friendly Uniqlo Reddit Rep) for This Kind Gesture on AskReddit." reddit, March 8, 2017. https://www.reddit.com/r/malefashionadvice/comments/5y8oz6/shoutout_to_umidnight1214_our_friendly_uniqlo/.

Skiba, Katherine. "Arrest Photo of Young Activist Bernie Sanders Emerges from Tribune Archives." *Chicago Tribune*, April 23, 2019. https://www .chicagotribune.com/news/ct-bernie-sanders-1963-chicago-arrest -20160219-story.html.

"Slaps Roof of Car." Know Your Meme, June 28, 2018. https://knowyourmeme .com/memes/slaps-roof-of-car.

Small, Deborah. "Hearts, Minds and Money: Maximizing Charitable Giving." Interview by Knoledge@Wharton. Wharton Education. Accessed January 11, 2020. https://knowledge.wharton.upenn.edu/article/maximizing -charitable-giving/.

"Snapchat Ad Examples & Success Stories: Snapchat for Business." Snapchat for Business. Accessed January 14, 2020. https://forbusiness.snapchat .com/inspiration.

"Snapchat Advertising Formats." Snapchat for Business. Accessed January 14, 2020. https://forbusiness.snapchat.com/advertising.

"SOMEONE PLEASE DRAW THIS ON R/LAYER! IT WON'T WORK FOR ME." reddit, September 10, 2019. https://www.reddit.com/r/greenday /comments/d2fz9e/someone_please_draw_this_on_rlayer_it_wont _work/.

"Sony Pictures' Venom Snapchat Campaign Drove 1 Million Incremental Movie Ticket Sales." Snapchat for Business. Accessed January 14, 2020. https://forbusiness.snapchat.com/inspiration/sony-pictures-venom -snapchat-campaign-drove-1-million-incremental-movie.

"SOS 073017 2130 EST TWTR 3x.5GAL." reddit. McDonald's, July 30, 2017. https://www.reddit.com/r/rickandmorty/comments/6qis8y/sos_073017 _2130_est_twtr_3x5gal/.

Sollosi, Mary. "April Fools' Day 2017: The Best Brand Pranks." EW.com, April 1, 2017. https://ew.com/news/2017/04/01/april-fools-day-2017-brand -pranks/.

Solorzano, Sergio. "Old Spice Creates New 'Gentleman' Class for Dungeons & Dragons (and Pathfinder!)." *TheGamer*, February 22, 2018. https://www .thegamer.com/old-spice-dungeons-dragons-pathfinder-gentleman -class/.

"Squatty Potty." Facebook. Accessed January 14, 2020. https://www.facebook .com/squattypotty/.

Squatty Potty. "This Unicorn Changed the Way I Poop." Facebook, October 2015. https://www.facebook.com/squattypotty/videos /925884884149638/.

"Target Celebrates 20 Years of Designer Partnership with an Anniversary Collection." Target Corporate, August 1, 2019. https://corporate.target.com /article/2019/08/20-years-anniversary-collection.

"Taylor Swift Foils Prank with Donation to School for the Deaf." *Rolling Stone*, June 25, 2018. https://www.rollingstone.com/music/music-country /taylor-swift-counters-4chan-prank-with-donation-to-school-for-the -deaf-102935/.

"Teachers of Reddit, What's the Saddest Thing You've Ever Found out About a Student?" reddit, March 7, 2017. https://www.reddit.com/r/AskReddit /comments/5y3ax2/teachers_of_reddit_whats_the_saddest_thing _youve/dene3x8/?context=8&depth=9.

"Ted Cruz Favorable Rating—HuffPost Pollster." *The Huffington Post*. Accessed January 17, 2020. https://elections.huffingtonpost.com/pollster /ted-cruz-favorable-rating.

"The Basic Bastard Wardrobe: British Budget Edition." reddit, September 18, 2019. https://www.reddit.com/r/malefashionadvice/comments/d5zhqw /the_basic_bastard_wardrobe_british_budget_edition/.

"The History of Word of Mouth Marketing." *The Free Library*. Accessed January 11, 2020. https://www.thefreelibrary.com/The history of word of mouth marketing.-a0134908667.

"The Ice Water Challenge." Cancer Society Auckland. Accessed January 10, 2020. https://web.archive.org/web/20140819082259/https://www .cancersocietyauckland.org.nz/newsandmedia.

"The Most Exciting Phrase in Science Is Not 'Eureka!' But 'That's Funny....'" Quote Investigator, November 26, 2018. https://quoteinvestigator.com /2015/03/02/eureka-funny/.

"The Passing of the Buffalo." *First People*. Accessed March 31, 2020. https:// www.firstpeople.us/FP-Html-Legends/ThePassingoftheBuffalo-Kiowa .html.

"The Power of Community: A Research Project by Reddit & YPulse." *YPulse*, September 18, 2019. https://www.ypulse.com/2019/09/18/ypulse -x-reddit-whitepaper-the-power-of-community/.

The TODAY Show Australia. "Reporter Can't Stop Laughing at Grumpy Cat." YouTube, August 18, 2013. https://www.youtube.com/watch?v= BW8Aleq2Hn0.

"Think Faster, the World's Fastest AMA." M/H VCCP. Audi. Accessed January 15, 2020. https://mtzhf.com/work/audi-think-faster-the-worlds-fastest -ama.

Thomas, Giles. "[23] Best Instagram Marketing Campaigns for Growth in 2019." RisePro, May 30, 2019. https://risepro.co/instagram-marketing -campaign/.

"Top Sites in the United States." Alexa. Accessed January 15, 2020. https:// www.alexa.com/topsites/countries/US.

Turner, Laura. "Is Twitter Making You More Anxious?" *The Atlantic*. Atlantic Media Company, July 19, 2017. https://www.theatlantic.com/technology /archive/2017/07/how-twitter-fuels-anxiety/534021/.

"u/hero0fwar." reddit, February 4, 2010. https://www.reddit.com/user
/hero0fwar.

u/mumbalakumbala. "Commenters—you are doing an awesome job, this is
all in all a pretty impressive . . . ." reddit, November 14, 2017. https://www
.reddit.com/r/promos/comments/7ct3se/we_did_it_reddit_cozmo_has
_finally_escaped_from/dptgvx2/.

u/Northern_Nomad. "r/Pics—Cheerios Will Send You 500 Wildflower Seeds
for Free to Help Save the Honeybee (Link in Comments)." reddit, March
15, 2017. https://www.reddit.com/r/pics/comments/5zmio2/cheerios
_will_send_you_500_wildflower_seeds_for/.

"U.S. Census Bureau QuickFacts: Kodiak City, Alaska." Census Bureau
QuickFacts, July 1, 2018. https://www.census.gov/quickfacts/fact/table
/kodiakcityalaska/PST045218.

u/Spencerforhire83. "I Have Been Invited to Red Carpet Screening for the
Movie LOGAN . . . ." reddit, February 15, 2017. https://www.reddit.com
/r/malefashionadvice/comments/5u7h86/i_have_been_invited_to_red
_carpet_screening_for/.

u/Spencerforhire83. "I Met Hugh Jackman in 2009, Fox Studios Heard About
My Story and Decided to Fly Me to the New York Premier of LOGAN.
Needless to Say, It Was AWESOME." reddit, February 26, 2017. https://
www.reddit.com/r/xmen/comments/5waowm/i_met_hugh_jackman
_in_2009_fox_studios_heard/.

u/Spencerforhire83. "Last Week I Commented About Meeting Hugh Jackman
in Seoul Years Ago . . . ." reddit, February 15, 2017. https://www.reddit
.com/r/movies/comments/5u7fwr/last_week_i_commented_about
_meeting_hugh_jackman/.

u/SpookyBlackCat. "This Is the Best Use of Obvious Advertising on the Internet!!!" reddit, November 14, 2017. https://www.reddit.com/r/promos
/comments/7ct3se/we_did_it_reddit_cozmo_has_finally_escaped_from
/dptguk9/.

Vasquez, Natalia. "11 Examples of Branded Snapchat Filters & Lenses That
Worked." *Medium*. Comms Planning, February 28, 2017. https://medium
.com/comms-planning/11-branded-snapchat-filters-that-worked
-94a808afa682.

"Watch the New LOGAN Big Game Spot below! Wolverine's Getting His
Claws out for the Last Time. What Do You Want to See?" reddit. FOX
Studios, February 1, 2017. https://www.reddit.com/r/promos/comments
/5ri3jc/watch_the_new_logan_big_game_spot_below/.

"We are Edward Snowden, Laura Poitras and Glenn Greenwald from the
Oscar-Winning Documentary CITIZENFOUR. AUAA." reddit, February 23, 2015. https://www.reddit.com/r/IAmA/comments/2wwdep/we
_are_edward_snowden_laura_poitras_and_glenn/.

Wendy's. "Thanks for Sharing Your Baby Pictures." Twitter, December 18, 2017. https://twitter.com/Wendys/status/942854646070235137.

Wendy's. "Buy Our Cheeseburgers." Twitter. Accessed January 11, 2020. https://twitter.com/Wendys/status/1012398470903291904.

"Wendy's Training Video Is What I Wish We Were Still Doing Today." reddit, November 10, 2019. https://www.reddit.com/r/videos/comments/ducbu2/wendys_training_video_is_what_i_wish_we_were/.

"Wendy's Training Video Regarding Hot Drinks." reddit, May 20, 2016. https://www.reddit.com/r/NotTimAndEric/comments/4k9dia/wendys_training_video_regarding_hot_drinks/.

"What Are Some Things That Guys Misinterpret from Women as 'She's Interested in Me'?" reddit, November 28, 2018. https://www.reddit.com/r/AskWomen/comments/a15seh/what_are_some_things_that_guys_misinterpret_from/.

"What Does 'Wealthy' Mean to You? Here's Where Some of the Top US Cities Draw the Line Between 'Financial Comfort' and 'Wealth' (from Your Friends at Charles Schwab)." reddit. Charles Schwab, June 14, 2018. https://www.reddit.com/user/Schwab_Official/comments/8r4yxg/what_does_wealthy_mean_to_you_heres_where_some_of/.

"What Is a Common Carrier?" Findlaw. Accessed January 17, 2020. https://injury.findlaw.com/torts-and-personal-injuries/what-is-a-common-carrier.html.

"Where Stories Are Born." reddit. Accessed January 12, 2020. https://www.redditinc.com/press.

"Which Marvel Super Hero Matchup Would Make the Best Big Game Commercial? (Most Persuasive Answers Win a Year of Gold)." reddit. Coca-Cola, December 22, 2015. https://www.reddit.com/comments/3xvstd/which_marvel_super_hero_matchup_would_make_the/.

Whittaker, Zack. "New York's Anonymity Ban: Why Should the Web Be Any Different?" ZDNet, May 26, 2012. https://www.zdnet.com/article/new-yorks-anonymity-ban-why-should-the-web-be-any-different/.

"William Lashua's Birthday." Know Your Meme, November 20, 2019. https://knowyourmeme.com/memes/events/william-lashuas-birthday.

Williams, Shawna. "Human Species May Be Much Older Than Previously Thought." The Scientist Magazine, September 29, 2017. https://www.the-scientist.com/news-opinion/human-species-may-be-much-older-than-previously-thought-30819.

Yarwood, Andrew. "A Brief History of 5 Iconic Oil Business Brands." Fircroft, March 27, 2019. https://www.fircroft.com/blogs/a-brief-history-of-5-iconic-oil-business-brands-98627135823.

Zak, Lena. "Healthy Year Ahead for Yoghurts." Food Mag, March 25, 2009. https://www.foodmag.com.au/healthy-year-ahead-for-yoghurts/.

Ziploc Brand. "Cheesecake Stuffed Strawberries." Facebook, March 9, 2015. https://www.facebook.com/Ziploc/photos/a.329236260422251/947546951924509/?type=3&theater.

Ziploc Brand. "DIY Tie-Dye Crayons." Facebook, September 18, 2015. https://www.facebook.com/Ziploc/photos/a.329236260422251/1049744868371383/?type=3&theater.

Ziploc Brand. "Easy Pomegranate Juice." Facebook, July 26, 2014. https://www.facebook.com/Ziploc/photos/a.329236260422251/820978114581394/?type=3&theater.

Ziploc Brand. "Pecan Pie Bark." Facebook, November 17, 2015. https://www.facebook.com/Ziploc/photos/a.329236260422251/1068198406526029/?type=3&theater.

Index

About the Author

Joe Federer is the former head of brand strategy at Reddit, where he helped reposition the platform's narrative to the larger world of advertising, helping to drive revenue growth of more than 10× in its first year in market. Prior to joining Reddit, he worked at top PR and advertising agencies, where his campaigns performed in the top 95th percentile of advertiser studies on Facebook, and led top-performing brands through the launch of Pinterest and Instagram ads.

With clients as diverse as Charles Schwab, Google, Amazon, McDonald's, Toyota, Audi, S.C. Johnson, Bud Light, and Coca-Cola, Joe thrives at finding the intersection between what brands stand for and what their social media fans are interested in seeing. He has developed a model for the way social media sites network together, an understanding of the value users derive from each platform, and the way ideas mutate and change as they are shared between different psychological environments.